Representing 'Race'

Representing 'Race'

Ideology, identity and the media

Robert Ferguson
Institute of Education,
University of London

A member of the Hodder Headline Group
LONDON • NEW YORK • SYDNEY • AUCKLAND

First published in Great Britain in 1998 by
Arnold, a member of the Hodder Headline Group
338 Euston Road, London NW1 3BH

http://www.arnoldpublishers.com

Co-published in the United States of America by
Oxford University Press Inc.
198 Madison Avenue, New York, NY 10016

British Library Cataloguing in Publication Data
A catalogue entry for this book is available from the British Library

Library of Congress Cataloging-in-Publication Data
Ferguson, Robert, 1941 July 15–
    Representing 'race': ideology, identity, and the media / Robert
Ferguson.
        p.   cm.
    Includes bibliographical references (p.   ) and index.
    ISBN 0–340–69238–3. — ISBN 0–340–69239–1. (pbk.)
    1. Race relations in mass media.   2. Ideology.   3. Ethnicity.
I. Title.
P94.5.M55F47   1998   98–13913
305.8—dc21   CIP

ISBN 0 340 69238 3 (hb)
ISBN 0 340 69239 1 (pb)

1 2 3 4 5 6 7 8 9 10

Production Editor: Liz Gooster
Production Controller: Sarah Kett
Cover Design: Terry Griffiths

Typeset in 10.5/12.5 Palatino by York House Typographic Ltd, Ealing
Printed and bound in Great Britain by MPG Books, Bodmin, Cornwall

Contents

Acknowledgements

I am indebted to many colleagues for the conversations and discussion they have engaged in over a number of years. There are too many to name them all, but I would include Phil Cohen, Jagdish Gundara, John Twitchen, Catherine Antomarchi, Gael de Guichen, Katriina Simila, Gladys Garcia, David Buckingham, and Roxana Morduchowicz. I also wish to thank the many students on the MA Media and Cultural Studies Programme at the Institute of Education for the stimulation, discussion and good ideas which they have furnished. Grateful thanks also to Crispin Jones for reading and commenting upon early chapters and to Gunther Kress for his consistent encouragement and support. None of the above can be held responsible for the deficiencies of this book, though they have contributed significantly to what is of value.

Thanks are also due to the editorial staff at Arnold, to Lesley Riddle and Elena Seymenliyska. Particular appreciation goes to Susan Dunsmore for her patience and good ideas.

I also wish to thank Shlomit, Galit and Dan for giving me more strength than they know.

The editors and publishers would like to thank the following for permission to use copyright material in this book:

Ron Whittaker for the *Twelve Factors in Newsworthiness* from his Television Production Course; The Princes's Youth Business Trust for permission to reproduce the advertisement on page 142 (please note the Trust now has a different telephone number which is: 0171 543 1234); Lord Tebbit for permission to quote from his address delivered to a meeting of 'Conservatives against a Federal Europe'.

Introduction

This book, as the title suggests, is about the representation of 'race' in the media. It is aimed at students, researchers and others who might be interested in considering the ways in which issues of ideology are relevant to our understanding of media representations of 'race'. The key factor around which the book develops its argument is the importance of sustaining a theory of ideology which can be productively related to any analysis of issues of 'race', identity or media representations.

There is no attempt to argue that there is a *right way* to analyse the ideological. There is, however, an insistence upon the role of the ideological in understanding how representation and the understandings of the representation of issues of 'race' have evolved and continue to evolve. I use the word in inverted commas throughout this book for two reasons. The first is to highlight the fact that the term has no reliable scientific status as far as I am concerned. The second is to guard against any intellectual complacency as I attempt to engage with a field which, though primarily discursive, has had and continues to have real material consequences and correlates. The issue of 'race' relates to a world where racism has demanded and continues to demand a debilitating and sometimes deadly toll. It is important to resist any temptation to *normalise* the term 'race'.

The media continuously and in a multitude of ways re-present to audiences, at the local, national and global level, issues which are concerned with how people of different backgrounds and ethnic origins inter-relate, clash or live in harmony. These representations may be of a documentary nature, part of the news and current affairs output, or advertisements. They may also be, most significantly, dramatic representations of a fictional or semi-fictional kind. In this book I will be examining in some detail a range of media texts from a variety of sources.

The first three chapters attempt to identify a theoretical, discursive and historical basis from which it may be possible to move towards the consideration and analysis of specific media representations. I believe that the issues raised in these chapters are important enough to warrant this amount of consideration. It is my contention that productive media analysis is rather like an iceberg. The tip which shows may be likened to the moment of media analysis. The vast bulk which is not immediately visible is the intellectual, historical and analytical base without which media analysis runs the risk of becoming superficial, mechanical or glib.

This issue is also important because, on most undergraduate courses, there is little time to engage with primary sources when dealing with intellectual debate. One is often forced to read summaries, or summaries of summaries. In relation to the media this is aggravated by the fact that one may be obliged to acquire a minimum of theoretical jargon and then spend much time juggling with it in an attempt, it sometimes seems, to please one's tutors. This is, perhaps, an unkind caricature of the situation, but it is a way of trying to focus attention on the fact that media analysis, as an academic activity, is part of a *process*. This means that media analysis skills have to be developed over time. Any media researcher is likely, however, to encounter the same theoretical or conceptual issues on more than one occasion. The most useful model for a media researcher to adopt in this respect is that of Jerome Bruner's 'spiral curriculum'. Bruner (1963) suggests that, in any field of study, one is likely to revisit particular topics or theoretical positions, but at a higher level. Using this model, one is always able to approach a particular research topic in a manner which is intellectually respectable, whatever one's own level of entry. This means that one does not have to spend years studying before one can begin any analysis. It also means, however, that one is never deluded into thinking that one has reached a level of understanding where further learning would be an irrelevance. Because of the unavoidable fact that study has to start somewhere, there have been many attempts by authors to offer introductory overviews of fields as disparate as postmodernism, genre, racism, psychoanalytic theory and many more. Such texts *are* crucially important and potentially useful, but they lose their potential when they become not introductions, but the students' only contact with the work of a particular thinker. This happened when Althusser's (1970) writings on Marx's *Capital* became a substitute for reading the original. This book is also about the various ways in which media representations have evolved which have dealt with 'race' across a range of generic forms. The emphasis throughout will be on media texts which are likely to have been popular or widely accessible. This means that some very important genres of representation will be left out, including avant-garde and experimental work. There will also be little reference to independent film-making. My emphasis on more popular media texts is based quite simply on their relevance in the sphere of ideology and the ideological. I am not attempting in this book to suggest alternative ways of representing matters concerning 'race'. I am more interested in the ways in which ideological relations are produced, sustained or challenged in the everyday and in the popular media.

There are other contextualising factors which need to be acknowledged before addressing the main subject of this book. They are the concerns of all media researchers in a period of theoretical and methodological instability. I will comment on just two. The first is the relationship between media representations and the material world, and the question of postmodernism. The second is a cluster of issues which centre around matters of identity, multiculturalism and cultural hybridity.

The material world has, from time to time, become a problematic issue for the media analyst. The question of its existence or non-existence is one which has, in the past, been mainly the concern of philosophers who have seldom found their way into the public sphere. Today this is not the case. Although the names of the philosophers may not be bandied about in public discourse, some of the ideas which challenge the materiality of the world are now becoming part of popular culture, often by implication rather than argument. Contradictions abound. Films which would once have been designated as science fiction are now discussed as though they were extensions of reality. Wars which might once have brought terror to the real stomachs of actual people have become media events. The armies, the victims, the aggressors become largely absent performers while *technology* wages war through and around them. The contradictions thrown up by media representations of (for instance) acts of violence, are well illustrated if two examples are considered. The Gulf War of 1991 has been described by many writers as a media war. It has also been suggested by Baudrillard, with his flair for ironic overstatement, that the Gulf War did not actually occur (Baudrillard, 1991; Norris, 1992). This is an example of the way in which media representations can be interpreted as the only 'reality' that there is. Yet there is another dimension to the relationship between media representation and lived experience. This is highlighted by the now world-famous videotape of the beating of Rodney King (Gooding-Williams, 1993). I refer to this in more detail in my chapter on Oprah Winfrey in Los Angeles. For the moment I only wish to highlight the way in which the Rodney King tape closed the gap between postmodern surface representation or simulacra and the signification of a material world which had always been part of the lived experience of a vast sector of the North American public. The tension between representations which become inter-textual and endlessly repetitive and which apparently deny the material world, and the harsh, metallic reality of lived experience, is one which will be explored in detail in the chapters which follow. I will argue that a substantial part of the enormous number of media repre-sentations of issues of 'race' play with these tensions for a variety of reasons. These include the possibility of generating fear, outrage, empathy or sometimes titillation for the mixed and changing audi-ences for particular media messages. I will also argue that the ideological dimensions of the majority of these messages work against both understanding and action in the public sphere.

The second major contextualising factor I wish to mention is that of cultural identity. Representations of issues relating to 'race' are now intertwined with issues of individual, group, national and ethnic identity. Stuart Hall (1992) has provided a summary of key debates on the issue of identity. He stresses the significance of narratives about national culture in relation to identity and difference. The key point which Hall highlights is that the once secure concept of individual identity is, as a result of social, political and philosophical upheavals, under threat. Identity, whether at the individual or national level, has become much more fragile nowadays than in previous generations. Insecurity can either lead to reappraisal and change, or to a reaffirma-tion in more stringent terms of one's original concept of self. Both these positions are to be found in a wide range of media representations, from advertisements to feature films, from newspaper editorials to chat shows. Such representations are often infused with implicit dis-course about 'race'.

Globalisation of the media has also meant that cultural represent-ation (along with implicit or explicit signification of issues of 'race') has often become fragmented, then recombined or reconstituted. This reconstitution is usually referred to as cultural hybridity. It can manifest itself in many forms, from popular music to food, fashion and narrative. So we have curry and chips, or Coca Cola with everything. All of these factors, in turn, are re-presented in the media. Zygmunt Bauman has clearly shown the way in which identity is linked with insecurity:

> One thinks of identity whenever one is not sure of where one belongs; that is, one is not sure how to place oneself among the evident variety of behavioural styles and patterns, and how to make sure that people around you would accept this placement as right and proper, so that both sides would know how to go on in each other's presence 'Identity' is a name given to the escape sought from that uncertainty.
>
> (Bauman, 1996, p. 19)

The representation of issues relating to 'race' should not, however, be reduced only to the matter of identity. The question of power is also of crucial importance. The ways in which relations of power and sub-ordination are signified with particular reference to media representations of 'race' need to be set alongside questions about individual or other forms of identity. The power to define specific issues in this field is also important, whether it be the power of the news editor to include or exclude a story, or the power of the film director to represent selectively national or international hero (they are usually men) figures. It will be apparent from the various factors which I have mentioned briefly, that I am approaching the issue of the representation of 'race' from a perspective which favours placing the concept ideologically rather than direct entry into debates about 'race' and racism. I believe it is necessary to situate the media and 'race' in at least three discursive and material fields: those of pleasure, politics and power. I will attempt to do this by the detailed consideration of a range of media examples. I will not attempt to privilege one form of representation of issues of 'race' over another, nor will I suggest that there should be a hierarchy to rank one form of racism against another. Ideological analysis is about much more than identifying or spotting the *negative* in any media representation. It is also about recognising the semiotic and discursive contradictions and tensions within a representation or set of representations. I will argue that, at the core of these contradictions and tensions, there is the potential to challenge particular power relations and concepts of identity. In need of most urgent challenge are those media representations which foster either racism or hopelessness. I will discuss and debate the ways in which these media representations are constructed and the implications, ideologically, of their modes of signification.

I wish to offer here the briefest biographical note. My interest in media research is that of a white middle-aged male educator who grew up in a small country town in the south of England. I learned, as a child, about racism and the concept of otherness without either term ever being mentioned to me. Over the years I, like anyone else who wanted to, have been able to observe racism in many forms and many contexts. The form in which I have personally found it to be most profoundly troublesome has been the ideological. Here the tendency has always been to naturalise relations of power and subordination in a manner which effaces the social origins of beliefs and judgements. This is a relatively trite manifestation of the ways in which racism can damage or destroy lives. I will be arguing, however, that the process of naturalising racist relations of power and subordination is still the key societal feature which needs to be undermined and eliminated. Denaturalisation of media representations refuses to accept everyday definitions and requires one to live in a state of what I call productive unease. The processes of naturalisation can take many forms in the media. I offer one example here as it indicates for the reader the modest, though I would argue profound, beginnings of my wish to question the media representation of issues of 'race'. In one of the early television documentaries about the British royal family, Queen Elizabeth II was presented with a black Labrador dog. She enquired of its keeper the name of the dog. He answered, 'Nigger, Marm'. Those two words have echoed over the years for me, as a reminder of the ease with which racist discourse can form the bedrock of normality for so many in so many contexts. It has also been a salutary reminder that racism, class, gender and economics are never far apart. Nor are racism and national identity. We have come a long way in media representation and in societal change from the relative comfort of the days when those two words could be uttered with impunity. The bedrock of racist behaviour still lies, however, in concepts of normality. Mapping the media field concerning 'race' and the characteristics of its ideological terrain are the guiding principles of this book.

In Chapter 1 I offer a selective overview of a range of theories of ideology and argue for the importance of gleaning certain features from several theories for the purposes of media analysis. Chapter 2 pursues the possibility of developing approaches to representation which draw upon different methodologies, operable from the micro to the macro level. The third chapter turns to the question of history and representations of issues of 'race', exoticism and Otherness, with particular emphasis on the significance of debates about the nature of 'Orientalism'.

The remainder of the book is devoted to more detailed consideration of examples. These include an Oprah Winfrey show, six feature films which in different ways addressed major issues relating to 'race', the press, news and current affairs reportage of issues of 'race', children's television, and international perspectives on reportage of 'race' issues. There is also a chapter devoted to the relationship between racism and normality. The book concludes with an critical examination of selected research paradigms relevant for those concerned with 'race' and the media, and offers some suggestions for future research.

A note on the reading of this book

I would like to offer a brief note on the order in which the reader may wish to approach this text. I have given considerable emphasis at the beginning of the book to debates about ideology and the significance of a historical approach to representations of 'race'. For those who are interested in addressing matters concerned with theorising and conceptualising the relationship between 'race', ideology and the media, this seems like the most suitable point of entry. If, however, the reader would prefer to consider the media examples and analyses offered before coming to the first three chapters, this is perfectly possible. The book has not been written as a mechanical aid to analysis. It is not about ticking off characteristics of media representations of issues concerning 'race' and awarding points. There *is* a relationship between the analyses and the theories and it is one of tension. It is my argument that this should always be the case. Once a theory becomes unquestioned it can easily slide into dogma, however much it is disguised in the jargon of the day.

It is my hope that this book can offer a bridge between texts whose role is to introduce ideas and debates and the act of engaging in primarily textual research and writing about issues of 'race' and the media.

PART I
Ideology and 'race'

1

On theories of ideology

The aim of this chapter is to explore a number of arguments and debates about ideology and, eventually, about ideology and the media. It is a central platform of this book that, without a working theory of ideology, it is unproductive and often counterproductive to try to make judgements and analyses of issues relating to representations of 'race' in the media. In order to give some substance to this claim, it will first be necessary to consider selectively some theories of ideology. I say 'selectively' because it is not the aim of this book, even if it were possible, to be prescriptive, except in one respect. It is my contention that there is no way that we can write about and research the media and representations of 'race' in the media and stand somehow outside ideology and the ideological. This is a conjecture which the reader may wish to refute. It is, however, important to recognise that theories of ideology and the ideological do not lead to a single or a necessarily fixed position for the reader or the researcher. The value of recognising the significance of ideology in our media work is that it produces and sustains what I will call a sense of *productive unease*.

Contemporary debates about the nature and influence of ideology have many of the characteristics of medieval scholasticism. They are carried out by a small group of intellectuals who are engaged in a pursuit unknown to the majority of the people, the very subjects of their debate. They utilise a language which is understood only by the closest initiates, and draw upon sources unheard of and unstudied by most graduates. These debates also went through a period of confident proclamations and virulent denunciations in the 1970s and early 1980s, while now there is a sullen reappraisal of all that implied certitude. The collapse of the 'communist' regimes in Eastern Europe has been the final blow. For some, another God has failed. For others, perhaps the more astute, there is a recognition that it is time to move on if one is not to be left holding an outmoded theory of ideology. This chapter will argue for a revised and perhaps uneasy interaction with the Enlightenment project. Garnham, (1990) has argued the case for Enlightenment thinking with rigour. More recently McLennan has provided a most dynamic engagement with the ideas associated with the Enlightenment project, whilst Callinicos has combined this approach with a critique of certain postmodern ideas (Callinicos, 1990; McLennan, 1992).

The major buffer against which debates about ideology have been shunted is surely that of postmodernism, which, while it may not be a unified movement, has spawned a large number of thinkers who have moved to positions of cultural, political and conceptual relativism. Books and learned articles in the last decade have featured the word postmodernism in their titles *ad nauseam*. There are numerous references in the literature to the disappearance of 'Grand Narratives' and concepts such as 'Totality'. There is also a finality in some of these rejections which highlights the paradox of postmodernism as a non-totalising movement which is driven to contradict its own methodology. For everything cannot be relative unless 'everything' is a totalising concept (Jay, 1984; Jameson, 1991, pp. 1–67; Bauman, 1992, p. xxiii).

The literature on postmodernism is large and still growing, and the impact of postmodernism has been keenly felt in the field of media and cultural studies. This impact will be discussed where it relates to the main thrust of my argument. For the moment it should be noted that the more thoughtful and constructive works on postmodernism have drawn attention to shortcomings and tendencies towards dogma in certain approaches to the ideological (Hebdige, 1988; Bauman, 1992). Others have taken a much more combative approach to debates about the postmodern, rejecting in particular any tendencies towards relativism (Callinicos, 1989; Norris, 1990; 1993). These debates have significance in relation to representations of 'race' where they impinge upon issues of truth and reason. Many of these writings have an important bearing upon debates about ideology to which this book will return. For the moment, however, it is important to identify as a key issue the centrality of establishing certain ground rules if debates about ideology, the media and representations of 'race' and the postmodern are not to become vacuous linguistic diversions. Norris puts it thus: 'one needs to reassert the basic claim that issues of truth and right reason are inescapably raised by any discourse that presents itself for serious appraisal in the mode of diagnostic commentary' (1990, p. 148).

Part of the main argument which will be put forward here is that the analysis of media representations, and issues relating to representations of 'race', require the evolution of complex and usable diagnostic approaches. It is certain that any 'truth' which is thus sought will not be easy to pin down or to make immutable, but it is equally certain that the media researcher has to be constantly concerned with such a search. The general search for truth within media studies and representations of 'race' has to be just as much concerned with the consequences of what is being identified as with the verifiability of any data. For while those who wish to do so, and are considered capable of doing so, engage in debates about the nature of ideology, the demise of the Grand Narrative, or propositions about the nature of truth, the (material) mass media and the material world which they either represent or reconstruct, continue to assert their presence. For those whose life is lived out in the reality which precedes the media representation, there is less likelihood that debates about issues relating to 'race' will be reducible to mere simulacra. There is, then, a tension between lived, material existence, and the endless stream of media representations of issues of 'race'. This is the context in which diagnostic commentaries on the ideological dimensions of such media representations have to take place.

There is now a very considerable literature concerned with definitions of and debates about the significance of ideology, some of which will be cited here. This will be done selectively in order to trace one line of development through the debates. It is a line which is potentially productive and has a bearing on the understanding of the mass media and their representation of issues of 'race'. The aim here is not to construct a 'new' theory of ideology, as much as to hold in productive tension some of the existing theories.

There is, however, one fundamental principle which will be put forward in the discussion of various theorists of ideology, and that is the principle of contradiction. It is certainly the case that to suggest that contradiction is important is to open the doors to all those who sense the influence of Hegel and are not amused. For as Dunayevskaya has noted, philosophers have never forgiven Hegel for placing contradiction at the centre of reality (1973, p. 23). Ollman comments usefully on the concept, particularly in relation to the work of Marx and Engels:

Either one grants that Marx and Engels ascribe to a philosophy of internal relations and then tries to discover the particular way things are related in their system, or the ways they say things are related will appear manifestly absurd. Hence the unqualified abuse levelled by most critics at Marx's dialectical method. The temporal relations of any entity, as we saw, are its ties to what it was and will be conceived of as its component parts. Each component of an entity is itself a relation whose development is a function of the particular configuration of circumstances in which it stands. It is the result of all these different developments (viewed as occurring within the entity) that determines what the entity as a whole will become. 'Contradiction' is a way of referring to the fact that not all such developments are compatible. In order to progress further in the direction made necessary by its own links of mutual dependence, a component may require that the probable course of change of another component be altered. The developments of the two (as internally related elements in the same covering structure) stand in contradiction, and it is through the working out of such contradictions that the larger entity takes on the form it does.

(Ollman, 1973, pp. 56–7)

The (necessary) abstraction here is of considerable value when approaching the empirical study of social formations and the media, and the discourses, whether about issues of 'race' or identity, that circulate within and between them. Even for those who cannot accept a philosophy of internal relations, however, the debates about the nature of ideology are relevant, bearing as they do upon the operations of the mass media. One other informing principle upon which the arguments offered here are based is taken from Marcuse's interpretation of Hegel, and is concerned with the concept of speculative thinking:

Speculative thinking compares the apparent or given form of things to the potentialities of those same things, and in so doing distinguishes their essence from the accidental state of existence. *This result is achieved not through some process of mystical intuition, but by a method of conceptual cognition, which examines the process whereby each form has become what it is.*

(Marcuse, 1972a, p. 46, emphasis added)

This is an argument which recognises the potential for change in any social formation. The social formation from which one writes is then not conceived as a fixed and stable entity or set of relations, but one in a constant process of becoming. Within certain changing limitations the social formation will always be subject to human agency. If this were not the case, the only purpose in identifying the workings of ideology would be for the functionalist textbook of social theory. The concept of ideology is approached here as necessarily encompassing a totalising engagement with both individual and social perceptions and understanding of 'race', structures of power and subordination, media representations and the question of identities. The choice of this phrase 'totalising engagement' is deliberate. It is important for the moment that the issue of totality is left as something against which theories of ideology are constantly 'tested' – bearing in mind that the very issue of totality is itself ideological! It is equally important that the concept of totality is invoked more as a dynamic process that a summative moment.

What is ideology?

Though the concept of ideology undoubtedly pre-dates Marx and Engels, it is with them that I shall begin this chapter. Larrain (1979) contains a useful overview of debates about ideology, particularly in Chapter 1. Terry Eagleton (1991) has also written a provocative intro-duction. I want to emphasise four major moments in the developing debates about ideology, which have lost none of their force with the invention of postmodernism and the recrudescence of writings about the end of history. The four moments are taken selectively from the work of Gramsci, Marcuse, Althusser and Hall.

Marx and Engels

The key relationship which Marx and Engels identified in their work on ideology was that between social being and consciousness, attribut-ing primacy to the former as a determining factor. They further argued that there was a direct correlation between the ruling ideas in a given period and the ruling class. So the ruling material force was also the ruling intellectual force:

> The individuals composing the ruling class possess, among other things consciousness, and therefore think. Insofar, therefore, as they rule as a class and determine the extent and the compass of an

historical epoch, it is self-evident that they do this in its whole range, hence among other things rule also as thinkers, as producers of ideas, and regulate the production and distribution of the ideas of their age: thus their ideas are the ruling ideas of the epoch.

(Marx and Engels, 1976, p. 59)

The relative crudity of this argument by the standards of contemporary theories and debates is often used as a way of skirting some of the central issues which it does raise. It is true that the argument has been used in the most reductive and destructive ways by those advocating Stalinist politics. It is also true that it has made an easy target for those who would miss the politics in Marx in order to play with the philosophy. It is not a formulation which needs to offer crude predictive insights in order for it to be important. What has to be retained, however, in any meaningful engagement with the concept of ideology, is the *relationship* between social being and consciousness.

There are, nevertheless, several weaknesses in the formulation. It can suggest that a ruling group or class in any period is able to conspire to dominate, even to fool the working class. Such conspiracy theories have been largely discredited as both simple-minded and as bearing little relationship to verifiable conditions in specific social formations. It is also difficult, if this approach is taken literally, to understand how the working class manage to generate any ideas of their own at all (Benton, 1984). There is, however, one important proviso to be made: in order for ideas to be the ruling ideas of the epoch, they do not need to be ideas which are agreed to by the majority of a given population. They are the ruling ideas because they are backed up by the force of law – law provided by those same groups who also furnish the ideas. This is not to say that there are not times when the working class can acquiesce to their own subjugation and exploitation. But whether they do or not is not as important as the power of the state to propagate or attempt to circulate those ideas as 'dominating'.

When the suggestion that social being determines consciousness has been used as dogma, it has led to the labelling of unwelcome or unwanted ideas as 'bourgeois'. This has, in turn, facilitated the removal of the purveyors of those ideas. In its milder manifestations it has been a means of avoiding serious debate or the recognition of political contradictions. It has also led others to suggest that the working class are inherently stupid as a result of social determination. And yet others, often but not exclusively of a Leninist persuasion, adopt a patronising leadership role in relation to the workers in order that those workers made be made to 'see the light'.

Marx and Engels argued that there is a relationship between the economic structures and organisation of a society or social formation (usually referred to as the base), and the social, political, religious and legal systems of that same social formation (usually referred to as the superstructure). There is also the suggestion, strongly put, that the former has a kind of determining effect on the latter. Thus, there is said to be some kind of correlation between the relations of production in a given social formation and the kind of ideas that are produced. The main problem with this aspect of Marx and Engels' concept of ideology has been over the notion of determination, particularly where it is seen as solely an economic determination from the base. It is another of the accusations levelled against Marx by his critics that this approach leads to mechanistic and formulaic interpretations of the operations of societies. It is, however, generally agreed by those not totally hostile to the thought of Marx and Engels that they argued for a dynamic relationship between the base and superstructure. They also argued that the production and reproduction of what Engels called 'real life' played the ultimately determining role in history. This is miles away from some of the opinions attributed to Marx and Engels and is summarised clearly in Engels' letter to Bloch:

> According to the materialist conception of history, the ultimately determining element in history is the production and reproduction of real life. More than this neither Marx nor I have ever asserted. Hence if somebody twists this into saying that the economic element is the only determining one, he [sic] transforms the proposition into a meaningless, abstract, senseless phrase. The economic situation is the basis, but the various elements of the superstructure – political forms of the class struggle and its results, to wit: constitutions established by the victorious class after a successful battle etc., juridical forms, and even the reflexes of all these actual struggles in the brains of the participants, political, juristic, philosophical theories, religious views and their further development into systems of dogmas – also exercise their influence upon the course of the historical struggles and in many cases preponderate in determining their form. There is an interaction of all these elements in which, amid all the endless host of accidents (that is, of things and events whose interconnection is so remote or so impossible of proof that we

can regard it as non-existent, as negligible), the economic movement finally asserts itself as necessary.

(Marx, 1973, p. 487)

The third and, it will be argued here, the most significant strand of Marx's thinking about ideology, is that concerned with real relations and phenomenal forms. This is also discussed by Marx under the categories of essence and appearance. At its most basic, one might characterise this approach as suggesting that things are not always what they appear. Marx argues unequivocally, for instance, that science would be superfluous if the outward appearance and the essence of things coincided directly (Marx, 1973, vol. 2, p. 419). With regard to economic relations, Marx suggests that there is a kind of masking process at work which makes relations of production appear as different from what they are. This may be illustrated by quoting from Benton's description of the wage-form and how it serves to draw a veil over the relationship between capitalist and labourer:

> In the comparable case of the wage-form, the exchange between labour and capitalist takes on the appearance of the buying and selling of a commodity, labour. But, as Marx shows, 'labour' cannot be regarded scientifically as a commodity. What is really being exchanged is a special property of the labourer which is distinguished from other commodities by the fact that its consumption creates a value greater than its own. This property is labour power. The discovery of this hidden reality enables us to distinguish within the working day a part during which the labourer works for himself [sic] (that part during which he creates a value equivalent to that of his labour power) and a part during which he produces value for the capitalist (surplus value). In short, what the wage-form 'disguises', and the concept of labour power 'reveals', is the essential relation of exploitation of the labourer by the capitalist.
>
> (Benton, 1984, p. 164)

This concept of relationships appearing as other than they are in their essence is important in the development of debates about ideology. It may take the form of (re)presenting an exploitative relationship such as the one described above, or it may take the form, for instance, of the media constructing a spurious concept of national unity in times of crisis. Such conceptualisations of the ideological process do, of course, beg many questions. Why, for instance, does not everyone notice the discrepancy between their lived practice and the 'real' foundations of that practice? Who or what brings about the 'appearance' of phenomenal forms so that they do not coincide with reality? Is it all a conspiracy by the ruling groups or classes to deceive those whom they exploit, or is it a 'natural' consequence of relations of production and exchange – a kind of self-perpetuating ideological aura of mystification? And, most important, how is it that not everyone is deceived by phenomenal forms, and some are able to get underneath them to that reality which is so elusive? All these questions are both valid and important to answer. However, the main point in identifying them here is to suggest that debates about ideology are by no means over.

The 'base and superstructure' and 'social being and consciousness' approaches to ideology have been briefly considered, along with that concerning the discrepancy between 'real relations and phenomenal forms'. These three elements or tendencies form the basis for all major debates about the role and function of ideology in relation to the mass media and the re-presentation of issues of 'race'. The debates about what Marx and Engels said and what they meant will continue. Meanwhile, their ideas have been taken up and used by a whole range of scholars and political activists. The thinker who made one of the most significant contributions to our understanding of the general operation of ideology within a specific social formation is the Italian theoretician, Antonio Gramsci.

Antonio Gramsci

Gramsci was born in Ales in Sardinia in 1891. His family were poor and Gramsci's childhood was somewhat lonely. He also had an accident at the age of three which caused him to grow up with a hunched back. He was a good student and studied eventually at the University of Turin, specialising in linguistics. His political activities led him, via membership of the Italian Socialist Party (PSI) to become a leading figure in the Factory Councils Movement which sprang up in Italy in 1917. Modelled upon the Russian Soviets, these councils were particularly concerned with educating and training workers for leadership by providing them with the necessary technical and administrative skills. These moves towards workers' democracy were eventually frustrated, and Gramsci came to recognise the need for a more structured and disciplined party of the working classes. He was a founder member of the Italian Communist Party (PCI) in 1924.

Gramsci's political activities as leader of the PCI lasted from 1924 to

1926, when he was arrested by the fascist government. At his trial in 1928, the Public Prosecutor pointed at Gramsci and announced that 'for twenty years we must stop this brain functioning'. Gramsci therefore spent most of the rest of his life in prison. It was here that he wrote what came to be known as the Prison Notebooks, which contain the bulk of his theoretical ideas. This very brief biographical note is intended as a reminder that Gramsci's political theories were born out of struggle as much as meditation. I will give brief biographies of the Marcuse and Althusser for similar reasons.

Gramsci's ideas are also of great pertinence to all those who are involved in debates about the significance of ideology, and the relationship of ideology to education and the mass media. Gramsci has, in turn, influenced some of the most important media theorists of recent decades.

In an introduction as brief as this, it is not possible to do more than indicate in basic outline some of Gramsci's ideas. I will do this by referring to two concepts which are of crucial significance to the arguments put forward in this text. The first is that of hegemony, the second that of 'contradictory consciousness'.

Hegemony

I have already pointed out that Marx and Engels argued for a determining relationship between ruling ideas and ruling classes in a given social formation. I have also noted that this was linked to an analysis of the relations of production – to an emphasis on the bedrock of the economic as the determining basis of both ideas and the law. Whilst Gramsci would not have disagreed with this basic thesis, he did place more emphasis on those facets of society which related to the ideological superstructures; to religion, the arts, education and the law.

Gramsci recognised the crucial inter-relationship of the state, civil society and the economic in the maintenance of a given social formation. These three categories or distinctions, as Bocock reminds us, are *analytical* (1986). Hence, at any one point it is possible that a given organisation may change its location and belong to one, two or even three of the categories. By the state Gramsci meant the apparatus of 'coercive power which "legally" enforces discipline' on those who do not consent to the relations of power in a given social formation. In other words, the state consists of the means of violence, via the army and the police, and of various spheres of influence of a more or less coercive character, such as the legal and welfare institutions, the civil service and education. Civil society is comprised of those institutions organised and run by people outside the formal sphere of the state and the economic. This would include religious organisations which are not of the state, and could also include certain communication organisations.

By the economic, Gramsci was referring to the mode and relations of production in a given social formation. It is important to remember that, while Gramsci was totally opposed to any simple reduction of the relationship of the state and civil society to determination by the economic, the economic is still there as a 'decisive' factor. Gramsci provides one of the most succinct comments on hegemony in his description of intellectuals as

> the dominant group's 'deputies' exercising the subaltern functions of social hegemony and political government. These comprise:
>
> 1.   The 'spontaneous' consent given by the great masses of the population to the general direction imposed on social life by the dominant fundamental group; this consent is 'historically' caused by the prestige (and consequent confidence) which the dominant group enjoys because of its position and function in the world of production.
> 2.   The apparatus of state coercive power which 'legally' enforces discipline on those groups who do not 'consent' either actively or passively. This apparatus is, however, constituted for the whole of society in anticipation of moments of crisis of command and direction when spontaneous consent has failed.
>
> (Gramsci, 1971, p. 12)

Hegemony is, then, a means by which some form of consent can be secured from those who are dominated to the domination under which they live. It is always backed up by the threat of the force of arms. Hegemonic domination is exerted, to a large extent, by ethical as well as political means. Notions of what constitutes right and wrong in relation to such fundamental issues as who owns the land and the issue of private property are thus often re-presented as purely ethical issues. As long as such questions remain unchallenged, or challenged only at the level of discussion and debate, there will be no need to invoke the repressive powers of the state. Gramsci also points out that, although the leading group in any social formation might be willing to make certain sacrifices in relation to the group over which hegemony is exercised, in order to maintain what he describes as 'a certain compromise equilibrium', economic domination must also continue 'for though hegemony is ethical–political, it must also be economic, must necessarily be based on the decisive function exercised by the leading group in the decisive nucleus of economic activity' (Gramsci, 1971, p. 161).

There is no suggestion by Gramsci that the 'masses' are suffering from some kind of 'false consciousness'. But, it has to be noted, as long as they consent to their domination, there would seem to be a thin line dividing their collective attitude or political disposition from those who had been previously considered as dupes of the dominant ideology. Gramsci answers this problem by suggesting that hegemony is not a natural state of affairs; that it has to be won and maintained and that it can be lost. He also points out that many people are possessed of what might be described as two consciousnesses, or a *contradictory consciousness*.

Contradictory consciousness

The question of whether or not the 'masses' are conscious of their subordination is a thorny one. It has led, in the past to one of two positions. Either they are seen (usually by mechanistic Marxists) as deceived or duped, unable to perceive their true condition, and hence in need of assistance by those who know better, or they are described by more reactionary or liberal thinkers as perfectly well aware of the 'state' of which they are a part – and are, with occasional reservations, quite happy with it. Both of these positions are questionable and difficult to defend by recourse to empirical data. At the very least, what is required is a conceptualisation of the consciousness of ordinary people as allowing for both contradiction and movement. In a sense, it must also allow for people to hold, at one and the same time, political and ideological positions which are incompatible. The crucial issue, if this argument has any validity, is whether and how such contradictions might be identified and overcome. Gramsci's comments on this dilemma are worth quoting in full:

> The active man-in-the-mass [*sic*] has a practical activity, but has no clear theoretical consciousness of his practical activity, which nonetheless involves understanding the world in so far as it transforms it. His theoretical consciousness can indeed be historically in

opposition to his activity. One might almost say that he has two theoretical consciousnesses (or one contradictory consciousness): one which is implicit in his activity and which in reality unites him with all his fellow workers in the practical transformation of the real world; and one, superficially explicit or verbal, which he has inherited from the past and uncritically absorbed. But this verbal conception is not without consequences. It holds together a specific social group, it influences moral conduct and direction of will, with varying efficacy but often powerfully enough to produce a situation in which the contradictory state of consciousness does not permit of any action, any decision or any choice, and produces a condition of moral and political passivity.

(Gramsci, 1971, p. 333)

Gramsci seems to be suggesting that the active political person has a practical sense of working with others in an activity of transforming. There is, however, a problem with what Gramsci describes as the superficially explicit, verbal explanations which people carry with them. These verbal explanations are, as he argues, not without consequence. Gramsci has also argued that conflict on the level of ideology is not psychological or moralistic. Instead, he places stress on its structural and epistemological character.

In this sense, then, the politically active person has to make an epistemological breakout. Gramsci also argues that what is needed is a philosophy which makes possible the construction of an 'intellectual-moral bloc which can make politically possible the intellectual progress of the mass and not only of small intellectual groups'. But this epistemological dilemma, this inherited and uncritically absorbed verbal understanding of the world can, says Gramsci, lead sometimes to political passivity. And he is writing here of the politically active person. It might, therefore, be not unreasonable to assume that the less-than-active person would experience moral and political passivity more often than those of whom Gramsci writes! I will be picking up on the concept of contradictory consciousness in relation to some of the major media representations of issues of 'race'. For the moment I would hope that the concept might offer fertile ground for pondering on a range of media representations and the ways in which we, our friends and others have made sense of them.

To overcome the dilemmas of contradictory consciousness it is necessary, according to Gramsci, to develop critical consciousness:

Critical understanding of self takes place therefore through a struggle of political 'hegemonies' and of opposing directions, first in the ethical field and then in that of politics proper, in order to arrive at the working out at a higher level of one's own conception of reality. Consciousness of being part of a particular hegemonic force (that is to say, political self-consciousness) is the first stage towards a further progressive self-consciousness in which theory and practice will finally be one.

(Gramsci, 1971, p. 333)

It is important to note, for the moment, that Gramsci was writing about people who are politically active. Such people have attained some kind of political consciousness, but are sometimes driven to a state of inactivity. The political realities in contemporary social formations in Europe and North America are such that many would seem not to have reached a state of political consciousness from which to experience contradictions. This is not to suggest for one moment that they are thereby deluded or unconscious. For the opposite of political consciousness is not political unconsciousness but apolitical consciousness. I would further suggest that the apolitically conscious usually side with the forces of domination in a given social formation – at least until their interests have been so threatened that their actions are no longer of immediate relevance. One has only to look at liberal opinion in Nazi Germany, or consider the fate of the liberals in Pinochet's Chile in 1973.

Although it leaves many problems yet to be resolved, Gramsci's concept of contradictory consciousness is a workable way of arguing for differing strata of awareness within individuals and groups, and for recognising the tensions and contradictions which exist within and between them as they encounter possibilities for change and the development of political understanding. This concept could form the basis of a workable and dynamic model of the relationship of audiences to the mass media and to representations of issues of 'race'. It is important to the media analyst precisely because it allows for complex, multi-layered readings of texts and does not fall back on a theory of ideology based on simplistic notions of deception. But if Gramsci provides the media researcher concerned with issues of 'race' with a relatively humane approach to the ideological, the next thinker I will discuss provides some sobering observations on the operations of ideology as capitalism goes from 'strength to strength'.

Herbert Marcuse

The name of Marcuse was publicised in the 1960s when he was represented in the media as the 'guru' of the protest movements, particularly in the United States of America. Paperback editions of his books were re-issued with lurid covers in the late 1960s and early 1970s. The jacket of the 1972 Abacus edition of *Eros and Civilisation* describes Marcuse as a writer 'whose biting analysis of the faults and failings of modern industrial states has made him the spokesman of radical opinion in America'. The front cover has a graphic rendition of a light-skinned, mini-skirted woman seated on a motor cycle, from the engine of which stylised red and orange flames belch out. On her lapel is a large badge which displays a purple heart; round her neck hangs an Iron Cross. The top she wears is black and fastened only at the neck, exposing the bottom curve of her breasts. One is immediately reminded of Marcuse's comments on the 'classics' of literature, philosophy and politics which, in becoming available as paperbacks in the local bookstore

> have left the mausoleum to come to life again ... but coming to life as classics, they come to life as other than themselves; they are deprived of their antagonistic force, of the estrangement which was the very condition of their truth. The intent and function of these works have thus fundamentally changed. If they once stood out in contradiction to the status quo, this contradiction is now flattened out.
>
> (Marcuse, 1972b, p. 24)

Whether or not one judges Marcuse's work as worthy of the designation 'classic', it is certainly the case that he, the Frankfurt School and Hegelian Marxism were not likely to be more widely disseminated merely because they were available in paperback. Indeed, there might have been customers who felt bitterly disappointed having bought the books on the basis of their covers.

Yet, as with so much of Marcuse's work, the short piece which has been quoted is open to the widest misinterpretation, particularly by those on the left or the right who are ill at ease with his analyses of the uncomfortable contradictions inherent in capitalist society. And these contradictions highlight the weaknesses of both the dominant and the subordinate in given social formations.

Marcuse's most quoted book is *One Dimensional Man* (Marcuse, 1972b). In relation to this work, Marcuse is generally described as a pessimist who leaves no space for action by ordinary people to escape their fate: that of total domination in the fields of economics, aesthetics, science and discourse. It is indeed a rather bleak analysis, but one which could usefully be interpreted as an act of *re-cognition* rather than a statement of unchanging and unchangeable reality. It is inconceivable that Marcuse, with his lifelong engagement with the concept of the dialectic, would want readers to merely take his writing at face value – or to ignore that he too was capable of generating productive contradictions in his analysis of the operations of capitalism. If it can only be accepted that, at the very least, Marcuse identified certain tendencies in capitalist social formations, this will be sufficient basis for the re-examination of his work in the 1990s. Before turning to a more detailed consideration of *One Dimensional Man*, I will offer a few brief biographical details about Marcuse.

Born in 1898 into a prominent Jewish family in Berlin, Marcuse was educated at the Augusta Gymnasium and the Universities of Berlin and Freiburg where he studied under Heidegger. His academic life in Germany was brought to an end by the coming to power of the Nazis and he left for Geneva where he taught for a year before emigrating to the United States of America. Here he worked, from 1934–40 at Columbia University in the Frankfurt Institute for Social Research which had been transferred there from Germany. His colleagues included Erich Fromm, Max Horkheimer and Theodor Adorno. His later academic life was spent in various universities, including Harvard, Brandeis and the University of California. He also spent periods as Director of Studies at the Ecole Pratiques des Hautes Etudes in Paris. He died in 1979.

Marcuse argued in *One Dimensional Man* that there was a strong tendency in contemporary society for domination to be exercised by technology rather than terror. He saw efficiency and the general rise in the standard of living as helping to provide the necessary environment for the development of what he described as one-dimensional thought:

> The means of mass transportation and communication, the commodities of lodging, food and clothing, the irresistible output of the entertainment and information industry carry with them prescribed attitudes and habits, certain intellectual and emotional reactions which bind the consumers more or less pleasantly to the producers and, through the latter, to the whole. The products indoctrinate and

manipulate; they promote a false consciousness which is immune against its falsehood. And as these beneficial products become available to more individuals in more social classes, the indoctrination they carry ceases to be publicity; it becomes a way of life. It is a good way of life – much better than before – and as a good way of life, it militates against qualitative change. Thus emerges a pattern of one-dimensional thought and behaviour in which ideas, aspirations and objectives that, by their content, transcend the established universe of discourse and action are either repelled or reduced to the terms of this universe. They are redefined by the rationality of the given system and of its qualitative extension.

(Marcuse, 1972b, p. 24)

Marcuse's prose style is not one which always wins him supporters. He has been accused of writing here a work which is a grandiose journalism of doom. Yet it is worth looking in detail at what is suggested here, for the language is, I believe, carefully chosen and not to be dismissed as mere bombast. To suggest that products produce a 'false consciousness'; that they 'indoctrinate', is enough to bring howls of derision from those who see themselves as defenders of the pleasures of the commodity. But to interpret this as Marcuse not wishing people to have washing machines or stereos is drastically to miss the point. For the false consciousness of which he writes is not that of a populace unaware of what they are doing. It is, in fact, the true consciousness of those who have adopted consumerism as a way of life to the exclusion of other possible ways. In the 1990s, in the United Kingdom at least, there is a sense in which consumerism is not as rabid as it was in the heydays of aggressive Thatcherism. But that does not mean that the ideology of consumerism has been superseded, merely that it has been tempered by recession and celebrated by many analysts of postmodernity. For one of the senses in which Marcuse speaks of falseness is the falseness of believing that the product is beneficial enough. Marcuse was wrong if he believed that capitalism would always produce the goods necessary for an ever improving standard of living. He was right, however, in suggesting that under capitalism consumerism would be seen as the good way of life. One of the main strengths of one dimensional thought is that it works to ensure that what is transitory, and comes about as the result of the actions of men and women and their relationships of power and subordination, seems timeless and natural.

One of the consequences of Marcuse's analysis is, he suggests, that if one tries to conceptualise the world differently, one's arguments will not be accepted as valid for consideration until they have been reduced to the terms of the existing universe of discourse. There have been many examples of this in broadcasting and a later chapter will consider in detail the operations of the existing universe of discourse in the representation of the 1992 Los Angeles riots.

Marcuse's interest in the development of various modes of discourse led him, unsurprisingly, to make enquiries about language use, in which he was influenced by the early work of Roland Barthes. Marcuse did not argue for any simplistic notion of a language of domination through which the people were controlled. Instead, he put forward the more paradoxical notion that control could be exercised through freedom of choice:

> Language not only reflects these controls but becomes itself an instrument of control even where it does not transmit orders but information; where it demands, not obedience, but freedom. . . .
>
> This language controls by reducing the linguistic forms and symbols of reflection, abstraction, development, contradiction; by substituting images for concepts. It denies or absorbs the transcendent vocabulary; it does not search for but establishes and imposes truth and falsehood. But this kind of discourse is not terroristic. It seems unwarranted to assume that the recipients believe, or are made to believe, what they are being told. The new touch of the magic-ritual language rather is that people don't believe it, or don't care, and yet act accordingly.
>
> (Marcuse, 1972b, pp. 91–2)

There are similarities between the suggestion that people do not care about the messages which they receive and yet still act upon them and the notion put forward by Gramsci of contradictory consciousness. The difference, however, is that Marcuse does not offer any way out of this dilemma, whilst Gramsci argues for the development of what he calls political consciousness.

We will see that the concept of discourse, while not new, becomes increasingly central to debates about media representations. I will say more about the importance of discourse and discursivity in the next chapter. Marcuse argued that there is often a process of transformation located within discursive processes. He suggested that, over time, texts and images are re-presented as other than they had been, particularly if what they had been contained opposition to the status quo. So, as noted earlier, the classics of bourgeois art may lose their oppositional function at the same time as they become widely available. In a similar vein, Marcuse comments on the characters to be found in literature whose role was oppositional, such as the prostitute, the artist, the adulteress, the outcast. These characters, according to Marcuse, stood for another dimension which was irreconcilably antagonistic to the order of business. This was also in opposition to the reputed 'good' in the figures of moral or spiritual leaders, who often sustained the moral order. Within the bourgeois moral and political order, such characters were indeed oppositional or antagonistic.

> To be sure, these characters have not disappeared from the literature of advanced industrial society, but they survive essentially transformed. The vamp, the national hero, the beatnik, the neurotic housewife, the gangster, the star, the charismatic tycoon perform a function very different from and even contrary to that of their cultural predecessors. They are no longer images of another way of life but rather freaks or types of the same life, serving as an affirmation rather than a negation of the established world.
>
> (Marcuse, 1972b, p. 59)

The representation of the world in fiction is not the only mode in which linguistic transformations take place. Marcuse cites from Roethlisberger and Dickson an interview with a worker about the level of his wages:

> Another example: a worker B makes a general statement that the piece rates of his job are too low. The interview reveals that 'his wife is in the hospital and that he is worried about the doctor's bills he has incurred'. In this case the latent content of his complaint consists of the fact that B's present earnings, due to his wife's illness, are insufficient to meet his current financial obligations. Such translation changes significantly the meaning of the actual proposition. The untranslated statement formulates a general condition in its generality ('wages are too low'). It goes beyond the particular condition in the particular factory and beyond the worker's particular situation. In this generality, and only in this generality, the statement expresses a sweeping indictment which takes the particular case as a manifestation of a universal state of affairs, and insinuates that the latter might not be changed by the former.
>
> (Roethlisberger and Dickson, 1947, cited in Marcuse, 1972b, p. 96–7)

In this way, the personalising of an industrial complaint tends to obstruct what Marcuse describes as 'the real concreteness' of the case, which is the universal character of the complaint. This type of analysis does not have the sophistication we have come to expect from more recent examples such as the work of Kress, Hodge and Fowler (Hodge and Kress, 1988, 1993; Fowler *et al.*, 1979). It does, however, have one distinctive characteristic: it is based upon a detailed consideration of the processes of transformation and disjuncture between linguistic forms and the relations of power and domination for which they stand but do not immediately articulate.

Marcuse's work is important for the contribution it can make to our understanding of the processes outlined above. His conceptualisation of the closing of the universe of discourse is probably of most significance to our understanding of the processes of representation utilised by the mass media. His suggestion that literature or history may reappear as other than they had been was borne out, for instance, in London in the 1980s by the existence of boutiques called simply 'Che Guevara' and hamburger houses called 'Strikes' which were decorated with elegantly framed images of industrial disputes from the past. That the examples are there to be seen is not as great a vindication of Marcuse's analytical approach as the fact that they are accepted by the consumer virtually without comment.

Marcuse's pessimism has been rightly attacked for being too suffocating. His perceptive insights have, on the other hand, often been ignored or adopted by others with little acknowledgement of their source. Many of the arguments which Marcuse made found an echo in the more structuralist approaches to language, ideology and the media found in our next thinker.

Louis Althusser

Louis Althusser exercised enormous intellectual influence in Europe and beyond in the 1960s and 1970s. Only those aspects of his work which can usefully be held in a productive tension with the other theories and ideas already cited will be drawn on here. There could hardly be – on the surface at least – two theorists of ideology who seem, more dissimilar than Althusser and Marcuse. Althusser was born in Algiers in 1918. After the Second World War he finished his education as a student at the Ecole Normale Supérieure where he worked under the supervision of Gaston Bachelard and was, subsequently, to become a prominent teacher. Althusser was a member of the French Communist Party from 1948. In 1980 he was admitted to St Anne's Psychiatric Hospital in Paris after he had confessed to the killing of his wife. He died in 1991.

There are three books for which Althusser is best known. These are *For Marx* (1977), *Reading Capital* (1970), and *Lenin and Philosophy and Other Essays* (1971b). In the latter volume is to be found the essay 'Ideology and Ideological State Apparatuses', which is the main source for his theoretical conception of ideology. Althusser declared himself to be totally opposed to humanist approaches to Marxism and to the various Hegelian manifestations of it. His intellectual trajectory is not a happy one, and it must be said that many of the sustained critiques of his work, some of which are laced with bile, tend to look more convincing as the years pass. A good short biography followed by reasoned critique can be found in Jay (1984, pp. 385–422), and a scholarly overview is provided by Benton (1984). It should be noted that many of those who were once disciples of Althusser have, as critiques of his work grew more convincing, been driven into silence.

Althusser drew upon Gramsci's concept of hegemony and developed the notion of what he termed the 'Ideological State Apparatuses' (ISAs). These included the family, the Church, the mass media and the school. For Althusser, the school had replaced the Church as the dominant ISA. All ISAs contributed to the same result: the reproduction of capitalist relations of production and exploitation. These ISAs are, of course, backed up by the Repressive State Apparatuses (RSAs) such as the police and the army. Of the ISAs he wrote:

> Each of them contributes towards this single result in the way proper to it. The political apparatus by subjecting individuals to the political state ideology, the 'indirect' (parliamentary) or 'direct' (plebiscitary or fascist) 'democratic' ideology. The communications apparatus by cramming every 'citizen' with daily doses of nationalism, chauvinism, liberalism, moralism etc., by means of the press, the radio and television. The same goes for the cultural apparatus (the role of sport in chauvinism is of first importance), etc. The religious apparatus by recalling in sermons and the other great ceremonies of Birth, Marriage and Death, that man is only ashes, unless he loves his neighbour to the extent of turning the other cheek to whoever strikes first. The family apparatus . . . but there is no need to go on.
>
> (Althusser, 1971a, p. 154)

A 'cramming' or banking model of media influence seems to be suggested here. In other places, Althusser is not as simplistic, though there is, as with Marcuse, a sense of identifying real issues without necessarily providing satisfactory answers. In the above quotation this is borne out by the reference to the role of sport in chauvinism. Althusser then goes on to discuss education in no less strident terms: 'Nevertheless, in this concert, one ideological state apparatus certainly has the dominant role, although hardly anyone lends an ear to its music: it is so silent! This is the school' (Althusser, 1971a, p. 146).

There are two aspects of Althusser's theory of ideology which are, with qualifications, relevant to the consideration of identity and the media, and representations of 'race'. These are the suggestions that ideology is based upon a *relationship*, and the conceptualisation of the material existence of ideology.

Ideology, for Althusser, is a representation of the imaginary relationship of individuals to their real conditions of existence. He explains this with relative clarity in a passage which carries traces of the earlier Marxist contention that real relations may be belied by phenomenal forms:

> So ideology is a matter of the lived relation between men [*sic*] and their world. This relation, that only appears as 'conscious' on condition that it is unconscious, in the same way only seems to be simple on condition that it is complex, that it is not a simple relation, but a relation between relations, a second degree relation. In ideology men do indeed express, not the relation between them and their conditions of existence, but the way they live the relation between them and their conditions of existence: this presupposes both a real relation and an 'imaginary', 'lived' relation.
>
> (Althusser, 1977, p. 233)

The most important aspect of this suggestion is that ideology is not a pre-existent body of beliefs which are somehow imposed upon, or merely inculcated, hammered in to an unsuspecting and innocent mass of people. It is, instead, a process and relationship of living. Inasmuch as there is any validity in this suggestion, it clearly points to the need for changing relationships of living if we wish to change ideologies. But it must also be remembered that lived relationships are not only those between people and people, but also between people and things. Here it is necessary to return to a consideration of the lived relationship of people with commodities, people with 'knowledge', people with institutions, people and power. In order to do so, it is essential to examine in detail the construction of the discourses through which these relationships are normally mediated, and to consider the possibility of working out alternative discourses. These discourses are not, however, to be conceptualised in a purely abstract way, and it is here that Althusser's suggestion that ideology has a material existence is helpful:

> I shall therefore say that, where only a single subject (such and such an individual) is concerned, the existence of the ideas of his [sic] belief is material in that his ideas are his material actions inserted into material practices governed by material rituals which are themselves defined by the material ideological apparatus from which derive the ideas of that subject.
>
> (Althusser, 1977, p. 499)

The materiality of ideological practice is something that should not be reduced to the discourses which are in play in any given social formation. Although discourse can be argued as an essential component in the ideological relationship, it is only one component among many. The materiality of other components in the relationship such as, for instance, the dole queue, the 'Last Night of the Proms', the family group or viewing 'unit', and television shows such as *The Price is Right* have all to be recognised. The latter, with its weekly call to contestants to 'Come on down!' might have been structured with Althusser's theory of ideology in mind:

> I shall then suggest that ideology 'acts' or 'functions' in such a way that it 'recruits' subjects among individuals (it recruits them all), or 'transforms' the individuals (it transforms them all) by that very precise operation which I have called interpellation or hailing, and which can be the most commonplace everyday police (or other) hailing: 'Hey, you there!'
>
> (Althusser, 1971a, p. 174)

A very selective aspect of Althusser's theory of ideology has been presented here. Where he has (rightly) come in for some of the strongest criticism has been over his tendency to write mainly about the reproduction of social formations. He could only get himself out of the strait-jacket he had assembled by insisting that change could occur, but that this would happen by means of the class struggle, the 'motor of history'. Such a struggle would take place, it may be assumed, outside the domains of ideological domination and in the field of revolutionary contestation. In the meantime, ideological domination is virtually total for the mass of the people. The problems with this kind of argument are enormous and have been highlighted by Althusser's critics. Althusser sometimes tipped over into open patronisation, as in his now infamous and ill-considered remarks about teachers who attempt to teach

> against the ideology, the system and the practices in which they are trapped. They are a kind of hero. But they are rare and how many (the majority) do not even begin to suspect the 'work' the system (which is bigger than they are and crushes them) forces them to do, or worse, put all their heart and ingenuity into performing it with the most advanced awareness (the famous new methods!). So little do they suspect it that their own devotion contributes to the main-tenance and nourishment of this ideological representation of the School, which makes the School, today as 'natural', indispensable-useful and even beneficial for our contemporaries as the Church was 'natural', indispensable and generous for our ancestors a few cen-turies ago.
>
> (Althusser, 1971a, p. 157)

While condemnation of Althusser's patronisation and pessimism is important here, it is counter-productive if we miss those dimensions of his theory which are both helpful and productive (Jay, 1984; Hall, 1996).

I will now discuss a theorist of ideology who is, in many respects, the most important for the purposes of this work, namely Stuart Hall. His writings represent a long-term engagement with ideology, popular culture, racism, the media, and education.

Stuart Hall

Hall was until 1996 Professor of Sociology at the Open University. Before that (1969–79) he was Director of the (then) Centre for Con-temporary Cultural Studies at the University of Birmingham. He was one of the founders of the *New Left Review* and has, over the last twenty years, written a great deal on theories of ideology. He has turned his attention to the relationship between various theories of ideology and political realities such as Thatcherism and what he has

termed 'authoritarian populism' in the sustenance of particular ideological relationships. The question of racism has also been one to which
he has returned many times. His most recent work has been concerned
with concepts of 'identity'.

It is not possible in this brief section to do justice to the breadth and
sophistication of Hall's writings. He is, however, of particular importance because of his constant appraisal and reappraisal of the theorists
already mentioned, and many more who have entered the field of
debate in recent years. Some of Hall's arguments in relation to ideology will be outlined before considering his approaches to the
ideological significance of the media.

A major influence on Hall over the years has undoubtedly been
Gramsci, particularly Gramsci's concept of hegemony. Hall's Marxism
is non-dogmatic and open to careful and considered development in
relation to particular conjunctures. He does not bring a formulaic
creed to the world in order to interpret it, nor has he ever been a party
hack. He has, indeed, written of 'Marxism without guarantees' (Hall,
1983), of the open horizon of Marxist theorising. Unlike so many
theorists of the recent period, Hall has always striven to relate his
theoretical excursions to concrete examples. These have varied from
the mundane or quotidian to the overtly political. One of his most
significant recent statements is bound up with his analysis of Thatcherism in Britain (Hall, 1988). He has also combined his analyses of
political conjunctures with an extensive engagement with and analysis
of theories of signification, representation and discursive practice.
Much of this work has taken the form of research into specific moments
of signification, from single programmes (Hall *et al.*, 1976) to a broader
engagement with the reportage of specific issues over a period of time
(Hall *et al.*, 1978).

It is precisely Hall's ability to hold together multiple developments
in theory in order to further the potential for change which makes his
work so important in relation to the construction of an open and
genuinely critical theory of ideology. Theorising, for Hall, enables us
'to grasp, understand and explain – to produce a more adequate
knowledge of – the historical world and its processes; and thereby to
inform our practice so that we may transform it' (Hall, 1988, p. 36).

Hall has written at some length on the issue of 'false consciousness'
and has asked how it can be that this condition always seems to apply
to others and never to those who identify it so clearly. The theory of
false consciousness assumes, says Hall, an empiricist relation of the

subject to knowledge. The empiricist relation suggests that the real world is available directly to our consciousness, where it can indelibly imprint its meanings and interests. If, therefore, people cannot perceive particular 'truths', there must be something obscuring them – a 'cloud of unknowing' (Hall, 1988, p. 44). Not only does Hall reject this formula, he also points out that it is one which presupposes a moment either could or will come when the veil will be lifted and true sight will be restored to those whose vision has been ideologically impaired. This moment would, in such formulaic approaches, have to be that of the Revolution. This is unacceptable to Hall intellectually: 'as if anybody would have time to reconstruct their vision, overnight ... '. He also interprets it as a model of the ideological process which is a 'confidence trick' view of how ideas are constructed and changed.

Yet, while at pains to reject mechanistic notions of false consciousness, Hall is well aware that there is a serious problem in relation to the social distribution of knowledge which is, in its very particular way, often 'false'. He addresses the issue through the notion of one-sidedness.

> One-sided explanations are always a distortion. Not in the sense that they are a lie about the system, but in the sense that a 'half-truth' cannot be the whole truth about anything. With those ideas, you will always represent a part of the whole. You will thereby produce an explanation which is only partially adequate – and in that sense, 'false'. Also, if you use only 'market categories and concepts' to understand the capitalist circuit as a whole, there are literally many aspects of it which you cannot see. In that sense, the categories of market exchange obscure and mystify our understanding of the capitalist process: that is they do not enable us to see or formulate questions about them, for they render other aspects invisible.
>
> (Hall, 1983, p. 73)

Here, one is a little nearer to the closing of the universe of discourse of which Marcuse has written. In more recent work, Hall has argued his case more fully. He suggests that ideologies may not be automatically and in total attached to their appropriate classes, 'but this does not mean that the production and transformation of ideology in society could proceed free of or outside the structuring lines of force of power and class' (Hall, 1988, p. 45). In other words, it cannot be predicted that working-class people will think one way and middle-class people another, particularly in relation to their political understanding, but neither can the very real power bases in social formations, which do leave power very much in the hands of a particular class, be ignored. Hall argues that there is no unitary logic of inference or deduction from one to another, though this does not negate the proposition that 'material interests help to structure ideas and the proposition that position in the social structure has the tendency to influence the direction of social thought . . . ' (Hall, 1988, p. 45). He also argues that the relations of power in a social formation are, to some extent, apparent in the 'symbolic power' of dominant ideas:

> The social distribution of knowledge is skewed. And since the social institutions most directly implicated in its formation and transmission – the family/school/media triplet – are grounded in and structured by class relations that surround them, the distribution of the available codes with which to decode or unscramble the meaning of events in the world, and the languages we use to construct interests, are bound to reflect the unequal relations of power that obtain in the area of symbolic production as in other spheres. Ruling or dominant conceptions of the world do not directly prescribe the mental content of the illusions that supposedly fill the heads of the dominated classes. But the circle of dominant ideas does accumulate the symbolic power to map or classify the world for others; its classifications do acquire not only the constraining power of dominance over other modes of thought but also the inertial authority of habit and instinct. It becomes the horizon of the taken-for-granted: what the world is and how it works for all practical purposes.
>
> (Hall, 1988, p. 44)

The classifications to which Hall here refers have clear epistemological implications which relate back to the arguments of Gramsci. Drawing heavily upon Gramsci's work, Hall re-stresses that hegemony is not a natural state of affairs. It is something which has to be striven for and won. And it is something which can be lost. Here Hall differs from Althusser, who argued that Ideological State Apparatuses simply reproduced already existing ideologies. For Hall, the process by which an ideology reproduces itself is a contested and contradictory one. But while Hall is critical of Althusser's functionalist tendencies, he is much more interested in his work on the construction of 'subjects' through ideology. Althusser's concept of interpellation or hailing has already been mentioned. Hall, following Pecheux (1982), suggests that subjects who are already formed may nevertheless be interpellated into new discursive relations. He gives as an example the way that Thatcherism depended for the logic and unity of its discourse upon the subjects being addressed adopting specific 'subject positions'. This means that the discourse of Thatcherism can

> only be read or spoken if it is enunciated from the imaginary position of knowledge of the self-reliant, self-interested, self-sufficient taxpayer – Possessive Individual Man [sic]; or the 'concerned patriot'; or the subject passionately attached to individual liberty and passionately opposed to the incursion of liberty that occurs through the state; or the respectable housewife; or the native Briton.
>
> (Hall, 1988, p. 49)

This concept of hailing to other discursive positions is something which will be utilised later in relation to the analysis of specific media texts. It is also something which, Hall argues, has not been adequately tackled by those theories of language and the creation of subjectivities which rely only on Oedipal identifications exemplified in and through language. Hall is thinking here of Lacan's re-reading of Freud and Althusser's appropriation of Lacan in his development of a theory of ideology.

The development of Hall's theory of ideology leads towards the questioning not only the social relations of production in a given social formation, but also the processes and discursive formations through which meaning is made, sustained or changed. This also involves the questioning of the relationship of individual subjects to the discourses which help to sustain or change their subjectivities. It is thus important, from the point of view of this book, to investigate the specific signifying practices employed in the mass media as they represent issues of 'race'. This does not mean, however, that reductive arguments should be utilised which suggest that discourse and ideology constitute the total ideological domain – thus ignoring the material relations and conditions of living of those subjects who are represented in and through media discourses.

The importance of Hall's reading of Gramsci's concept of hegemony as something which must be 'constantly renewed, re-enacted', needs to be stressed. For, as Hall reminds us, this 'implies a conception of the process of social reproduction as continuous and contradictory – the very opposite of a functional achievement' (Hall, 1988, p. 54).

Hall on ideology and the media

Most of Hall's research has been concerned with explaining, at various levels of complexity, the workings, manifestations and implications of ideology through both the media and the educational process. Two key pieces here are 'Culture, the Media and the "Ideological Effect"' and 'The Rediscovery of "Ideology": Return of the Repressed in Media Studies' (Hall, 1977; 1982). In these pieces, Hall traces a tentative but sure line of development through from Marx and Engels to Gramsci and on to the more recent rediscovery of Volosinov's work on language, and of Poulantzas on political theory. Once again, Hall is at pains to avoid simplistic or reductive arguments or claims about the influence of the media.

In the former of the two pieces cited, Hall extracts key moments in the development of the thought of Marx, Engels and Gramsci. He spends some time considering Marx's description of the market as a representation of 'a system which requires both production and exchange, as if it consisted of exchange only' (Hall, 1977, p. 325). This representation means that the foundations of capitalist production are not immediately visible. Hall argues that it is necessary to conceptualise the operations of ideology in a similar way. For, he argues, ideology is not something hidden, concealed, but 'what is most open, apparent, manifest – what takes place on the surface and "in view of all men" [*sic*]. What is hidden, repressed or inflected out of sight, are its real foundations. This is the source of its unconsciousness' (Hall, 1977, p. 245).

Very often, ideology works though what is known as common sense. Following Gramsci, Hall argues that common sense helps us to classify our world in simple but meaningful terms.

> It is precisely its 'spontaneous' quality, its transparency, its 'naturalness', its refusal to be made to examine the premises on which it founded, its resistance to change or correction, its effect of instant recognition, and the closed circle in which it moves which makes common sense, at one and the same time, 'spontaneous', ideological, and unconscious.

> (Hall, 1977, p. 325)

Again and again, Hall attempts to establish a viable framework for comprehending the necessary contradiction embedded in a theory of ideology which does not speak of 'false' consciousness, but of unconsciousness as the basis upon which ideology can operate openly.

Echoing in another register the concept of the closing of the universe of discourse, Hall suggests that we cannot learn through common sense how things are, but only where they fit into the existing scheme of things. This is clearly an attempt to move away from the problematic associated with theories of ideology which describe the mass of the populace as duped. It is significant because it allows that one may choose, both logically and openly to act in specific ways according to specific criteria, but still ignore the bases upon which one's thought and action are founded. These are, as Hall argues, 'hidden, repressed or inflected out of sight'.

There is, some might argue, an implication here that if the real foundations of ideology were brought to the surface, the human subject would change – and presumably move towards the construction of and participation in an alternative ideology. This is a thorny question for all theorists of ideology, for it does seem to return, in another guise, to a notion of misinformation or absence of information which is not so very far removed from having a consciousness which is false. Against this possibility, it can be argued that there is a fundamental difference between conceptualising the operations of ideology as based upon false or 'incorrect' consciousness, and arguing that thought and action may be undertaken, for much of the time, on the basis of clear reasoning and a common-sense understanding of the world. The former conceptualisation implies a deceit of the 'ordinary' person by a class or power group in a given social formation. The latter suggests that consciousness is only partially rooted in ideological matters because it is oblivious to its own foundations.

Both these positions have considerable implications for the present work. The former (that which is associated with 'false consciousness') can lead towards an understanding of the media which is based upon a moralising or evangelising approach. The researcher is the one who has 'seen through' the falseness of ideological operations and can expose the trick which is being played. The second position (that which conceptualises the foundations of ideology as unconscious – or less controversially 'out of consciousness') suggests a very different approach to Media Studies.

Hall, drawing heavily upon the work of Poulantzas (1965), goes on to develop theoretically the concepts, first discussed with regard to the operation of the market, of a process of masking and displacing of real relations of production and exchange. There is, Hall suggests, a tendency for the class nature of the state to be masked through a series of 'characteristic inflexions'. First, there is shifting from an emphasis in social formations upon the importance of production, towards an emphasis upon the process of exchange. Second, there is a tendency towards fragmentation in the way in which various classes are represented in popular and official discourse as individuals. Third, in terms of political economy, there is a tendency towards binding individuals into a community of consumers. A similar process can be identified in the juridico-political field, where 'political classes and class relations are fragmented into individual subjects (the citizen, the voter), and then recombined into a new "unity" as the Nation' (Hall, 1977, p. 337).

The tendency towards shifting, fragmenting and binding is then related by Hall to Gramsci's concept of hegemony, and he reiterates the importance of securing legitimacy for these tendencies and winning consent for the ways in which they are represented in and to particular social formations.

> Here, in the structures of political representation and of 'separate powers' and of liberties and freedoms, which lie at the core of bourgeois-liberal formal democracy, both as superstructures and as lived ideologies, the operation of one class upon another in shaping and producing consent (through the selective forms of social knowledge made available) is rendered invisible: this exercise of ideological class domination is dispersed through the fragmentary agencies of a myriad of individual wills and opinions, separate powers; this fragmentation of opinion is then reorganised into an imaginary coherence in the mystical unity of 'the consensus', into which free and sovereign individuals and their wills spontaneously flow.
>
> (Hall, 1977, p. 339)

It is only after considering the complexities of the economic and juridico-political spheres that Hall moves on to an attempt at situating the media and their ideological potential. He rejects the possibility of any unitary ideological discourse into which a range of social knowledge can be processed, arguing instead that many more 'worlds' than that of a 'unitary ruling class' have to be 'selectively represented and classified in the media's apparently open and diverse manner' (1977, p. 341). This process becomes, Hall suggests, the site of an enormous ideological labour. Through such a process of ideological work, the media can be observed to actively rule in and rule out certain realities, 'offering the maps and codes which mark out territories and assign problematic events and relations to explanatory contexts, helping us not simply to know more about "the world" but to make sense of it' (Hall, 1977, p. 341).

This process of the classifying in and out of various 'realities' is not, Hall stresses many times, related to a single discourse but to what he terms a 'plurality of dominant discourses'. He also recognises that not all audiences will take from the media the messages which those who are involved in the encoding process attempt to provide. Nevertheless, the overall intention of what Hall calls 'effective communication' must be to move the audience towards the preferred reading, 'and hence get him [sic] to decode within the hegemonic framework'. In this sense the concept of active readership would have to be conceptualised as not so much 'natural', but constrained or effected through complex histories and complex relationships with texts.

Finally, and perhaps most important, Hall argues that it is unhelpful to try to understand the operations of ideology in relation to media through reference to concepts of partisanship or bias. Instead, he concentrates upon the paradoxical situation whereby there has to be an overall 'unity' in a given social formation which will bind together opposing positions. It is necessary, says Hall, for certain limits to argument, presuppositions, terms of reference, etc. to be shared in order for disagreement to take place.

> It is this underlying 'unity' which the media underwrite and repro-
> duce: and it is in this sense that the ideological inflexion of media
> messages are [sic] best understood, not as 'partisan' but as funda-
> mentally oriented 'within the mode of reality of the state'.
>
> (Hall, 1977, p. 346)

The move by Hall and others towards understanding how the complex processes of 'winning consent' are accomplished or sustained leads one to a growing recognition of the importance of the discursive, of discourse. Hall would not wish to suggest that discourse is the central feature of hegemonic domination, or that there are not extra-discursive factors which play a crucial role in the maintenance or change of specific social formations. It is, nevertheless, only possible to make sense of the world through the appropriation of language in discourse (Hall, 1982, pp. 70–1). Hall also argues that discourse can have the effect of 'sustaining certain "closures"', of establishing certain systems of equivalence between what could be assumed about the world and what could be said to be true'. Deflecting argument away from an emphasis on the necessary intentions of those who produce media messages, Hall suggests that, in the critical paradigm, ideology is more a function of the discourse and of the logic of social processes, rather than being directly linked to the intention of the agent.

Hall has also taken careful account of developments in theories of discourse, but is still drawn back to the writings of Gramsci in order to relate the concept of hegemony to the contemporary operations of ideology. The most important advances in the theoretical under-standing of how ideology functions are well encapsulated here: 'That is the contemporary revolution: the notion that the arena or medium in which ideology functions is one of signification, representation, dis-cursive practices. That is the intervening term that has changed the nature of the debate' (Hall, 1988, p. 73).

Finally, in a recent piece, Hall has acknowledged the influence on his thinking of key arguments put forward by Althusser. I offer it as the final quotation in this chapter because it draws us back to the impor-tance of recognising a trajectory which can be traced through from Marx and which still wishes to insist that there are 'real conditions' out there in a world beyond the re-presentations offered in the mass media.

> Finally, let us consider Althusser's use of this phrase, 'the real conditions of existence' – scandalous (within contemporary cultural theory) because here Althusser commits himself to the notion that social relations actually exist apart from their ideological repre-sentations or experiences. Social relations do exist. We are born into them. They exist independent of our will. They are real in their structure and tendency. We cannot develop a social practice without representing those conditions to ourselves in one way or another, but the representations do not exhaust their effect. Social relations exist independent of mind, independent of thought. And yet they can only be conceptualised in thought, in the head.
>
> (Hall, 1996, p. 25)

It is appropriate to leave this overview of Hall's work with his refer-ences to discursive practices and real social relations. There is much more to be said about this development in the analysis of the opera-tions of ideology in relation to the representation of issues concerned with 'race'. Before doing so, however, I will summarise the various epistemological, political and re-presentational implications of the theoretical developments which have been discussed so far.

Towards a working definition of the ideological process

Conceptualisations of the workings of ideology are notoriously difficult to formalise without some kind of reductionism. E. P. Thompson
(1978) has made great sport with the theoretical approaches of Louis
Althusser, characterising them as orreries or analogies which tell us
more about their author than about their object of reference. Thompson
also warns against analogies which can become petrified into concepts,
such as has often happened to the analogy of base and superstructure
in Marxist theory. As Thompson rather grandly proclaims, 'The grave-
yard of philosophy is cluttered with grand systems which mistook
analogies for concepts' (Thompson, 1978, p. 296). With this warning in
mind, it might still be suggested that the process or lived relationship
which is ideology is best described as a state of political, psychic,
economic, aesthetic, pedagogic and discursive tension. It is, of course,
possible that objections might be raised to this apparently all embrac-
ing collection of epithets. The stress, however, needs to be put upon the
state of tension existing between them. They may be considered as a
force field, the strength and impact of which depend upon relations of
power and subordination. This ideological force field is sustained or
challenged by those very subjects upon which and through which it
acts, and by the structural and subjective conditions under which they
live and interact at the personal and social level. It is also a force field
which exists only in time and is manifested in the lived relationships of
human beings and their social organisation. 'Ideology' is not directly
visible, but can only be experienced and/or comprehended. What is
visible is a range of social and representational manifestations which
are rooted in relationships of power and subordination. Representations of 'race' are an integral part of this range.

The formulations gleaned from various theorists thus far will now
be drawn together into some kind of order. The exposition here is of
necessity linear. The possible importance of the points, however, can
only be gauged if they are held in productive tension.

Speculative thinking is a central factor in any workable theory of
ideology. A materialist theory of ideology has to recognise a determi-
native relationship between social being and consciousness, although
this does not mean that, at any one point in any one social formation,
the relationship is singular or unitary within social groups and classes.

The relationship between social being and consciousness is both changing and changeable, though the former is more likely to effect a change in the latter.

The formulation, first put forward by Marx and Engels, that ruling ideas are ruling class ideas, needs qualification – for ruling ideas do not have to be agreed to in order to operate successfully. A great deal of confusion has been caused, mainly in the form of theories associated with 'false consciousness', by those who seem to think that domination is the result of an enormous trick perpetuated by the ruling class as they propagate their ideas and values. It would be more appropriate to reconceptualise this issue around relationships of power and subordination. Ideas may 'rule' because the subjects of ideology recognise and temporarily accept their subordinate role. Ideology may operate differently in different contexts with different subjects. There is no single unitary subject of ideology and there is no single unitary context in which ideology operates. This is why any theorist of ideology should beware of reducing ideological analysis to a game of recognising the ideology in the message and, in effect, prescribing a given reading to a given subject. Instead, what is required is the development of various methods of identifying a changing and fluid relationship of power and subordination which is likely to operate in a multitude of ways and contexts.

The concept of contradictory consciousness, put forward by Gramsci, is extremely useful in allowing for the fact that people sometimes take up positions that they know not to be in their own best interests in the long run, but which make life more tolerable in the short run.

In order to develop a working theory of ideology, particularly in relation to 'race' and the media, it is necessary to refer constantly to the potential differentiation between real relations and phenomenal forms.

Any workable theory of ideology has to take careful account of Gramsci's suggestion that the relationship of consciousness to ideology is not psychological or moralistic in character, but 'structural and epistemological'. This means that it has to do with the ways in which knowledge and understanding are constructed and defended.

Ideology has to be conceptualised and studied as a lived relationship rather than a set of beliefs which are shared or imposed. It is a relationship of power and subordination/subjugation which is socially and historically situated and which is, within identifiable parameters, changeable. A working theory of ideology has to be applicable not only to the social relations of production in given social formations, but also and with equal intensity, to the discourses, linguistic structures and formations, and the specific signifying practices utilised by the communication media.

For media researchers, the processes of ideology have to be understood as concerned with the (necessary) reproduction of society; a process which is both 'continuous and contradictory'. There is, however, no place in a theory of ideology for notions of conspiracy. Conspiracies do indeed take place from time to time, but they are more likely when there is a crisis in the hegemonic balance of a given social formation. When we consider representations of issues relating to 'race', we have to be concerned with understanding the ways in which what Hall calls 'the modes of reality of the state' are constructed and sustained. This involves a long-term engagement with modes of signification, representation and discursive practices. In the next chapter I will consider some of the paradigms and methodologies which may take us a little nearer that possibility.

2

Questioning research

The analysis of representations of 'race' in the media requires more than a consideration of theories of ideology. It also requires the investigation and eventual use of practicable methodologies. This chapter will consider a range of approaches to research which are based on attempts to analyse the operations of ideology at both the macro and the micro levels. I will consider first the ambitious conceptual outlines offered by John Thompson (1990) and then the stress in the work of Michael Billig and his associates on the significance of contradiction and dilemmatic thinking. I will also feel free to import a range of analytical tools from a wider variety of sources, drawing upon the work of social semioticians such as Kress and Hodge and discourse analysts such as Potter and Wetherell and Fairclough. The chapter will finish with a brief critical consideration of the importance of Michel Foucault to those concerned with media representation of issues of 'race'. The purpose of this chapter is to form a bridge from the consideration of ideology as a general issue to the analyses of issues relating to 'race' and the media. To use a culinary metaphor, I would suggest that the researchers from whom I will take examples and paradigmatic instances provide the media researcher with a range of high quality cooking and carving implements. It is Thompson, however, who has concentrated his eye on the structure of the (ideological) menu.

The representations of race with which I will be concerned in the following chapters originate from a variety of sources and span a variety of generic categories. For many media and cultural analysts it would seem odd or even perverse to group all representations together, whether they are from newspapers, television, cinema or magazines. It has been argued in the past that media often utilise 'specific signifying practices' (Heath, 1977). I also wish to argue for the

importance of particular modes of signification, but not before I have
gone as far as possible with a consideration of those aspects of representation which are relevant across a range of media. This will mean
that I shall not be distinguishing between generic forms such as
documentary, feature films or television drama until later in the book.
First, I want to deal with some broad conceptual outlines.

Looking for a conceptual approach

Thompson has argued that ideology is best approached as an issue
which concerns the relationship between meaning and power. The act
of constructing or deconstructing meaning, I wish to argue, is no more
or less valid ideologically because it belongs to a generic form associated with 'fact' rather than 'fiction'. The relationship between
meaning and power is a recurring factor *within* media discourses and
in the utilisation of those discourses in the lived experiences of audiences. Representations of issues relating to 'race' are, as we will see,
very much concerned with power and meaning, whether in the form of
news bulletins, documentaries, advertisements, popular music or
forms of drama. For Thompson, relations of power are 'systematically
asymmetrical', which is another way of saying that some people have
more of it than others, and that this may not be entirely accidental.
Drawing on the work of Paul Ricoeur, Thompson gives considerable
weight to the importance of depth hermeneutics.

> The value of this idea is that it enables us to develop a methodo-
> logical framework which is orientated towards the interpretation
> (or re-interpretation) of meaningful phenomena, but in which dif-
> ferent types of analysis can play legitimate and mutually supportive
> roles. It enables us to see that the process of interpretation is not
> necessarily opposed to types of analysis which are concerned with
> the structural features of symbolic forms or with the social-historical
> conditions of action and interaction, but that, on the contrary, these
> types of analysis can be linked together and construed as necessary
> steps along the path of interpretation.
>
> (Thompson, 1990, p. 21)

There is an openness here which is important because it is neither
prescriptive nor proscriptive in terms of approaches to research. What
Thompson offers us is a framework against which we can test our
media research and analysis. He suggests that there are three aspects of

mass communication which we have to recognise and analyse. These are: 'first, the production and transmission or diffusion of mass-mediated symbolic forms; second, the construction of media messages; and third, the reception and appropriation of media messages' (1990, p. 23). There is nothing particularly new in this for the media researcher, but it does put down a useful marker if one wishes to check one's orientation when studying representations of 'race'. Thompson also identifies three phases of depth hermeneutics as a methodological framework. The first of these involves a socio-historical analysis and is concerned with 'the social and historical conditions of the production, circulation and reception of symbolic forms' (1990, p. 22). The importance of social history will become increasingly apparent as we consider a range of media examples. One has only to think, for instance, of the *contexts* from which forms of advertising have arisen, such as the use of black bodies to sell products which purportedly made the user or their possessions more 'white' (Pieterse, 1992). A specific example would be the historical conjuncture which saw the creation of an advertisement for a soft drink offering us a multicultural myth with national-costumed adults standing together but separate on a hillside, united by the bottles in their hands (Pendergrast, 1993, p. 306).

Formal or discursive analysis, for Thompson, involves the study of symbolic forms as complex symbolic constructions which display an articulated structure. He is arguing here that there *are* certain formal features of texts, whether visual or audio-visual, and that these formal features are identifiable and important in the construction of meaning. He is equally adamant that these formal features should not be studied in isolation, but that they have to be related to their socio-historical context. We will see, later in the chapter, that other analysts have taken this procedure a stage further by actually undertaking specific forms of analysis.

The third phase of the depth-hermeneutical framework, according to Thompson, is that of 'interpretation or re-interpretation'. This phase is, in many ways the most significant for the purposes of this book. It is also the one about which we know the least. What has to be remembered is that all media representations have to be recognised as just that – as re-presentations. Interpretation is, then, the process of making sense of something which is *already* an interpretation. This would be as true if it related to news coverage of civil unrest in the streets of Los Angeles, or if it was a feature film about a young black man who wants to marry a white middle-class woman. I am referring, of course to the well-known and now rather jaded plot of Stanley Kramer's *Guess Who's Coming to Dinner* (1967). Let me stress once more that any interpretation of these messages would be, according to Thompson, an interpretation of an interpretation. In the context of depth hermeneutics, it would also be a 'creative' interpretation. I take this to mean that there would be a *conscious* engagement, on the part of the interpreter, with the text under consideration, and that they would not necessarily take any text at face value. Here we will need to question, as we proceed in our analyses, whether there are any differences between the creative depth-hermeneutic approach of the media student or researcher, and that of the non-specialist reader. The latter, whose media consumption is part of their everyday existence, may or may not engage in *creative* interpretation. I will be exploring this issue closely in relation to everyday representations of matters concerning 'race'. Thompson argues that we must guard against what he calls the myth of the passive recipient. He is referring here to those who would argue that media consumers are simply the helpless inactive dupes of ideology. Thompson suggests that receivers of messages are 'actively, sometimes critically, engaged in a continuing process of self-formation and self-understanding, a process of which the reception and appropriation of media messages are today an integral part' (1990, p. 25). This formulation does not deal with the complexity or range of response which may be identified in the active decoding of media messages, not all of which might be typified as 'creative', and some of which may be structured in and through ideological discourses. I will be arguing, throughout this book, that no single model is adequate to describe or facilitate research into the processes of reception. I will be sceptical about any acceptance of readers as *either* the helpless dupes of ideology *or* the creative or ironic decoders of anything and everything that comes their way. I will also be sceptical about the extent to which, when viewing, reading, or listening to media messages concerning issues of 'race', the audience is concerned with self-understanding. While Thompson's general conceptualisation of the reception of media messages is very valuable, he does occasionally adopt an almost naïve approach to reception. It is necessary for the media and cultural studies student or researcher to engage with the active and progressive dimensions of activities of readership, but it is equally important to entertain the possibility that some readings might be regressive or reactionary. There are no guarantees here. While we may, on occasion,

TABLE 2.1
Modes of operation of ideology

General modes	Some typical strategies of symbolic construction
Legitimation	Rationalisation
	Universalisation
	Narrativisation
Dissimulation	Displacement
	Euphemisation
	Trope (e.g. synecdoche, metonymy, metaphor)
Unification	Standardisation
	Symbolisation of unity
Fragmentation	Differentiation
	Expurgation of the other
Reification	Naturalisation
	Eternalisation
	Nominalisation/passivisation

Source: Thompson, 1990, p. 60

be involved in a process of 'self-formation', it is less likely that we may be engaged in a process of self-understanding as we receive media messages.

The other major schema which Thompson offers which is valuable in our context is that which deals with the modes of operation of ideology. He identifies five modes of operation: legitimation, dissimulation, unification, fragmentation and reification. I am making use here of the schematic outline provided by Thompson and illustrated in Table 2.1. I am allowing myself, however, the chance to creatively reinterpret Thompson where necessary.

Each of these modes of operation is articulated through specific strategies of symbolic construction. I will say a little about each because they will be of some significance to the analyses in later chapters. In the history of racism there have been many occasions when the issue of legitimacy has been of prime importance. One of the most extraordinary and chilling examples of this was the way that the Nazi Party in Germany documented, within their own established legal frameworks, their systematic extermination of Jews (Bauman, 1989, especially Chapters 1 and 2). The keeping of records was one way of seeking legitimacy. Another was the production of media messages which sought to legitimise anti-Semitism within a popular ideological discourse. The speeches of Hitler recorded in Riefenstahl's documentary, *Triumph of the Will*, are a first-class example of such a strategy, which, through the medium of film, appeals to God as the highest form of legitimation. Within the production of media messages concerned with issues of 'race', the producers may seek to construct a chain of reasoning designed to win support for a particular way of making sense of things. There may also be occasions when a state of affairs which serves the interests of small groups of people is re-presented as serving the interests of all. Chapter 4, on Oprah Winfrey in Los Angeles, will deal with this in some detail. The third strategy of symbolic construction which Thompson mentions in relation to legit-imation is that of narrativisation. The issue of narrative is something which will arise on numerous occasions throughout this book. For the moment, however, it is sufficient to note that the telling of a good story is one very important way of legitimising asymmetrical power rela-tions. I will be discussing later how important the process of narrativisation is in films such as *Cry Freedom* or *Malcolm X*.

The second general mode of operation of ideology identified by Thompson is that of dissimulation. In Chapter 1 discussed how Marx had made, at the epistemological level, a distinction between real relations and phenomenal forms. When we come to dissimulation, however, this involves a process whereby relations of domination are glossed over or deliberately misrepresented in order to justify the status quo. It can sometimes involve what Thompson calls *euphemisa-tion*. Euphemisation involves the selective redescription of power relations in order to attempt to elicit a positive valuation of what is being described. This can vary from calling a concentration camp a 'rehabilitation centre' to describing brutal and unjustified police vio-lence as 'the restoration of law and order'. Other forms of dissimulation may be much more subtle. A now classic example of this phenomenon is the (almost certainly unintended) outcome of NBC's *The Cosby Show*. This television series, with an African American cast, was for some time in the late 1980s at the top of the ratings in the United States. Research by Jhally and Lewis has suggested that the programmes gave rise to a kind of 'enlightened racism', whereby many whites were able to look at the success of a tiny number of African Americans and read it as an indication of the absence of racism and discrimination in the Unites States of America (Jhally and Lewis, 1992).

The third mode of operation of ideology suggested by Thompson is that of unification. A sense of unity may be represented in the media in such a way as to elide differences in social or financial power. Once again we will find examples of this in the wake of the civil unrest in Los Angeles, including the indignant voices of some African Americans who were apparently impervious to the vast differences in wealth and hence job and education prospects between middle-class professionals and the urban poor. Other examples would include the ways in which the inhabitants of countries at war are somehow called upon, through a range of media messages, to 'unify', irrespective of the causes for which the nation may be fighting, or the justice of their position. Unification as a mode of operation of ideology in the media covers a wide range of possibilities, from downright lying to the subtlest forms of suggestion or inference.

The fourth mode of operation is that of fragmentation. It is an intriguing phenomenon as a companion to unification and may sometimes be identified as a parallel ideological mode of operation. It involves the emphasising of differences rather than similarities. In terms of the media, it has often resulted in sections or sub-groups in a society or community being represented as separate even from the rest of their own group. They can be differentiated because of their alleged actions, their attitude and sometimes their looks. Rastafarians have often been represented in the media as the personification of the alleged threat which young black British people have posed to the stability of society. On other occasions it has been the Moslem community which has been represented as different and apart from the very 'British' society of which, on other occasions, they may be represented as an integral part. The operations of ideology may manifest themselves through a process of representation where fragmentation is simply the first stage in reconstructing either the 'public' or 'youth' or 'the nation', once the perceived threat or alien force has been expurgated. In its extreme form, expurgation can argue for the total elimination of alien forces or 'cancerous growths' from society. At the more everyday ideological level, it is usually accomplished by forms of representation which demonstrate, often over a period of time, that there are some very bad apples in the barrel. Such bad apples must either be treated to stop their decay, or thrown out.

Finally, Thompson considers the concept of reification as significant. This is a complex term which indicates how

relations of domination may be established and sustained by representing a transitory, historical state of affairs as if it were permanent, natural, outside of time. Processes are portrayed as things or events of a quasi natural kind, in such a way that their social and historical character is eclipsed.

(Thompson, 1990, p. 65)

The typical strategies associated with this mode of operation of ideology include naturalisation and eternalisation. In terms of re-presenting 'race', this is a crucial strategy. The history of the media representation of blackness, for instance, is full of examples of the ways in which white imperial society has undertaken ideological work to eradicate certain key historical issues in order to eternalise its own claim to dominance as part of the natural order of things. Such ideological work might, on occasion, include the conscious planning of the most suitable way of communicating such messages. This is often referred to as a conspiracy theory of ideology and it implies some kind of plotting by small groups anxious to retain their power and influence. Much more often, however, such media representations came about as a result of the already established power relations in particular societies. As such, they required no conspiracy, for the makers of such messages would usually recognise (and regenerate) their own identity in the re-presentation of their personal or national superiority. This could be accomplished, for instance, through advertisements which illustrated the glorious and proud aspects of the Empire while selling us tea. It could also take the form of travel brochures and posters which provided exotic otherness as the perpetual presence and backdrop against which the lives of the (white) tourist could be played out.

Discourse, the media and dilemmatic thinking

Thompson has offered a most useful and thought-provoking conceptual outline for the media researcher concerned with aspects of ideology. One must turn elsewhere, however, to find researchers who are concerned with the complex and contradictory ways in which 'race' is dealt with in everyday life. This requires an approach which is not reducible to a single epistemological or methodological principle, for it involves the media researcher in dealing with perceptions relating to 'race' as part of the lived experience of media audiences, *and* the ways in which issues related to 'race' are represented across a range of media and genres. It is often necessary, to avoid confusion and endless complexity, to separate the perceptions of media messages by specific audiences from the potential meanings on offer in a given text. But this should be recognised as a strategy for understanding rather than some kind of binary distinction between text and audience.

The work of Michael Billig and his colleagues has provided a rich resource for the student of media representations of 'race'. (Billig, 1982; Billig *et al.*, 1988; Billig, 1991). Billig recognises the significance of ideology and the ideological in everyday life, but suggests that the operations of ideology are far from being linear or without contradiction. It is his introduction of the concept of dilemmatic thinking which is crucial to the media researcher who is trying to explore the relationship between text, audience and context in media representations of issues of 'race'.

> In stressing the dilemmatic aspects of ideology, we hope to oppose the implications of both cognitive and ideological theory, which ignore the social nature of thinking. In contrast to cognitive psychologists, we stress the *ideological* nature of thought; in contrast to theorists of ideology, we stress the *thoughtful* nature of ideology.
>
> (Billig *et al.*, 1988, p. 2)

Billig argues that ideology is not a complete or unified system of beliefs. It contains contrary themes through which we all, in Billig's words, 'puzzle over' our social worlds. This is an important conceptualisation because it suggests that audiences have to negotiate meaning in the face of often contradictory evidence or contradictory personal perceptions of a given situation. Representations of 'race' and racism in the media provide numerous examples of dilemmas in both textual formation and the decoding of texts by readers. It is the business of the media researcher to identify these dilemmas and to provide a range of readings and analysis which explore their operations. Billig has elsewhere referred to thinking as a process of internal arguing (Billig, 1991, p. 31ff.). Whether conceived as the negotiation of dilemmas or as arguing with oneself, this is an important methodological step. It moves away from understanding representations of 'race' as either acceptable or unacceptable and audience behaviour as either enlightened or blinkered and constrained. Whether we are considering advertisements, or feature films, comic strips or documentaries, it suggests that the meanings which audiences make from texts as part of their social life are likely to require constant negotiation of dilemmas and contradiction. It will also become apparent that this approach provides a serious challenge to any semiotics which supposes that signification takes place without contradiction and the generation of dilemmas. Meaning becomes a dynamic phenomenon rather than the end product of a mechanistic or linear chain of signification. This has profound implications for the understanding and study of issues relating to media representations of 'race'. One final quotation from Billig will, I hope, encapsulate his conceptualisation of the dilemmatic aspects of ideology.

> According to this conception, ideologies, as lived practices and commonsensical beliefs, contain contrary themes. One implication of this position is that ideological subjects do not typically possess the sort of internally consistent 'belief-system' which is assumed in many conventional social psychological theories and, indeed, in a number of critical theories of ideology. Instead, a discursive variability is to be expected, for ideological subjects possess contrary interpretative repertoires for talking about the world. Thus, what people say, think and argue will vary across time; the recourse to one repertoire rather than another, may depend upon the functions of the discourse and the context in which it occurs.
>
> (Billig, 1990, p. 18)

This also suggests another important methodological issue for the media researcher. On the one hand, it is important to recognise that the meaning of a media text is, to a certain extent, negotiated socially. It is also negotiated, within the reader. Some contradictions are worked through in private and may influence future social interaction. The negotiation of meaning takes place as both a public and a private activity.

There is a useful comparison to be made between the views of Billig on dilemmatic thinking and those of Gramsci on contradictory consciousness. But it is in the work of Potter and Wetherell that we find another directly useful tool for the analyst of media representations of 'race'.

Languages of racism

In drawing attention to the work of Jonathan Potter and Margaret Wetherell, I am also highlighting for the first time in this book the ways in which specifically racist discourse may be generated and sustained. It is important to remember that when one is considering the ways in which 'race' and racist discourse are represented in the media, one has also and at the same time to consider the ways in which similar discourses circulate in everyday life. It becomes increasingly difficult (and undesirable) to separate off the textual representation of issues concerning 'race' from the context in which they are likely to be received. Every text presumes an audience and, in relation to the mass media, every audience requires and presumes a text.

Potter and Wetherell are discourse analysts with a strong base in social psychology. Their main interest is not with language as a formal system of signification, but with *language use* (Potter and Wetherell, 1987). They are not interested 'in the dictionary definition of words, or abstract notions of meaning, but in distinctions participants actually make in their interactions and which have important implications for their practice' (1987, p. 170). In analysing discourse, they argue that one needs to look at what the participants in any discursive activity see as consistent and what they see as different. Analysing discourse about 'race' is not, then, an examination of the literal content of discourse. It is about the ways in which the discourse or interpretations of a discourse are *used*. It could be argued that the (ideological) issue of 'race' is *constituted* in and through discourse. It could be argued further that discourses are sustained through the utilisation of *interpretative repertoires*. The process, however, is not linear. In most media representations, discourses are constructed around previously existing interpretative repertoires, in this case the repertoires of the producers of messages. These discourses may be regarded by those producers as simply good professional practice. The description and placing of certain minority groups as *ethnic* minorities are, for instance, an example of media discourse constructing and, to a large extent sustaining, an interpretative repertoire. The potential absurdity or invidiousness of what seems a perfectly normal characterisation become apparent only if one considers the possibility of frequently inserting the phrase *ethnic majority* into media discourse. One has also to ask of such discourses, and those who sustain them, whether *non-ethnic* groups of any size exist. The non-problematic, naturalised utilisation of such words or phrases provides the foundations upon which interpretative repertoires can be erected and re-erected. The utilisation of interpretative repertoires is, however, usually undertaken without reflection or consideration.

The recognition of the ways in which judgements and evaluations are constructed and sustained by the readers of media messages is also an important step in the development of media analysis techniques. Potter and Wetherell argue that, in order to evaluate and characterise events, actions and other phenomena, interpretative repertoires are necessary. Such repertoires are, they say, often organised around a limited range of terms and stylistic and grammatical constructions. The use of such repertoires has to be studied in context, including the way that concepts of 'race', 'culture' and 'nation' are mobilised, 'paying close attention to their specific construction, to their placement in a sequence of discourse, and to their rhetorical organisation' (Wetherell and Potter, 1992, p. 93).

The study of interpretative repertoires has to be undertaken in relation to a variety of media texts as well as audiences. This will involve, eventually, the analysis of implicit and explicit racist discourses as well as the analysis of discourses about 'race'. As mentioned above, Potter and Wetherell place considerable emphasis on the importance of the ways in which repertoires of interpretation are used *in context*. For the media researcher or media student, it is often necessary to actively simulate different contexts where participatory research is not always possible. What this means is that the media student may need to try to read a media text adopting a range of interpretative repertoires. This is, of course, a delicate and potentially dangerous activity. It requires from the student or researcher the development of a critical and reflective empathy with identifiable reading positions. These may include the recognition of interpretative repertoires which are abhorrent to the student. It may also involve the media researcher in having to move into new academic fields of enquiry in order to accumulate the necessary skills and knowledge which might facilitate the adoption of alternative interpretative repertoires.

It is useful, here, to compare Potter and Wetherell's emphasis on interpretative repertoires with Norman Fairclough's approach to the ways in which differently located groups or individuals might make sense of messages (Fairclough, 1989). For Fairclough, we all enter into any act of interpretation by drawing upon what he calls *'members' resources'*. This rather quaint-sounding concept is of crucial importance because it involves 'an active process of matching features of the utterance at various levels with representations you have stored in your long-term memory' (Fairclough, 1989, p. 11). For our purposes, we may consider any media text to be constituted as a pattern of 'utterances' of greater or lesser complexity. Just as we have to interpret the statement of, for example, a friend or an official in any communicative context, so we have to interpret a media text which may be written, audio, visual, audio-visual or a combination of all of these. Fairclough also stresses the social dimensions of message interpretation when we draw upon our members' resources (MR):

> The MR which people draw upon to produce and interpret texts are cognitive in the sense that they are in people's heads, but they are social in the sense that they have social origins – they are socially generated, and their nature is dependent on the social relations and struggles out of which they were generated.
>
> (Fairclough, 1989, p. 24)

The strength of the arguments put forward by Fairclough and Potter and Wetherell lies in the way they insist on the dialectical relationship between the context in which a message is received and the social sedimentations of meaning potential upon which individual readings are constructed. Meaning making becomes a *process*, but it is a process which takes place within specific (potentially changeable) contexts. These rather abstract statements will become of central importance to the analysis of a range of media texts, which are concerned, with issues of 'race' as the book progresses.

Social semiotics

The importance of semiotics and semiotic analysis has been recognised by media researchers for many years. It is not my intention to go over many of the well-rehearsed arguments for their significance. Robert Hodge and Gunther Kress have argued for the centrality of what they describe as social semiotics (Hodge and Kress, 1988). Semioticians have often placed emphasis on the system of signs as an abstract and hence static structure. Social semiotics is different in that it is concerned with the ways in which the *semiosic* process occurs. Semiosis is the social process by which meaning is constructed and exchanged. For Hodge and Kress, the system of signs is constantly reproduced and reconstituted in texts. Texts become, in effect, the material realisation of systems of signs. But the system in which signs are used is also subject to change over time. There is a tension or dialectic between text and system which can be found in semiosic acts, that is, in discourse. It is through discourse that the meaning of signs is established, negotiated or struggled over. Discourse is also the means by which subjects are constituted. If we consider the way in which a news broadcast or a newspaper's front page describes a specific issue pertaining to matters of 'race', it will be clear that specific forms of discourse will be called up or reconstructed through the choice of particular signifying practices. If, for instance, a newspaper carries a banner headline which reads simply 'BLACK WAR ON POLICE' over a picture of ranks of riot police, it does suggest a particular discursive agenda. The word 'war', for instance, is not used in the literal sense, for no war has been declared. The use of the word 'Black' is, in this context of civil unrest, more of a provocation than an elucidation. In this sense, the basic discourse of a newspaper which purports to be reporting on a specific happening is also *constructing* that happening. It should be noted, however, that discourse is not something found only in news report-age or documentary. The same or very similar discourses may circulate in texts which are intended as fictional. The line between fiction and non-fiction can, in the field of discourse, sometimes appear blurred. Discourses about issues of 'race' may then slide from fiction to doc-umentary reportage and back again. It could be argued that different generic forms such as documentary or drama or news can inform and sustain each other at the level of discourse. If this is a possibility, it raises another difficult question for the media researcher, which is that of trying to understand whether or where there is truth in representa-tions of issues of 'race'.

Hodge and Kress, as social semioticians, are well aware of this problem of the truth status of messages. They address it primarily through reference to the concept of *modality*. They borrow the term from linguistics, and for them it refers to 'the status, authority and reliability of a message, to its ontological status, or to its value as truth or fact' (Hodge and Kress, 1988, p. 124 and all of Chapter 5). Modality is indicated verbally by the use of specific words or phrases, usually referred to as modal auxiliaries. In terms of media messages, they could include such contextualising commentary as 'According to a govern-ment spokesman ... ', or 'It is more than likely that ... ', or 'Unnamed sources in Whitehall have suggested ... ', or 'Every responsible citizen knows that ... ', or 'We say unambiguously ... '. The list could go on, for our daily media intake is positively peppered with modal auxiliaries in one form or another. They all refer to questions of status and reliability in media messages. Roger Fowler has offered a parallel definition of modal structures in fiction which is helpful here. He suggests that:

Modality is the grammar of explicit comment, the means by which people express their degree of commitment to the truth of the propositions they utter, and their views on the desirability or otherwise of the states of affairs referred to.

(Fowler, 1986, p. 130)

Fowler is writing here in relation to literature and the novel, but it is clear that the question of modality is relevant to the discursive structures of both fiction and non-fiction texts. Again and again the media analyst of issues relating to 'race' has to ask about the precise modality of a comment or a commentary, whether in a documentary or a feature film. This is not to suggest for one moment that fiction and 'fact' should be construed as synonymous. The key point to note is that modality statements have to be considered with the same care irrespective of their point of origin, because the modality of statements or messages is intimately bound up with their ideological status.

Social semiotics can offer a great deal to the media student or researcher because it provides an approach which allows for analysis at the micro and the macro level. It is also possible to broaden the emphasis on the verbal nature of modality statements in order to consider visual and audio-visual messages. We know, for instance, that the literal content of a statement can be totally undermined by the tone of voice in which it is delivered. Spoken messages are also susceptible to almost endless modal subtlety once they are linked with the visual image. The image may be of the person speaking or of anything else. If it is of the speaker, her or his body language, or the slightest movement of an eyebrow can be combined with intonation to offer a whole palette of expressive forms. If the spoken word of an identified character or speaker is linked with images other than the speaker's face, another vast range of meaning potential is made available. In all these instances, the factor of modality will be of central importance. This will be seen to be particularly relevant in relation to matters of 'race' in situations where the media language (and hence its modality) in use is subtle rather than crass or stringent.

There is one other approach to discourse and power which needs to be mentioned before turning specifically to matters concerning representations of 'race'. This is the significance of the work of Michel Foucault.

Foucault, discourse, power

Michel Foucault is regarded by some as the heir to the mantle of Sartre as the leading French philosopher of the 1970s. He has also been described as the historian of the present (Merquior, 1985). From the multi-layered and complex intellectual work which Foucault undertook, I propose to extract two key issues. There are two reasons for this. The first is that Foucault has had a considerable impact upon teaching in the field of media and cultural studies, and that this impact has seldom been based upon a critical consideration of his work. As a consequence, a few concepts associated with his name have become common currency in the field of media and cultural studies. These include the question of power, a sceptical and sometimes downright cynical attitude to concepts of truth, and a particular understanding of the concept of discourse. The second reason for concentrating on selected moments from Foucault's intellectual output is that I believe that much can be learned by the student of 'race' and the media from selective and critical engagement with some of Foucault's thought.

When one considers the numerous ways in which issues of 'race' have been defined, redefined, excluded, eliminated, exaggerated, underplayed or ignored in the media, it is very easy to hypothesise that the operation of power is a central feature of these phenomena. This would be equally though differently true of representations which are fictional as much as those which lay claim to be factual. There is a power in telling stories, whether they be the news stories of the day or the latest episode of a soap opera. Foucault interpreted the operations of power in a very particular way. He argued that power should not be thought of as something emanating from a given point. Instead he argued that 'power means relations, a more-or-less organised, hierarchical, co-ordinated cluster of relations' (Foucault, 1980, pp. 198, 199). Rather than trying to erect a theory of power, he suggests that we should provide ourselves with 'a grid of analysis which makes possible an analytic of relations of power'. There is much potential for the media researcher of issues concerning 'race', in attempting to systematise investigations of representation and in recognising the structuring processes both within and between representations. This is likely to have an impact upon the ways in which investigation is conceived and carried through, and is a strong antidote to over-zealous conspiracy theorists. There is a weakness, however, in Foucault's approach which also needs to be addressed. For if power (including, for instance, the power of the media to define) is concerned with hierarchical relations, there are likely to be at least plateaux, if not pinnacles in these relations. It is important, therefore, that the investigation of power should not be reduced to either a concentration on the 'sources' of power *or* the structures or relations within which power can exist. It is about both. This means that the media researcher has to develop methodologies which allow for a recognition of the significance of structures and relations of power, but that there should also be an awareness of the need to problematise the concept of responsibility/agency in relation to representations of issues concerning 'race' in the media. Whether or not Foucault intended his readers to draw such a conclusion, the way in which his writings on power have tended to be interpreted in media studies suggests that power is all-pervasive, ubiquitous, anonymous. This, to say the least, makes the concept of agency somewhat problematic. It is in the tension between the suggested ubiquity of power and the possibility that some body or bodies may generate, sustain or even change modes of representation that we find an evolving debate for all analysts of culture and society. In relation to the general theme of this book, it is a core issue.

The matter of truth is also of significance, although it is not always something which is considered of primary importance for those concerned with representations of issues concerning 'race.' For some, this may be because they believe they possess an unproblematic truth in relation to issues of 'race' which allows them to inflect any media representation towards proof of that truth. There are others who experience justifiable indignation or sometimes repulsion in the face of racist modes of media representation which makes truth something which requires some form of action rather than some form of debate. The material, lived existence of those who are subject to racism does not usually result in a scepticism on their part about whether there is anything beyond representation. How those truths are mediated, however, becomes an issue of central importance in media research. Not all representations of issues concerning 'race' are immediately repugnant, and some may be intended to amuse or to enlighten. The question of the truth of a wide and varied field of representations needs to be addressed by any media researcher. For Foucault, truth is something produced via constraint. It is, in effect, imposed by a structure of power which in turn cannot be traced to any source beyond reference to its own anatomy. We need to take careful note of Foucault's comments on regimes of truth:

> Each society has its regime of truth, its 'general politics' of truth: that is, the types of discourse which it accepts and makes function as true; the mechanisms and instances which enable one to distinguish

true and false statements, the means by which each is sanctioned; the techniques and procedures accorded value in the acquisition of truth; the status of those who are charged with saying what counts as true.

(Foucault, 1980, p. 131)

A critical reading of the above paragraph may make one wonder how Foucault can be so hostile to the potential of a critique of power/truth relations based upon an evolving theory of ideology. It is my contention that it is only when Foucault is appropriated by those who do wish to undertake ideological analysis that he retains a significant potential for the researcher concerned with media representations of 'race'.

The first two chapters have been concerned with mapping out a series of conceptual and theoretical issues which, I have argued, are important to engage with before and during any sustained engagement with representations of issues concerning 'race'. I have suggested that it is important for the media researcher to develop a viable theory of ideology in order to undertake analyses across a variety of representational modes. It will be clear to the reader that this process involves the making of many choices and that, for me, theorising the relationship between 'race' and ideology is a central issue.

I have not attempted, however, to construct some kind of visual representation of this relationship in the form of a model. The reason for this is that, although I have suggested that one has to work towards a viable theory of ideology, it is the act or *process of theorising* which is most important. Any worthwhile theory is likely to resist diagrammatic representation. Diagrams or models tend to be or become static and eventually reified representations of a dynamic cluster of relations. Thompson's conceptual outlines, though evocative and productive, are still susceptible to becoming a rigid, formulaic interpretative tool unless invoked with extreme care.

The range of thinkers I have introduced most certainly does not presume to be inclusive or prescriptive. What I am suggesting is that the theoretical or conceptual choices one makes in approaching a specific field of media representation can facilitate modes of analysis more productively if one is constantly working to identify the tensions, contradictions and dilemmas which such choices inevitably raise.

This is clearly no more than a beginning. It is also necessary to consider something of the historical background and present context of media representations concerning issues of 'race'. It is also necessary to consider the possible relationship between forms of representations and the context in which they have arisen. This is why social semiotics, with its emphasis on the social negotiation of meaning , is so important. The next chapter will consider another cluster of issues more specifically concerned with representations of 'race', with an emphasis on debates on Orientalism, Otherness and exoticism.

3

Otherness, Eurocentrism and the representation of 'race'

This chapter will explore questions about Otherness as they have been discussed in some influential texts which relate to media representation and issues of 'race'. The purpose of the chapter is to demonstrate that the field is one which is intellectually as well as politically volatile. It is also designed to highlight the importance for both student and researcher of engaging with the often contradictory positions argued by theorists of 'race' and the media. The first two chapters mentioned the importance of the concept of contradiction and the significance of the possibility that a person may possess what Gramsci calls a 'contradictory consciousness'. I will now consider some ways in which tensions, contradictions and occasional dilemmas are very much part of the necessary investigation of Otherness in relation to media representation. The reason for beginning with this broad discursive and representational category is that it offers numerous examples of the ways in which dilemmas of meaning highlight the semiotic dynamism which informs so many media representations of issues of 'race'. Rather than present this dynamism through a series of binary oppositions, I wish to argue that it has to be conceptualised as the interplay of a range of fluctuating and often apparently incompatible interpretative repertoires. These repertoires are structured through, although they may not be dependent upon specific signifying practices. They may be utilised in an individual reading through what Billig has called 'internal argument', or may be contested and contrasted as readings are socially negotiated. In practice it is likely that they are developed in both the internal and the external arenas of semiosis. I will first discuss this possibility at the abstract level, and then move towards the consideration of some examples. The chapter will conclude with a more detailed engagement with debates on the concept of Orientalism and media representation.

Binary opposition or dynamic contradiction?

Structuralist thinkers based a great deal of their work on what they saw as the fundamental significance of the binary opposition (Hawkes, 1977; Sturrock, 1979). Through binary oppositions the notion of *difference* could be established, and the recognition of difference is essential, they argued, for the creation of meaning. We only know that something is hard because we can compare it with the concept of softness. We know that someone is an insider because we have a concept of an outsider. We only have a concept of 'blackness' because we can contrast it with its 'opposite' which is white. Hall has offered a lucid summary of four key theoretical accounts of the concept of difference (Hall, 1997, pp. 223–79). The first is related to the concept of difference outlined above, and stems from a theoretical position which considers the workings of culture as analogous to the workings of language. The second account suggests that 'we need *difference* because we can only construct meaning through a dialogue with the *Other*.' The third describes the argument which suggests that culture depends upon the erection of classificatory systems and that 'the marking of *difference* is thus the basis of that symbolic order which we call culture.' The fourth rests upon a psychoanalytic explanation of 'difference' in our psychic life. While these arguments do demonstrate that meaning is dependent upon identifying differences, they each present problems because they either lack subtlety, or because they utilise the basic premise about difference and meaning until it becomes rarefied or attenuated. It is to the concept of the *Other* that I will return in a moment, because it is so important in debates about media representations of 'race' and the exotic. First I will explore a little further the significance of binary oppositions in debates about culture.

The anthropologist Claude Lévi-Strauss wrote, in *The Savage Mind*, of the 'multi-conscious' mind which was capable of responding to an environment on more than one level simultaneously. This involved the development of complex classificatory systems which operated as systems of meaning. He referred to what he called 'analogical thought' which worked by imposing on the world a series of structural contrasts or oppositions (Lévi-Strauss, 1966, cited in Hawkes, 1977, pp. 32–58). These binary oppositions were often concerned with the regulation of conduct through, for instance, notions of diet. Hence the well-known opposition raw / cooked. The importance of this type of insight is that it could be developed from an initial pairing to various levels of interpretative and hence behavioural sophistication, whereby raw/cooked could be linked to edible/inedible and eventually to native/foreign. Meaning could thus be produced by dividing the world into a whole range of such oppositions, from culture/nature to man/woman or good/bad. Lévi-Strauss was writing, usually, about so-called primitive societies and the ways in which these societies utilise myth within their ways of living. His ideas have also been adapted, sometimes creatively, to the study of media representations. Will Wright's now classic study of the western is one example (Wright, 1975). Wright was interested in demonstrating a relationship between the structure of myths in a particular society, and the way in which those myths could communicate a sense of conceptual order to members of that society. There is no doubt in Lévi-Strauss's case, that he made his argument with scholarship and carefully modulated argument supported by fieldwork. Binary oppositions were, however, part of a complex methodology for research or theory of meaning and signification, and they have somehow returned to haunt many theorists of the media concerned with issues of 'race'. A structural overview of a wide range of media representations which is based upon binary oppositions, however sophisticatedly they are re-packaged, is more likely to facilitate the mechanical application of pre-existing conceptual categories than the exercise of critical thought. In this sense, structural analyses act somewhat as analytical templates which are somehow imposed on a wide variety of texts. When considering media representations of 'race', there is then a tendency to derive explanatory force from the degree of 'fit' which any particular representation offers. It does not matter whether one is dealing with narrative structures, generic structures, character structures, or even something like the star system in the cinema. Once the template has been designed, it can only be marginally modified, discarded, or clung to. It cannot evolve in response to specific historical, social or economic conditions. Nor can it easily respond to the specific activity of specific agents. Structural analyses also tend towards ahistoricism. They tend to underplay or ignore the complexities of human communication as they constantly seek underlying structures which, 'naturally', are there to be discovered.

I do not for one moment presume to suggest that there is no value in structural analyses. In fact they are essential, because they offer the possibility of testing various hypotheses about the ways in which meaning is generated and circulates. They should not, however, become reified. The question of binary oppositions is also problematic both theoretically and methodologically because it cannot cope with contradiction. The evolution of classificatory systems certainly helps us to recognise patterns and order where they exist, but they may also lead us to impose order where there is none. Conceptualising culture (or issues of 'race') as a system of classifications is more suited to explaining how a culture remains as it is than considering the question of change. If any tensions do arise in classificatory systems, they tend to be around what to do if something comes along which does not fit into prescribed categories. These issues bear heavily upon debates and research in relation to representations of issues of 'race'.

Pursuing the 'Other'

The relationship between the making of meaning and the category of the Other was well understood by Mikhail Bakhtin, the Russian linguist (Holquist, 1981). He argued that meaning was negotiated socially between two or more speakers. The activity of meaning making also involved some kind of dialogue. This productive insight into the ways in which language might operate in relation to the Other has not retained its initial dynamic. In many debates about representations of 'race', the concept of the Other is used as a means of imposing meaning rather than negotiating meaning through dialogue. As we shall see, this has meant that the concept of the Other has become an ideological signifier of considerable discursive power.

Once the *negotiation* of meaning has been relegated in importance, the category of otherness becomes something against which I can measure myself, usually as a representative of the normal. The 'African' in need of aid, the fundamentalist who is usually an 'Arab', or the 'Indian' who is usually starving, all become Others to 'my' normality. Otherness, then, may relate to conceptions as diverse as social or sexual deviance, or national or regional identity, or 'race'. A key issue has been the way in which the global Other has become something, in media terms, which is paired with the West as its (binary) companion. These two are not, however, equal discursive partners. They are, as Hall has pithily put it, 'The West and the Rest' (Hall, 1991). The almost entirely negative discursive construction of the Rest (Other) is seen as rooted in the arrogant certainties of Enlightenment thinking. Enlightenment discourse had attempted to establish universal norms. These norms, according to critics, were not so much universal, as Eurocentric.

It was then only a small step, analytically, to argue that Eurocentric thinking was likely to be racist thinking.

There is much to substantiate this line of reasoning in the representations of issues of 'race' which abound in the mass media. These would include the ways in which popular histories are constructed, the numerous adventure stories which tell of daring deeds in distant places (distant from Europe or the USA), or the Euro–North American emphasis which still predominates in news broadcasts and reporting. These matters are of crucial importance and will be explored in later chapters. They do not, however, tell the whole story. They do not allow for the complexities and contradictions which are a structured part of many media representations, nor do they allow for the problematisation of the subject or 'self' which is posited in opposition to the Other. This self or subject is, for the purposes of this book, a reader of media messages and/or part of a media audience.

Another problem with the concept of Otherness, when invoked in relation to cultural issues and media representations, is that it often tends to essentialise its object. Characteristics are thus attributed to certain groups which are apparently timeless and frequently demeaning. Kenan Malik has argued that the category of the Other 'eternalises human modes of perception. It takes historically specific ways of constructing identity and endows them with an eternal validity' (Malik, 1996, p. 222). This can result in negative stereotyping by the media. The problem, for Malik, does not lie with the tendency of Enlightenment thinking towards universalism. He argues that it is precisely the insistence on *difference* and the 'degradation of universalism which has given rise to the discourse of race'. He further argues that the politics of difference is the 'intellectual embodiment of social fragmentation' (1996, p. 219). Malik's emphasis here is clearly on Marx's dictum that it is social being which determines consciousness and not the reverse. This begins to identify the serious and important intellectual divisions which have to be addressed in the understanding of the present social, economic and context for representations of issues of 'race'. It is clear that the celebration of difference is the dominant ideological trope of many media analysts in the last decade of the twentieth century. This is linked to the importance of questions of identity as one posits one's 'self' against a whole range of Others. The extent to which media representation of difference facilitates either social understanding or hostile social fragmentation will be considered in later chapters, and at the end of this chapter in relation to the concept of 'identity'.

Orientalism and the media

One of the most influential texts on the development of our under-standing of media representations of issues of 'race' has undoubtedly been Edward Said's *Orientalism* (1978). I wish to give the book and its influence some detailed consideration because of the way in which it utilises the concept of the Orient and the Other. Said suggests that Orientalism, as a discourse, arose from the certitudes of Enlightenment thinking. It is worth quoting in full his well-known position at the opening of the book:

> My contention is that, without examining Orientalism as a dis-course, one cannot possibly understand the enormously systematic discipline by which European culture was able to manage – and even produce – the Orient politically, sociologically, militarily, ideologically, scientifically and imaginatively during the post-Enlightenment period. Moreover, so authoritative a position did Orientalism have that I believe no one writing, thinking, or acting on the Orient could do so without taking account of the limitations on thought and action imposed by Orientalism.
>
> (Said, 1978, p. 3)

The influence of Foucault on Said is clear and acknowledged. It becomes even more apparent later in the work:

> In a sense Orientalism was a library or archive of information commonly and, in some of its aspects, unanimously held. What bound the archive together was a family of ideas and a unifying set of values proven in various ways to be effective. These ideas explained the behaviour of Orientals; they supplied Orientals with a mentality, a genealogy, an atmosphere; most important, they allowed Europeans to deal with and even to see Orientals as a phenomenon possessing regular characteristics.
>
> (Said, 1978, p. 42)

The sweep of this theorisation is impressive, and it suggests all kinds of ways in which writings about the Orient might work to create and sustain a range of understandings about people from the Orient as Others. There is, also, a relationship between what Said is arguing and the concept of the interpretative repertoire. The only difference is that, in Said's case, there is an implicit claim towards exclusivity. It is true that he argues against any unilateral determination by Orientalism about what can be said of the Orient, but the general tenor of the remainder of the book does not substantiate his claim. This presents the researcher with a serious and challenging problem. Said, on the one hand, is undoubtedly identifying a whole range of (mainly literary and historical) representations which had and continue to have a powerful impact on readers in the West and elsewhere. On the other hand, he does not offer a model of analysis which allows for any tensions or contradictions in the meanings to be negotiated from the literary or historical texts he studies. His sophisticated theorisation of the operations of Orientalism as a discourse tend to utilise a mode of interpreting messages which is less convincing. This can be best illustrated by considering a passage where Said is referring specifically to film and television representations.

> In the films and television the Arab is associated either with lechery or bloodthirsty dishonesty. He appears as an oversexed degenerate, capable, it is true, of cleverly devious intrigues, but essentially sadistic, treacherous, low. Slave trader, camel driver, moneychanger, colourful scoundrel: these are some of the traditional Arab roles in the cinema. The Arab leader (of marauders, pirates, 'native' insurgents) can often be seen snarling at the captured Western hero and the blond girl (both of them steeped in wholesomeness), 'My men are going to kill you, but – they like to amuse themselves before.' He leers suggestively as he speaks: this is a current debasement of Valentino's Sheik. In newsreels or newsphotos, the Arab is always shown in large numbers. No individuality, no personal characteristics or experiences. Most of the pictures represent mass rage and misery, or irrational (hence hopelessly eccentric) gestures. Lurking behind all of these images is the menace of the *jihad*. Consequence: a fear that the Muslims (or Arabs) will take over the world.
>
> (Said, 1978, pp. 286–7)

Once again it is the sweeping generalisation which works to undermine the power of Said's argument. Many of the assertions put forward would be equally applicable to certain film and television representations of native Americans, of 'Africans', of Indians, of the Chinese, and in the Cold War period, of the Russians. If we exclude the 'menace of the *jihad*', it would seem that Orientalism in film and television is virtually synonymous with a generic form of melodrama where any imperialist or post-imperialist can celebrate their power (or lost power) through their representation of the Other. Some of the claims he makes would be hard to verify empirically, for instance, the reference to all Arabs being shown in 'large numbers'. But there are more problems. Said suggests that England and France were the main constructors of the discourses associated with Orientalism. Why he does not wish to include other powers with imperialist and colonial histories – the Dutch in the East Indies come to mind – is not made clear. There is also the danger, not of playing down the significance of a whole range of influential discursive strategies associated with Orientalism, but of making Orientalism seem like a case worthy of special pleading. The matter is not made any easier by the fact that Said does not seem entirely clear in what he means by the Orient. Malik (1996) suggests that Said seems to be referring mainly to the Middle East.

Said also argues that Orientalism demonstrated 'a proclivity to divide, subdivide, and redivide its subject matter without ever changing its mind about the Orient as being always the same, unchanging, uniform, and radically peculiar object' (1978, p. 98). There is here a strong smack of ahistoricism. For Malik it is ahistoricism which leads Said sometimes to 'mimic the very discursive structures against which he polemicises' (Malik, 1996, p. 228). This, according to Malik, allows Said the licence to suggest that there is a Western tradition which can be traced all the way from the Ancient Greeks through the Renaissance and Enlightenment to modernism. The beliefs and values associated with Western identity have, thus, remained unchanged for over two millennia. This, says Malik, is the myth of 'Western civilisation', and he associates it with such advocates of Western superiority as Gobineau and Goebbels. On another occasion in the book, Said falls prey to a form of argument which he is, elsewhere, at pains to castigate. When discussing the work of the Comte de Volney and his *Voyage en Égypte et en Syrie*, Said notes that the climax of the book occurs in the second volume where Volney gives an account of Islam as a religion.

> Volney's views were canonically hostile to Islam as a religion and as a system of political institutions; nevertheless Napoleon found this work and Volney's *Considérations sur la guerre actuel de Turcs* (1788) of particular importance. For Volney was after all a canny Frenchman, and – like Chateaubriand and Lamartine a quarter century after him – he eyed the Orient as a likely place for the realisation of French colonial ambition.
>
> (Said, 1978, p. 81)

It may seem a trifling point to question the reference to a 'canny Frenchman' but I think not. Said is here attributing characteristics to 'Frenchmen' which apparently transcend specific historical contexts. He is also helping to add to a wider discursive pool of references which suggest that the construction of the Other may not be limited to the Orient.

Another challenge to Said's work on Orientalism has come from John Mackenzie, who is particularly interested in the reference at the beginning of *Orientalism* to the Orient's role in defining Europe (Mackenzie, 1995). Mackenzie points out that Said never follows through the possibility that the Orient might 'become the means for a counter-western discourse, that it can offer opportunities for literary extension, spiritual renewal and artistic development' (1995, p. 10). Mackenzie argues that the Orient, 'or at least its discourse, has the capacity to become the tool of cultural revolution, a legitimising source of resistance to those who challenge western conventions, introspection and complacency'. This is indeed a serious and suggestive challenge, though it does not necessarily invalidate some of the main points argued by Said; it simply puts them into a wider context. Mackenzie goes on to identify the main areas in which Said's work has been challenged. These include, among other issues, Said's binary approach to the category of the Other. Mackenzie's own criticism of Said comes as a serious caveat to those media analysts who might rely mainly on a kind of 'spot the racist or demeaning representation' approach as an end in itself. He suggests that Said demonstrates

a historicism which is in itself essentially ahistorical, an unwillingness to grapple with political economy, with class, and the contrasting economic and social circumstances of different territories; and difficulties in connecting representation to agency, establishing the precise relationship between scholarly Orientalism and imperial instrumentality.

(Mackenzie, 1995, p. 11)

Perhaps the key issue which remains problematic for media analysts concerned with representations of 'race' is to find a way of reconciling two apparently irreconcilable arguments in Said's approach. The first is that which suggests that Orientalism as a discourse is stifling and tends to dissolve all resistance. The second is Said's interest in the work of Gramsci and the concept of hegemony and the struggle over meaning. I will be arguing throughout this book that the problem which Said has generated is one which recurs wherever there is reliance on binary modes of analysis as a way of studying representations of 'race'. This can only be adequately addressed by insisting that there is dialectical relationship between the discursive strategies and signifying practices associated with media representation, the materiality of the processes of signification, and the material world to which both refer.

Eurocentrism, racism and the media

In a work of considerable breadth and scholarship, Ella Shohat and Robert Stam have addressed the question of Eurocentrism and its relationship to multiculturalism and the media (Shohat and Stam, 1994). Their book has much to say that is both interesting and contentious about a wide range of media representations, but I will concentrate here on an interpretation and discussion of their opening chapter. In it they begin by questioning the triumphalist discourse of what they describe as Plato-to-NATO Eurocentrism. They remind the reader that Europe itself is a synthesis of many cultures, and that the West is 'a collective heritage, an omnivorous mélange of cultures' (1994, p. 14). They highlight the fact that much of science and technology, though popularly conceived as originating in the West, was borrowed from outside Europe. Knowledge of the West is idealised in ways 'flattering to the Eurocentric imaginary'. They suggest that Said's concept of Orientalism points to the Eurocentric construction of the East within Western writing, and is complemented by Martin Bernal's argument that Eurocentric construction of the West virtually 'writes out' the East and Africa (Bernal, 1987). For Shohat and Stam, however, just about the whole of the world can now be described as a 'mixed formation'.

They describe colonialism as 'ethnocentrism armed, institutionalised and gone global' (Shohat and Stam, 1994, p. 16) and argue that it is still alive and well as a discursive force. They also describe *neocolonialism* as 'a conjuncture in which direct political and military control has given way to abstract, semi-direct, largely economic forms of control whose linchpin is a close alliance between foreign capital and the indigenous elite'. There is, in this approach, an initial recognition of the determining force of material power relationships and the dominance of capital. They wish, however, to go beyond 'political economy *per se* to the role of discourses in shaping colonial practices' (1994, p. 18). Discourse they define in 'the Foucauldian sense of a transindividual and multi-institutional archive of images and statements providing a common language for representing knowledge about a given theme' (1994, p. 18).

Their commentary on race and racism is instructive for the media researcher. They point out that while racism is not unique to the West or dependent upon colonialism, it has nevertheless been historically allied with colonialism. They insist that racial categories are not 'natural' but constructs which have developed historically and sometimes *changed*. Above all, they argue that racism is a social relation which is 'anchored in material structures and embedded in historical configurations of power' (1994, p. 19). It is, in fact, both individual and systemic and is a structured part of the individual psyche and the system in which that individual has her/his being. Racism is not seen as a phenomenon which exists in a vacuum. It is often manifested in the companionship of sexism, or classism or homophobia. Racism also offers, they suggest, its own perverse pleasures in providing the racist with an easy and unearned feeling of superiority and a superficial sense of solidarity based upon antipathy to a chosen group. Many of the arguments which they make about racism can and perhaps should form the basis for evolving research questions about media representations.

The question of Eurocentrism is, as previously noted, closely related to Orientalism. The Eurocentric discursive repertoire includes more than passing out the wisdom of the West to the Rest. It also involves the consumption, at one or another level of sophistication, of imagery, narrative and values presumed to represent the East. The European and Eurocentric interests in the Orient also involve a consideration, often pleasurable, of the exotic. The exoticist has been compared to the racist in a way which suggests that the former is a person who has been mollycoddled whilst the latter is somehow poverty-stricken:

> While racists are threatened by difference, the exoticist finds it amusing ... . Racism is like a poor kid who grew up needing someone to hurt. Exoticism grew up rich, and a little bored. The racist is hedged around by dangers, the exoticist by used-up toys.
> (Rose, 1989, cited in Shohat and Stam, 1994, p. 21)

The above formulation is seductive but very problematic. It could be interpreted as an apology for those pampered individuals who wish to indulge themselves with a little 'Eastern Promise', as the advertisement for Fry's Turkish Delight would have it. It could also be seen as a justification for reactionary views which see the poor as racist (merely) because they develop a culture of envy and hence need a scapegoat for their resentment. It is also an example of the potential for media research into issues of 'race' to become trivialised in its slickness. I hope that I have already demonstrated that there is, at the very least, a possibility that an alternative conceptualisation of Orientalism might offer to the 'West' philosophical and scientific insights, understanding and cultural enrichment – and there may be those in the West who seek or have sought these in good faith. From this it follows that to essentialise Orientalism as a phenomenon which its subjects can neither escape nor resist drastically limits both readings and representations. It is also positively short-sighted, dangerous, and flies in the face of empirical evidence to associate racism with poverty in this glib manner. The fact that Shohat and Stam quote from Rose without any further comment is worrying.

They also discuss the importance of the concept of cultural hybridity, a phenomenon which has already impacted upon any remaining comfort which Eurocentrists might take from their cultural insularity. Hybridity has manifested itself in post-colonial contexts with the coming of complex and often multiple identities. So we may find Palestinian-Lebanese, Indo-Ugandan-Americans, etc. Hybridity, suggest Shohat and Stam, is dynamic and mobile and is constituted through an 'unstable constellation of discourses' (1994, p. 42). It has also led to the creation of numerous media texts which manage to combine a range of signifiers previously associated with particular generic forms into discourses which are, thereby, not only dynamic but fragile. One has only to think of the ways in which early forms of cultural hybridity produced representations of the 'African' servant who wore a bowler hat and waistcoat, or Native Americans shown with cigars and an occasional 'illegal' drink. More contemporary forms of cultural hybridity may be less immediately insulting to their subjects, but are still fragile in the sense that they explore social worlds which are volatile and evolving. They may, for instance, be concerned simultaneously with issues of 'race', of cultural identity, of sexuality and of popular culture, such as in the film *My Beautiful Laundrette*. Shohat and Stam resist the possibility of using hybridity as a catch-all term, because it 'fails to discriminate between the diverse modalities of hybridity: colonial imposition, obligatory assimilation, political cooptation, cultural mimicry, and so forth' (1994, p. 43). Once again this is a salutary reminder for the media researcher that studying representations of issues of 'race' in relation to cultural hybridity requires careful contextualisation and a recognition that hybridity is both 'power-laden and asymmetrical'.

In contrast to Eurocentrism, they offer not universalism but polycentric multiculturalism. This requires some consideration because of its implications for media research and analysis of issues of 'race'. Multiculturalism has spawned a whole literature of its own, and has become a polysemic hot potato in the United States. Shohat and Stam highlight the various culinary metaphors which have been used to describe multiculturalism, from 'ethnic stew' to 'bouillabaisse' and 'stir-fry'. They are well aware that the term has become problematic:

> The concept of 'multiculturalism', then, is polysemically open to various interpretations and subject to diverse political force fields; it has become an empty signifier on to which diverse groups project their hopes and fears. In its more coopted version, it easily degenerates into a state of corporate-managed United-Colors-of-Benetton pluralism whereby established power promotes ethnic 'flavours of the month' for commercial and ideological purposes.
>
> (Shohat and Stam, 1994, p. 47)

They argue that the term 'multiculturalism' has no essence, but rather points to a debate. It is a debate which they would hope to 'prod' in the direction of a critique of power relations leading to a 'rallying cry for a more substantive and reciprocal intercommunalism'. By this time they have certainly gone a long way beyond (or away from) political economy *per se*, and entered a discursive world which is heavily coded and occasionally opaque. They differentiate polycentric multiculturalism from liberal pluralism in the following ways: (1) polycentric multiculturalism sees all cultural history in relation to social power; (2) polycentric multiculturalism does not preach a multiplicity of viewpoints, but gives its sympathies [*sic*] to the underrepresented and oppressed; (3) polycentric multiculturalism is celebratory and thinks and imagines 'from the margins', seeing minoritarian groups as 'generative participants at the core of a shared, conflictual history' (1994, p. 48); (4) polycentric multiculturalism grants 'epistemological advantage' to those obliged by historical circumstances to negotiate both 'margins' and 'centre', who are thus better placed to deconstruct 'dominant or narrowly national discourses'; (5) polycentric multiculturalism sees identities as unstable, multiple, and historically situated; (6) polycentric multiculturalism 'goes beyond narrow definitions of identity politics, opening the way for informed affiliation on the basis of shared social desires and identifications; and (7) polycentric multiculturalism sees acts of verbal or cultural exchange taking place between permeable, changing individuals and communities.

It is clear that recognising these characteristics of polycentric multiculturalism may lead to productive investigation of media representations of issues concerning 'race'. There is, however, a serious flaw in their argument generated by the retreat from any serious engagement with economic or class issues. The political economy of the media and of society needs to be reinvigorated if debates about Eurocentrism, polycentrism and Otherness are not to become the deckchairs moved around on an ideological *Titanic*.

How many Others are there?

Most of the examples cited so far have concentrated on issues relating to Orientalism and Eurocentrism. It is clear, however, that there is much more to representations of issues of 'race' than this. The whole question of the representation of black people has to be considered. In saying this, I am aware that there is immediately a problem over the choice of words to describe particular groups of people, and that descriptive terms in this area are often contested and changed. We know, for instance, that there has been a move, for many, away from reference to the binary distinction between 'black' and 'white' to describe Americans towards the choice of 'African Americans' and 'European Americans'. We also know that that there are others in Europe and in the Middle East and elsewhere who still prefer to describe themselves as black. For the moment I will use the term 'black' as it relates to the work of Jan Nederveen Pieterse and consider some of the ideas he puts forward in *White on Black: Images of Africa and Blacks in Western Popular Culture* (Pieterse, 1992). The purpose in doing so is neither to review the book, nor to attempt a précis of his ideas. I wish, rather, to offer an interpretation of some of the issues he raises which are potentially productive or problematic for the media researcher.

The first point to note is the significance of adopting a historical perspective if one is to avoid studying representations of 'race' as though they were either arbitrary or 'natural'. Pieterse places emphasis on the fact that the images he discusses are produced by white people,

almost without exception from a position of dominance over those represented. Images, whether drawn or painted, photographed, or
presented as film or video, have to be decoded or interpreted in at least
two ways. First, they need to be understood, as much as is possible, in
the context in which they were produced. Second, they need to be
understood and 'placed' in a contemporary context.

Pieterse notes, for instance, that the whole range of racist discourse
about black people, from that of the savage to the 'animal' and the
heathen, has a prehistory. This prehistory belongs to Europe, where in
the Middle Ages 'the forests were the domain of beings on the border-
line between human and animal, myth and reality, like the *homo ferus*
who was raised by wolves or the *homo sylvestris*, or man of the woods'
(1992, p. 30). Pieterse points out that, to the Greeks it was the peoples
of the north, that is, those now called Europeans, who were barbarians.
In the Middle Ages, for instance, it was Hungarians who were referred
to as ogres and savages, and from the twelfth century the English
began to speak of the 'wilde Irish'. As eighteenth-century thinkers such
as Locke and Montesquieu turned their attention to the New World,
discussed and pronounced on the 'savage' and whether or not there
was the possibility of a 'noble savage', Pieterse argues that the agenda
to which they were working was, in fact that of European interest.
There was, according to Pieterse, an optimistic anthropology which
was adopted by the supporters of revolutionary change, and a pessi-
mistic one adopted by those who supported the status quo. The New
World was, in fact, invoked as a philosophical and political counter-
point to Europe. After the French and American Revolutions, by the
end of the eighteenth century, the debates about 'noble savages' no
longer had an ideological relevance and faded in significance. It was
around this period, at the turn of the century, that European nations
turned their attention to establishing a different kind of relationship
with the New World. Pieterse cites the *Edinburgh Review* of 1802 to
illustrate the different relationship: 'Europe is the light of the world,
and the ark of knowledge: upon the welfare of Europe, hangs the
destiny of the most remote and savage people' (1992, p. 34). While this
is a summary and telescoped version of events, more detailed consideration of the histories of the period does not suggest that it is,
overall, an incorrect appraisal of the situation. The key point to note
here is that debates about and descriptions of 'savage' people can be
seen to be closely related to European political and philosophical
purposes. As the change in attitude towards and perception of black

people became established, along with the expansion of slavery and a generally more aggressive or condescending attitude to the New World, so any ambivalence was eradicated. The totally negative construction of the savage which ensued was to form the basis for a multitude of representations of Africa and black people over the next century.

Pieterse has provided a most useful collection of visual reminders of the kinds of representations which evolved to meet the needs and perceptions of the empire builders and entrepreneurs. Such representations did not go completely unchallenged, however, as the abolitionists made their case against slavery. Pieterse argues that contending images of Otherness 'form part of the social construction of reality and the negotiation of the future. Images of others are a form of cultural polemics; they are contested and are themselves a form of contestation' (1992, pp. 231–2). This notion of contestation, particularly in relation to contemporary popular culture, will be explored in more detail in the following chapters.

The question of who constitutes the Other, and whether it is a category that transcends history, extends beyond considering the representation of any single group. I have spent some time discussing Orientalism and the ways in which black people have been represented. It will not be possible in the space available here to give necessary attention to other forms which racism may assume, the subjects of such racism, or the variety of media representations with which they may be linked. Phil Hammond (1997) has edited a collection of essays which trace the evolution of media discourses about Japan and the Japanese. Stuart Hall has provided a complementary text to that of Pieterse which also considers the historical context in which representations of 'race' and empire were produced (1997, pp. 223–79). The way in which the values and norms of the European way of life were exported through representation, and the values associated with 'the civilising mission' of the Europeans were brought home are illustrated well by Hall. He notes that the English explorer Henry Stanley was so interested in the importance of the civilising mission of spreading commodities across Africa that he named his native bearers after the products they carried on his late nineteenth-century explorations (Bryant and May, Remington, etc.). At the same time, the exoticism or Otherness of the lands and people of the empire were 'brought home' as products such as matches, biscuit tins and sheet music were generously illustrated with images of imperial heroes.

Otherness was becoming softened and commercialised, and this was only the beginning of a process of re-presentation which would undergo many more changes and mutations as contexts and social forces changed. It might be argued that in the face of so much cultural interchange and hybridity, to borrow from Mackenzie, what we need now is not so much a theory of 'Otherness' as a theory of cultural cross-referencing (Mackenzie, 1995, p. 55).

Identity, self and Other

Questions of identity and difference have become more and more prevalent in debates about the media and culture. The word identity crops up in the title of books almost as often now as postmodernism once did, and Marxism did before it. This book is no exception and I make no apology for highlighting the fact that specific signifiers have their historical moments or levels of cultural currency. Perhaps the only qualification I would wish to make is that I am interested in the relations between identity, self and Otherness precisely because of the challenges they pose to the researcher interested in media representations of issues of 'race'. What one has to conceptualise here is, in fact, a three-way relationship, involving 'self', Other and identity. Pieterse has argued, following Therborn, that 'an ideology of *alter* involves an ideology of *ego*' (Pieterse, 1992, p. 232). What this means is that we cannot seriously consider the identities or representations of others without considering the representations or identities of what we call 'self'. Identity is a relational concept rather than an essence. It is also a dynamic concept in which its two contributory dynamics change in themselves and in relation to each other. Identity is a relationship analogous to the relationship which constitutes the sign. The difference is that self and Other (the 'signifier' and 'signified' in this relationship) are seldom singular or unitary and are likely to change places and relative ideological weight as identities are formed, adjusted or destroyed, and as power relationships are contextually or historically changed.

Why is this significant for the researcher concerned with representations of 'race' in the media? First, because it is important to consider identity in a way which goes beyond the binary pairing of it with 'difference' (Woodward, 1997). There is a need to recognise that the (binary) opposite to identity is not difference but 'non-identity'. Second, individual identity needs to be conceptualised more dynamically as formed through a process which involves the recognition and confirmation of relative 'sameness', the negotiation of multiple and often contradictory positions on a range of issues, and, from time to time, the external imposition of undesired or unacceptable norms. It also needs to incorporate an awareness that difference is possibly more relevant, in relation to ideology and the media, when identified in terms of (changeable) material conditions, of general social conditions, of territorial claims, of wealth and poverty, of issues of power and subordination.

A beginning

This book is an exploration of a range of media examples which may illustrate, complicate and even sometimes contradict the concepts of identity which I have been discussing. It is also an attempt to hold in tension a range of theoretical positions in order to demonstrate the ideological significance of the identities which may be on offer in the chosen media representations. Underlying the investigation is a belief that secure identities are the possession of the ideologically numb. The next chapter is about questions of identity, but it is also an example of what happens when the politics of identity takes over completely from any politics of class.

Part II
Case studies and examples

4

Winfrey in crisis

The Oprah Winfrey Show on the Los Angeles riots broadcast by Channel 4 on 14 May 1992 was a remarkable piece of television. It is not that it was so different in structure or presentation from many other North American programmes which deal with emotive human issues. Oprah Winfrey specialises in challenging and stirring both participants and audiences with matters of perceived mutual concern. But this time there were signs of strain in the generic form as much as in the strong emotions expressed by the participants. The reason, I will suggest, was that what Marcuse once referred to as the 'established universe of discourse and action' proved to be an inadequate means of dealing with the issues in hand (Marcuse, 1972b). An established universe of discourse acted, for Marcuse, as a kind of shield. It ensured that 'ideas, aspirations and objectives that, by their content, transcend the established universe of discourse and action are either repelled or reduced to terms of this universe' (1972b, p. 24). The remarkable feature of the programme I will be analysing is that it, and its spokesperson Oprah Winfrey, precisely *failed* to deliver the reductive process described by Marcuse. The participants offered judgements and comments which broke with accepted codes of morality, attacked certain power structures, and above all raised issues about the nature of capitalism, that all too familiar ghost at the feast.

I aim to outline in brief several dynamics of television and ideology. My contention is that there are at least two kinds of televisual literacy. The first involves the comprehension of television's specific signifying practices, the second requires the identification and analysis of discursive strategies (intended or unintended) in the text. This is the domain of literacy, I contend, with which media research needs to concern itself at all levels. The narrative structure or emplotment of the programme is crucial here. I will suggest that Winfrey introduces inaugural and terminating motifs which bear little relation to the confused and vituperative montage of argument, assertion and counter-assertion that constitutes the main body of the programme. I will further suggest that the agenda which Winfrey reintroduces throughout the programme is one which is retrograde and reactionary and refuses (or is unable) to recognise publicly the central contradictions generated by the 'race'/power and economy/power relations informing most of the issues represented.

The programme contains the views of many of the citizens of Los Angeles as they struggle for space to confirm or deny the discourse inferred or openly asserted through Winfrey's questions. Those who are given space to speak do so with varying degrees of anguish and anger, and with varying degrees of discursive expertise. They are angry and operating in a discursive field in which most of them never find a voice. Thus they often become confused as they struggle to find words which fit into the fragmentation of a debate carried on at such speed, a fragmentation common in the televisual discourse (Postman, 1986). Winfrey is much more likely to empathise with the emotional drift of contributions than she is to pick up on their analytic or substantive content. Finally, I will suggest that it would be mistaken to look only to Oprah Winfrey for the origins of the discourse which is under such stress in the programme. It is the discourse of a free America, of the American Dream, of postmodern capitalism. It is a discourse shared in some way by the majority of the participants in the programme – if only it would work for them. Because it does not, they are confused, hurt, angry. Oprah Winfrey is in the impossible position of trying to maintain her credibility as an African American while defending the hopes and aspirations of entrepreneurial capitalism against the onslaught of the dispossessed and the disillusioned.

Presences and absences

Oprah Winfrey:

> We are on location in Los Angeles today, and over the last week I have, just like I know many of you have, felt a sense of shock and a sense of anger and a sense of, of course, outrage – and some tears – as people died and cities burned. What will be written into history books for our children and our grandchildren – the beating of Rodney King, came into our living rooms and smacked us in the face. And now we must ... we must ... listen to each other.

Before the credits Winfrey makes three points. First, she registers her shock and pain at the death and destruction which have occurred, and confirms it by her presence, with her show, in Los Angeles. This is a motif which will recur as several African Americans declare a minor victory in having gained the attention of Winfrey and hence of America; gaining attention seems to be a metaphor for rekindling some kind of black struggle which is never clearly articulated. The second point before the credits concerns the beating of Rodney King, which she refers to as something that will be written into history books. She suggests that it came into our homes and 'smacked us in the face', but most viewers had seen the tape many times before, during the trial, and some participants in the programme try to make it clear that this was no isolated incident. The programme later contains video of another example of police brutality, when Don Jackson has his head pushed through a plate glass window by a police officer. Winfrey's opening demonstrates the indignation which one might associate with the discovery of a single, unexpected and rare happening. For some, I suggest, it was not a slap in the face, nor even a last straw breaking the camel's back.

The titles

The title sequence lasts 18 seconds and consists of twenty shots and an accompanying sound montage. The complexity of this segment is belied by its purpose, which is not only to take us in to the show, but, in the context of US television, to serve as a means of securing the place for another batch of TV commercials. In this case they allow a show which has just started with Winfrey's piece to camera to just start all over again. The order prefigures in microcosm the patterns of representation which inform the mode of reality of Winfrey's show and, in this case, of the USA under stress.

The first shot is in black and white and is a simple sans serif upper-case type face superimposed over an image of the American flag. The first caption reads THERE IS BUT ONE RACE followed by a dissolve to HUMANITY. The second shot is of Martin Luther King, and we move in very rapid succession to the burning cross of the Ku Klux Klan, a group of religious Jews, Winfrey in the studio, a Black Power meeting, a black and white bleached-out shot of a crowd, over which is superimposed WE HOLD THESE TRUTHS, followed by a crowd sequence where an arm is holding a smouldering US flag. We then see a black and white shot of a white racist speaking, a black and white caption TO BE SELF-EVIDENT, American neo-fascists marching and carrying placards, one of which reads JEWS OWN ALL THE MEDIA, followed by shots of demonstrators and a black and white caption THAT ALL MEN. The Reverend Al Sharpton and entourage are then seen, linked to a shot of a black man shouting at Winfrey in the studio, which gives way to another black and white caption superimposed over a shot of a statue of Abraham Lincoln, reading ARE CREATED EQUAL. The final caption reads RACISM IN 1992 and includes the logo for The Oprah Winfrey Show in the top left-hand corner of the frame. After 18 seconds of televisual reality we are back with Winfrey, talking to camera.

A detailed textual analysis of this sequence would be necessary to unravel the layers of meaning packed into this narrow ambit. The complexity of association and relative opacity of the montage would, however, make such an analysis both lengthy and leave it always incomplete. It would also intervene in a process which is designed to be a preparation for a show which most viewers will have seen many times before. The titles provide, in effect, a metaphoric backdrop against which Oprah Winfrey, and by extension we the viewers, will play out their existence for the time of the show. In this context they are a dramatisation of what Jameson has described as 'psychic fragmentation' (1991, p. 90): postmodern popular television offering the viewer a renunciation of control or the possibility of being out of control. In the context of domestic viewing it would be an aberrant act to dwell on these images. No-one could make coherent sense of what they mean, though some may attempt a (desperate) reading. There is no time. Indeed, there is very little time for the whole show. What the titles do offer through all this miasmic confusion is the presence of Oprah Winfrey as 'our' representative.

Opening the debate

The urgency of the discussion, the gravity of the events, is curtailed and constrained by the need for the next round of commercials. And, in the midst of our anxieties about those who loot and plunder, we are constantly reminded of the commodities for which we exist and about which the show is concerned, by commercial breaks. The commodities mentioned or signified in the show itself include pairs of trainers and televisions and the stores in which the trainers and televisions are sold.

Property is also quantified and commodified by representatives of the black and Korean business communities. Confusion sets in, however, with the recognition that some do not have such easy access to the commodities as others. And those who do have access – the store owners and Oprah Winfrey – are more inclined towards a moralism which is of the old order.

They argue that viewers should remember the sanctity of the family, of hard work in order to 'make it' and above all the need to keep our hands off other people's property. But for the looters there is another discourse in play and it is much nearer to the ethics of postmodernity discussed by Bauman. He suggests that with the postmodern we have seen the deposition of universal reason but no reinstatement of a universal God: 'Instead, morality has been privatized; like everything else that shared this fate, ethics has become a matter of individual discretion, risk-taking, chronic uncertainty and never-placated qualms' (Bauman, 1992, p. xxiii).

Winfrey first informs us that many of the scenes we will observe are both haunting and unforgettable, and involve 'blatant, unapologetic' looting. We see a young African American leaving a shop and he urges us (the viewers!) to go inside and find some shoes which are our size.

The first montage sequence of the programme proper is concerned with the violation of property; violation of the body comes second. Winfrey's words are the words of a shocked, numbed capitalist, displaying solidarity with other shocked and numbed capitalists. The infringement of property rights transcends race as an issue. The decision to put a reference to looting before showing scenes of extreme violence cannot be unmotivated. Perhaps it could be argued that violence is not newsworthy because it is a daily occurrence in Los Angeles; looting is less common and hence deserves a higher priority. But this reading lacks conviction. It is possible that looting is perceived as a serious threat to the system, whereas violence is actually a means whereby the system is sustained. The issue of Rodney King is serious, but not so serious that it cannot be relegated to second place if citizens or members of the community begin to undermine the conventional means of making a profit. Cracking skulls, shootings and, beatings can all be understood as a norm, but stealing televisions and trainers is an unacceptable deviation.

The semiotics of horror

The events which we see are portrayed in long shot or through the flattened perspective of the telephoto lens. Most of the material of the violence in the riots was shot from the air, so there is little chance to identify any facial expression. Body language is all we have and it is from this that we may construct a reading. The horror is somehow accentuated by the distance. No close-ups are necessary. Any shots which are framed more tightly have a nightmarish calm accentuated by an absence of synchronised sound. The last time we saw similar sights was when the Israeli troops were spotted trying to break the arms of Palestinians by pummelling them with rocks. But in that case there was an acknowledged political dimension to the horror.

We watch, as outsiders, with abhorrence and, if we are honest, with a ghoulish fascination – here is what unchoreographed violence looks like. There is nothing of the organised flow of blow and counter-blow found in dramatic representations. There is also an aesthetic of terror in these sequences. First there is one in which a truck driver is mercilessly beaten by a group of men. They kick him when he is down. Finally, one man throws what appears to be a can at the truck driver's head from very close by and scores a direct hit. The truck driver drops and lies motionless. The assailant does a small celebratory dance and we move on to the next sequence. But in that brief moment we are offered something of the aesthetic of terror. There is a dream-like inevitability in its silent commentary on the violence. It also has the disturbing charm of a Rauschenberg in its fortuitous yet almost classical multi-media compositional elements.

The second sequence, that of King's beating, is an image straight from hell. It has no low sunlight or colour to give it a romantic air, just darkness and light with the moving figures wielding their batons over a hapless silhouette. The figures in the dark cannot be identified except as deliverers of violence. They have none of the Los Angeles chic to be found in so many of the shots of looting. There is nothing but a chiaroscuro of pain in long shot. There is no cathartic end to the violence in this scene. The date of the event is burned into image by the domestic video camera, and the violence is perpetual. These images will become part of a repertory of horror which defies us to deny them. We might remember the bodies at Kent State.

But Oprah Winfrey is wrong. These are scenes of *believable* brutality. What makes us hold our breath is the absence of that Hollywood crack

as fist hits face or baton hits skull. Just silence, distance and the absence
of make-believe. Absent but encroaching reality is an affront to the
simulacrum recognised for what it is – a representation of a world
beyond itself. Winfrey reminds us that when George Halliday filmed
the beating of Rodney King the truth was something which was hard
to ignore.

This seems a plausible judgement, but Oprah Winfrey does not say
for whom the truth was hard to ignore. Many knew that truth from
bitter experience. It would be very foolish to try to compare the
violence displayed in the two sequences. How could one be more
justifiable than the other? It might be better to consider that the
violence of the police and the violence of the people in the street are
politically explicable. And in such explanations we might have found
the 'justifications' of both the racists and the oppressed. But that is not
a road down which Oprah Winfrey goes. Instead she poses the audience a question which is one she has heard a lot of white people ask.
She wants (us) to know why black people are so angry.

This first substantive question places Winfrey at the centre of an
ongoing debate. She has made other programmes on racism and the
key question raised again and again comes from white people. Why
are black people so angry? She shares the perplexity of the white
populace in many ways. Winfrey's stance requires her to remain a
'sister', but also to show redneck indignation at the restlessness of the
natives. Her question also ignores the fact that the looters were not all
black and that the poor and exploited of Los Angeles include a large
central American population.

It is no wonder Oprah Winfrey looks perplexed. Opening questions
which she might have posed are too numerous to list, but they could
have radically affected the ways in which the programme developed.
If Winfrey had offered a formulation such as: 'One question which I
hear asked a lot is, how can America hold itself up as an example to the
rest of the world when it is riven with racial hatred, poverty and ever-
increasing urban decay?' Or perhaps: 'What can we do about our
society – a society in which black people can be treated with such
disdain by a legal system which purports to be egalitarian and an
economic system which perpetuates the lie that anyone can make it if
they try?' Winfrey's presentation, however, establishes a universe of
discourse which excludes or marginalises such issues.

The questions she now poses are linked to her own television
viewing of what occurred. She expresses disbelief that looting shoes or

televisions could have anything to do with Rodney King, then turns to one of the young African American members of the audience and asks him directly why he did it.

This second substantive question put by Winfrey moves the discursive ground considerably. The 'white' question about black anger carried with it an implicit reprimand which might have been better expressed (on behalf of the non-black population) as 'Why are these black people, who live in such a wonderful country as ours, so ungratefully angry?' or in another and more likely vernacular formulation: 'Why the fuck are these blacks so angry?' Either way, the question is judgmental and superior, put by a black presenter to the black people in the audience – but on behalf of the white audience. It is also a racialisation of a question which has historical precedents, as when rulers (ruling classes) were concerned about the conduct of the 'poor' or the 'slaves'.

It is now linked with a further judgement by Winfrey, before we hear from any of the participants. The second judgement is a (grudging) recognition that black people might have a just reason for anger, but not the right to go out and steal. Violence is not mentioned at this point. Winfrey is baffled at the way in which black people – and it is black people whom she has now definitively singled out – would show indignation by removing property (looting). She does not speak of 'poor' black people. While in no way questioning the sincerity of Winfrey's argument, there is a bitter irony in the way she insists that she sat at home and watched television 'like so many of you did'. Oprah Winfrey, it is not unfair to comment, inhabits a qualitatively different world to those who live in South Central Los Angeles, and her conditions of viewing are likely to be somewhat different in the literal and metaphorical sense.

The young man to whom she has posed the question suggests that it is important to try to understand why he and others acted as they did. Winfrey says she is trying to understand. This first interchange with a programme participant is one where Winfrey speaks for herself and the Nation. There is more than a hint in her response that she may be trying to understand, but so far she is not having much success. The young man says that he was after what he calls 'self-satisfaction'. He says that he and many others had no satisfaction from the beating of Rodney King or from the murder of Latisha Harlins. He suggests that, as far as he is concerned, he is being told that his own life is worthless. He feels that he is being told by the media that he can be beaten whenever those who wish to beat him feel so inclined. He says that he feels he is supposed to accept that and just be glad that he can go and vote to make things better. He suggests that voting does not make things any better. He goes so far as to say that by the time he has cast his vote the President has already been elected.

This man is not named, perhaps to avoid recrimination, though he is seen quite clearly enough to be identified by the police. He is someone to be looked at by the audience with fascination, as the 'innocent' stare at the condemned. He is a looter brought in from the heat of the street to the heat of the studio. Winfrey does not attempt to unravel the meaning of a term like 'self-satisfaction'. Instead she pursues her schoolteacherly line of thought and tests, on our behalf, the credibility of this unidentified man, by asking him if he is registered to vote. He says that he is, and Winfrey answers simply 'OK.' In this context it would be possible to read 'OK' as meaning 'You got past this one, but I'm not finished with you yet'.

The young man restates his point that the President is already elected before he gets to vote. The political implications of arguing that one's vote is of little significance in the United States of America are considerable. Whether right or wrong in his analysis, this man represents the views of many of those who do not vote. This could have led to a most important debate about the relationship between social unrest and the perceived efficacy of the electoral system. But this is not the way the debate is to be structured and Winfrey's response is brief and sharp. She says that he was out looting and wants to know if he got any stuff. There is almost impatience in her line of interrogation which suggests that she is not impressed by the analytical turn which the man's contribution has taken. She has not come to Los Angeles to discuss politics. She has come to practise it.

The young man verifies that he did indeed go out looting and that it made him feel 100 per cent better. He tells her that it gave him self-satisfaction, and he believes that everyone who was out in the streets felt the same satisfaction, which they could get no other way. 'Self-satisfaction' is thus invoked once more, though it is now reduced from its original context suggestive of a seeking for justice to the level of gratuitous and immediate gratification. Winfrey confirms what the man says by asking him once again and in the confirmation there is no vestige of empathy or understanding. There is nothing in the discourse of which she is a purveyor which has any space for this alien 'self-satisfaction'. She does not pursue this any further, but turns to another African-American man and simply says: 'You too?'

This is the beginning of the show and the first participant is allowed a considerable number of responses. The general tone is not too heated, but Winfrey's manner is cold and, in the context of her show, clinical. Her question to the second man is brief to the point of scorn. His response is much more complex and most of the substance of what he says will be ignored. He points out that the brothers and sisters do not 'have it' in the same way as those who go out to work every day, with their nice cars and nice houses. It may be that one could read what the young man says as envy, but it is more likely that it is plain resentment that he cannot get such a job. He reminds Oprah that he comes from the streets and that to come from the streets is to live in hell. He says that when something like the Rodney King verdict brings about a partic- ular situation, and the town is burning, and you don't know whether you will have enough groceries, then you go out and get whatever you can.

Winfrey asks him if that was why he went out on the streets, to look for food for his family. It is clear from her response that she is sceptical about the answer she has received. Whether or not this man is telling the truth, Winfrey has effectively cancelled out the possibility that anyone might have been out on the streets looking for food. This an important point because it draws the discourse of the programme closer to a debate about property rights than one about hunger or poverty. The suggestion that people like him live in hell is not picked up, and the silence on the matter is telling. The young man says he was out there looking for food. Winfrey then changes tack slightly and muses for a second or two on the fact that it is interesting that the young man has used the terms 'brothers and sisters'. She says that she considers herself a sister, but that it did not mean that she went out on the streets looting.

The use of the phrase 'it's interesting' can be best understood in its situational context as suggesting something quite different from its usual meaning. What Winfrey is doing in her response is opening out the definition of 'brothers and sisters' to include rich and poor African Americans. The argument is presented as an appeal to all decent, law- abiding brothers and sisters. It also introduces a fleeting possibility that is almost totally excluded from debates about poverty and depri- vation, the possibility that there might be a difference between the rich and poor, the haves and the have nots which transcends race. This is no more than the glimmer of a possibility and it is pushed away by the simple phrase 'it's interesting'.

The shift in the direction of the debate is accomplished by the simple device of introducing a half-baked syllogism which links Winfrey to the majority of African Americans who, she says, were not out there looting. She has now implied quite clearly that there is no justification for looting (poverty having been expunged by ignoring it) and her questions from now on will try to identify why her looting interviewees acted wrongly.

The young man responds to her point somewhat defensively. He says that if she was not out there on the streets, then she cannot speak for those who were. He has lost a little confidence and produces a standard response which lacks conviction. Winfrey pursues her line of questioning, while admitting that she was not out on the streets. She tells him that most of the brothers and sisters were not out on the streets. The young man persists that he still represents the majority of African Americans. Here there are contradictory arguments in play. The man is arguing that he does represent the majority of the people from the streets. Winfrey is arguing that he does not represent the majority of the people who stayed at home!

Once again Winfrey puts down her discursive marker with a simple OK which she uses as a means of closing off a debate that might prove complex or not fit easily into the pre-ordained but implicit discursive structure of the show. There is also a sense in which one feels the momentum of US television gaining force; she has to move on because the show requires it. This time she does so with a point of the microphone to another person, and a third man speaks. This third man suggests that it was necessary to be out there and to be caught up in the intensity of the event. He suggests that he had no intention of becoming involved at first, but rather went out to see what was happening. Winfrey says that what she is concerned about is the fact that most African Americans are hard-working, attempting to take care of their children every day. For this she receives a round of applause from the audience. If ever there was a clear manifestation of a struggle over the ownership of a sign, it is found in the struggle over who has the right to use 'brothers and sisters'. It can be used as an emotional appeal for solidarity, as a cynical riposte, or as a knife in the back. Here Winfrey drives home her first ideological advantage. She has won an audible approval from many in her audience and she has appealed in a populist way to the wider viewing public. The case she is now putting is one which congratulates the majority in order to be able to condemn what would doubtless be called a small number of 'bad apples' if it were an enquiry into police brutality. What it means is that most black people are 'good citizens', that they are trustworthy and honest. The problem with this argument is not that it is untrue, but that it is ideologically loaded. By stressing black participation in the looting and the 'normality' of most black citizens, Winfrey has strengthened the discourse of racists. It is now established that the people under discussion are either good citizens or looters *as black people*. It is very close to an apology for black people, and it is smacks of potential guilt or special pleading. Either way it is probably unintentional, but it does ignore the fact that black people were certainly not the only looters. The same young man makes one last effort to explain his activities, by telling Winfrey that he works hard every day too, but that the events of the day were enough to make him change his rules of conduct for a while. For this he receives a round of applause from another section of the audience. This time it comes from those in the audience who clearly perceive some justice in the case being made. But there is no probing follow-up by Winfrey, just the ubiquitous 'OK'.

Winfrey admits that she was not out on the streets, but suggests that the events were 'sadly amazing', and offers the viewer a chance to see what the cameras took 'for us'. In doing so she affirms the status of the recorded data. Phenomenal forms are more important here than real relations.

The wrong man and woman

The sequence which follows is a pre-edited segment which was put together by the programme makers to illustrate the kinds of things which went on during the looting. It is made up of five short pieces. The first is an interview with a man whose arms are stuffed with the goods he has just looted. He continues walking as he is interviewed. He is not African American. The fourth piece is, literally, a running interview with a woman who is reluctant to face the camera. She is not African American. This fact is not referred to once by Winfrey. It seems to have little to do with the first question posed by Winfrey about why black people are so angry, nor with the contribution later in the show by Ralph Wiley, the author of a book entitled *Why Black People Tend to Shout*. There is clearly an agenda which has been pre-set, which has a lot to do with the alleged rowdiness of black people, and which does not address wider political issues, including those of poverty and social deprivation. Hence it is possible to ignore the fact that those people who are seen looting and being interviewed just happen *not* to be African Americans!

The interview with the man in the street must be unique, for it is unusual to interrupt someone considered to be performing a criminal act to ask whether they are concerned about its legality. It is also clear that the man does not consider himself to be a criminal; he is, rather, inconvenienced by the interviewer. This is important because I do not believe that any interviewer would approach a common criminal with such questions for fear of endangering herself. The questions she asks are worth pursuing. Is what the man is doing wrong? Doesn't he care? The sequence is not, however, intended as a precursor to such debate, nor is it intended to prove the guilt of the looters; after all, they are in the act of looting and further proof would seem superfluous. What the interviewer wants to do is to shame and humiliate them. The horror of it is that they will not admit they are wrong, and it is this which puts too much strain on the hegemonic balance.

The sequence ends with a shot of an elderly (white) woman who is, understandably, very emotional. The emotion takes our interest away from the il/legality of looting to the suffering of this person. It is another nodal point in the narrative structure which has been pre-planned. We move from emotional shock to emotional shock. She tells us that this is the United States and wonders how 'they' could possibly let this happen. The woman is elderly and she has no food in the house. It is time for a commercial break.

Who says you're supposed to have it?

At various further points in the show Winfrey either changes the direction in which the discourse is evolving, or ignores the substance of a contribution in order to return to her own agenda. A young African-American woman is given time, for example, to explain how and why she looted. This she does with considerable dignity, though it is by definition impossible for her to justify her actions within a discourse where they have been pre-judged as wicked. Within the space of a few seconds, and flying in the face of other interjections, Winfrey asks three times: 'OK, but the question a lot of people want to ask, I'm one of those people, is who says you're supposed to have it? I mean, what's a TV got to do with your life?' The tempo and temperature of the show are such that Winfrey is not always able to complete her questions without interruption. But she insists on making her point. This time it is a question 'a lot of people' want to ask. It is no longer racialised. The authority of Winfrey's phrasing, however, slips with repetition. She attempts to make the question more succinct or accessible, until it becomes absurd – or bitterly ironic. 'I mean, what's a TV got to do with your life?' The ridiculousness of the situation is deflected by a more militant contribution which is well beyond the programme's remit. It is spoken with more authority than Winfrey is able to command and generates considerable applause. It is made by another African-American man, who mentions the genocide of the Indians and finishes with a suggestion that the White House has to be Painted Black. Other unseen voices join in at this point asking who has the right now to tell them that they are wrong.

This more militant contribution is backed up by the first African-American man to have spoken. The logic which suggests that 'America is a loot' may be hard to stomach, but it is also hard to say that it is wrong. The conclusion of the argument for this contributor is clearly to follow the path of black militancy – on the premise that no democratic reforms for 400 years have delivered anything worthwhile for black people. The point is taken up by the first man who highlights the hypocrisy of those who would dare to tell the oppressed that they are wrong to behave like oppressors. It is a complex and important political argument which directly addresses the questions which Winfrey has asked, but her response is to suggest that they have not addressed the question. She turns elsewhere to get some sense which she – and by extension, the viewer – can understand. In doing so she changes her mode of address, 'You're a business owner, sir ... '

I was upset too

The person she addresses is indeed a black business owner and he is puzzled and perplexed by the situation. His is a second-generation black-owned restaurant and he points out that he lost three stores in the fires and several of his stores were looted. He points out that it is hard enough to get insurance at the best of times, and that he could not even pay his 350 employees at the end of the week. Winfrey asks the black business man what he would like to say to the young African American. He is troubled, and turns to say that it may be possible to get televisions and some clothes in these circumstances, but where are people going to get their jobs from? Amidst applause, he asks where he is going to get the business which his parents started.

The discourse is now firmly back on track. The black business owner has spoken his piece with quiet conviction. His gentle persuasiveness ignores the line of argument which justifies radical action by the oppressed in favour of a quietism which provides a pay packet to those who have a job. It does not answer the radical argument, it simply bypasses it. The first young man is now firmly trapped in a discourse which has excluded any action of the kind which he has already admitted to being a part of. He goes through verbal torment as he tries to justify himself; in the end he has to resort to racism in the absence of any class dimension to his case. He says it was a mistake that black businesses were burned. The black businessman rubs some salt into the moral wound by his final contribution. Once again, it is a contribution based upon the 'proven' wrongness of the looters. It is unlikely, however, that he and the first man are neighbours.

> Black Businessman: I was upset too, I was upset too. I was as upset as everyone else, but I didn't go out and destroy your home, or where you live … (Applause)

The Korean dimension

The Korean business community lost a great deal of property and goods in the social unrest. The first contribution by a Korean business-man makes a valid point, followed almost immediately by a revealing value judgement on the attitudes attributed by the Koreans to the African-American population. A Korean businessman asks how burn-ing down a Korean store has anything to do with the oppression of African Americans. In a highly charged atmosphere, he points out that 50 per cent of the businesses which were burned were Korean. He suggests that the Koreans are not oppressors and that they were hurt 'just as much' by what happened. Koreans, he suggests, cannot justify three hundred years of oppression. Then his logic slips, as he says that they have only been in the USA for twenty years and 'you expect us to solve all of your problems'.

It would be naïve to suppose that there is no racism against the Koreans in the United States, just as it would be naïve to ignore the gradations of intensity of racial prejudice which are so often based on the darkness of skin colour. What this means is that the Korean community may on some occasions find itself the victim of racist ideology, but at other times may perpetuate that very same ideology. The suggestion by the businessman that the Koreans might be expected to solve the problems of the black community implies that the black community is one socio-economic group. Statistically it would be accurate to perceive it this way, were it not for the fact that the hurt parties here are the minority of better off black citizens. They are united in colour with their fellow African Americans but divided by class. As class is not a category allowable in the show, this debate is not on the agenda. Oprah Winfrey introduces a further complicating factor by reminding viewers of the killing of Latisha Harlins. This is a harrowing narrative, followed by an equally moving account by an African-American woman of how she feels that the Korean business owners are rude to her when she goes shopping. It is here that the second Korean businessman enters the debate. His comments do little to alleviate the mounting tensions.

This businessman stresses the importance of respect, but suggests to the African-American community that they cannot demand respect, but have to earn it. He goes on, in an apparently patronising manner, to suggest that with freedom comes responsibility, concluding by suggesting that the young African American who had spoken at the beginning of the programme did not represent 'the entire perspective'. When mentioning the demand for respect, he links it with the name of an African-American preacher named Cecil Murray.

At this point another African-American man steps forward and says that he does not demand respect, but that if he shows respect towards Koreans he expects this to be reciprocated. He goes on to say that if he walks into a Korean shop and greets the owner, he would like the greeting returned. He says it is not very reassuring to be followed around the store being observed as though he is someone about to steal.

This series of challenges and responses allows the debate to become more complex once again. It is clear that the Korean businessman has to temper his rather high-toned introduction ('There's a couple of things I want to address') when he is challenged by the unidentified African American. To suggest that the black community has to earn respect is to tacitly endorse the position that they have not done so as yet. The African American is clear in his response that he believes that respect is something that has to be reciprocated and that he does not feel that this is always the case with the Korean shop-owners. There is the basis here for some serious and probing discussion. But the dictates of the programme are such that Winfrey has to intervene and allow for another commercial break, which is done by using another piece to camera by a member of the community, in this case an unidentified woman of colour.

Winfrey talks the viewer out of the scene with a piece to camera in which she acknowledges the high tensions between the black and Korean communities. Winfrey says, with perhaps a little resignation, that she will be right back. Before the break we are shown a single shot of a woman who describes herself as a woman of colour. This woman is weeping and she talks to the camera and she tells the viewer that she has paid a high price to be an American. She says she understands the black community, having herself been a victim of prejudice. She points out that as a woman of colour she is doubly oppressed and closes with an unfinished sentence: 'I can still say this is the best country ... '. Apart from fulfilling the necessary purpose of fragmenting the programme in order to make space for the interests of advertisers and consumers, this break also provides another point of emphasis: irrespective of the suffering which racism or possible deprivation might bring, this is still the best country. It is a threadbare, tattered version of the American Dream, but it is a crucial part of the narrative unfolding before us for which the ending has already been written.

A world together

After the break there are several contributions, mainly from representatives of the Korean business community, arguing for a more conciliatory approach to the social and economic issues which Los Angeles (or a part of it) faces. There is reference to 'the depravity of mankind, starting from the White House', and from the author of *Why Black People Tend to Shout* a suggestion that the present situation is one of anarchy because representatives of the law are placed above the law. One African-American man is still unimpressed by the need to co-operate with the Korean community until each has their own house in order. Oprah Winfrey tries to guide the unfolding narrative, disregarding the contradictory positions being put forward. She pleads with the unimpressed African American, asking him whether or not we all live in a world together. His response is direct and overtly political. He tells her that when she leaves the show, she can go to a lavish home, but that many of 'us' go home to empty refrigerators, no diapers and crying kids. He tells her that not everyone has a job to go to, although he has a job himself. This is one of the most overtly political contributions to the programme, delivered without malice. Winfrey listens and her face shows real anguish, but she does not respond. It is not an issue over which the facts might be disputed; it is another moment when some serious questioning could have led to a more considered analysis. But, as usual, it is not to be, for an ideological saviour steps forward in the shape of another young African-American man. He has to speak very loudly to make himself heard, and Winfrey asks him twice what it was that he said. He states unambiguously that he is not a thief and reprimands the previous speaker, telling him that he is able-bodied and should get himself a job.

At one level it is important that the show is seen to be made up of contributions from the people. This means that it is generically snug when a contributor pursues the line of thinking along which Winfrey has been moving. The contributions which follow attack the African-American man who has dared to justify looting on the basis of poverty or for suggesting that some people 'ain't got it like everybody got', or that looting was the only way that 'we could have some action right now'. Once again, the debate is moving out of control as righteous indignation obscures any of the premises of political analysis. Once again, Oprah Winfrey brings the discourse back to a more acceptable generic structure. She simply asks the young man who had told her that she would be going to a lavish home after the show whether or not he wants peace. His response is that he does want peace, but . . . . After that his response is swallowed in the tension and the general hubbub. Winfrey's question is delivered to him in a conciliatory but weary manner. The man answers in a way which clearly indicates that there will be a price to be paid for such peace. But he is generically barred from attempting to develop his argument. He has served his purpose in the show by offending and by boosting the emotional temperature. The next person to speak does not let up the pressure, but turns towards the more overt forms which racism can take for the black person who happens to have a higher education. Like all those before him, he is not given a name.

He tells Winfrey that he has a degree in Quantitative Economics, and that he lives in the back room of his parents' house with his two kids. He says the reason for this is that he is too dark for corporate America. Once again the realities of racism are becoming painfully apparent. This is clearly an edit point in the show because when Winfrey next speaks there is a change in the ambience. The young graduate's contribution is a long way from the *LA Law* version of life. It calls, once again, for a serious reappraisal of the way in which the American

Dream has been represented in popular television. Perhaps that reappraisal took place and perhaps it did not. It is clear that tempers were running high in the studio. But this was overcome by simply editing. When we cut to Oprah Winfrey, she is making a generically appropriate comment about getting along in the studio. Once again, two major contributions have been deflected or ignored.

After the next break for advertisements, the studio has returned to relative calm. Winfrey calls upon a woman who is to play an important role in the generic structuring of the programme. She is also named. Isola Foster speaks with some authority, as the head of an organisation called Black Americans for Family Values. She says that it is important to start from where we are today because we can't go back to the years of slavery. She points out that we were not here at that time, but that many of those in the audience were around in 1965, when it was said that they could not get along with the Jewish community. She suggests that the problem now is that more money is being asked for programmes in the community. More money, she says, has been made available and implies that it has been poorly utilised by the leaders of the black community. For this she receives a round of applause. She moves immediately to the trial of Rodney King and suggests it was the black community leaders who encouraged riots and pillaging – and that this leadership put all these ideas in the minds of the young people. At this point the level of jeering in the audience is such that Winfrey has to make an appeal for Foster to be heard. Foster proceeds. She tells viewers how Bobby Kennedy calmed the black community when Martin Luther King was assassinated: 'He said my brother was white and he was assassinated. This is not the way. There was calm.' This is a most unusual argument, whether or not the words attributed to Bobby Kennedy were actually spoken. It seems to imply that even when someone as important as a white person is assassinated, it is important to stay calm. Foster is not deterred by the apparent hostility from the younger African-American men, and continues her attack on those (unnamed) leaders of the community who, she says, encouraged the rioting. It is important, for the analysis I am attempting, to note that Isola Foster does not mention family values once in her in initial contribution. She gives a passionate account of the mistakes of the leaders of the black community in Los Angeles. Her words are sufficiently disliked to cause pandemonium in the studio once again. Winfrey tries to bring in the next speaker over the now animated Foster. The structure of the programme suggests that this is a pre-ordained running order, rather than Winfrey attempting to pursue the question of family values, which Foster has yet to mention. Winfrey calls on another African-American man called Don Jackson. Foster, meanwhile, is continuing to interject with comments about how everyone saw 'it' on television. The 'it' referred to would seem to be the alleged incitement to violence. The programme is about to move into a sequence which hovers somewhere between tragedy and farce.

Winfrey informs us that Don Jackson, an African American, is a former policeman who went undercover and discovered that police brutality 'does indeed exist'. This is an extraordinary phrase, which implies either naïvety or a bad choice of words. The fact that Jackson is an African American might also have something to do with his experience when he went underground. Winfrey also has to attempt to link the planned contribution of Jackson with that of Foster. Jackson has, understandably, a different perspective on the recent events. He has also inhabited a somewhat different world to that of Isola Foster.

Jackson begins by saying that Foster has a pacifist view of things. He suggests that she sees the recent events in Los Angeles as acts of random violence, and that she is confused. He points towards the young African-American men who have spoken earlier, and says that they are not confused. Perhaps their anger should not have been directed at the Koreans, Jackson says, but he is tired, in 1992 of holding hands and singing 'We shall overcome.' He says that his contribution is a wake-up call, and then tells his own story. He says that he has already tried to do things 'the peaceful way', presumably as a police officer. He points out, with justification, that he was risking his life in his job, particularly when he went underground. The viewers at home are shown a copy of a black and white video which shows two men standing near a shop window. One of the men is a uniformed police officer and the other is Jackson. The police officer turns Jackson around, grabs his head and with one swift movement pushes it through the plate glass window. We see the window smash to the ground. Winfrey offers an interpretive commentary:

> The tape that you're seeing right now is Don Jackson being smashed through a plate glass window, uh, as he, uh, attempted just to prove that police brutality did indeed exist.

Her comments are greeted by derisory laughter off-screen. It comes from the young African Americans. Jackson points out that, having had his head pushed through the window, a jury of eleven white people and one black person voted for an acquittal. Only the black jurist voted against acquittal. Jackson is, by this time, ready to give a more extended interpretation of his experience. He gets as far as 'Now what I want to say is ... '.

The scandalous story which Jackson tells must surely rank as an abuse of justice equal to that experienced by Rodney King. It involves an act of vicious brutality. Winfrey's comment this time is fatuous and results in derisory laughter from an unseen audience member. She might have drawn upon Jackson's comments as a means of linking violence from the police with the Rodney King issue, or to give a historical perspective which would indicate that police violence and racially motivated violence by the police are regular occurrences for the black population of Los Angeles. Instead, Winfrey moves the debate in a way which is risible but generically and narratively necessary.

> But, but, Don, Don – what Isola is saying she stands for is Black Americans for Family Values – how can you argue against family values?

Jackson responds with another political contribution, delivered over the increasingly shrill voice of Isola Foster. He denies that he is against family values, but the ideological work has already been accomplished by Oprah Winfrey. The issue of police brutality and racism is slipping away. There are several other contributions by members of the Korean community, most of which seek peace and conciliatory measures. There is also a single contribution from a white woman who points out something which is never addressed by the programme, although it is obvious from the interviews with the looters: that the looters were by no means all black people. But there is one other angle which has to be covered before the programme finishes, and this requires further comments by black business owners. A man and a woman speak, though I will discuss only the woman's contribution.

She begins by explaining to the young brothers and sisters that the black business owners in the community are having a hard time surviving even without the social unrest. She says that the root of the problem does not stem from any minority group, but from the government, the system. She does not specify precisely what the government has or has not done, but concentrates on telling the audience about the various taxes she has to pay, including sales tax. She also has other debts and has to pay rent, with her six Burger King restaurants shut down because of the social unrest. Her contribution is not the first to single out the 'system' for criticism. One Korean citizen has pointed to what she sees as the moral deprivation which the system manifests. This time the critique comes from a black business person worried about paying sales tax and rent. This woman is so worried about these issues that Rodney King, Don Jackson and the exploitation of the poor are pushed aside in order to address what she perceives to be the real issues.

With remorseless logic, she asks if she can make just one more point, and she is allowed the time to do so. It seems that many people are coming into her restaurants, slipping, then suing her. Even her employees are claiming workers' compensation. She says it is the mentality of the people of Southern California who are 'suing us to death'. She says they (the black business owners) are being killed from every angle. Once again the show is approaching farce. It is the customers who slip and fall in black-owned burger houses and the workers (black, one presumes) who are claiming compensation who are the real enemy. But this farce is not noticed by the audience nor commented upon by Winfrey. This reactionary claptrap is ignored just as surely as any of the radical comments offered earlier.

There has to be a way of moving towards the end of the show. Time dictates it. Winfrey has had her arm around an African-American woman who has been waiting to speak. She does so following a contribution from an African-American man who has pointed out that the present violence and unrest would never have happened had it not been for the jury in the Rodney King case. The woman's contribution is suitably apolitical and emotive: we all have to look to ourselves for the solution to this issue of racial violence and economic exploitation.

Winfrey's final piece to camera clearly marks an edit point. It may have been shot before the previous contribution; it was clearly not shot immediately afterwards, because many of those standing in the previous shot are now quietly seated and watching the monitors above their heads.

> I don't, uh, uhm, pretend to know a whole lot about the world. I do know ye shall know the truth and the truth shall set you free. And I'm hoping that, uh, everything that has been said here today, that we will take into our hearts and be willing in our own selves to make a difference. There's a time for healing. There's a time for healing. This is our prayer.

The final appeal is religiose. It is a piece of easy rhetoric invoking the words of Christ from the Gospel according to St John (chapter 8, verse 32). The choice of this particular biblical quotation is linked to taking into the heart a series of mutually incompatible statements made from mutually incompatible positions. It is an impossible task, linked through religiosity with the world of Martin Luther King. The end title montage includes King's image and his voice advocating non-violence. It is intercut with angry voices of the black citizens of Los Angeles. The overall message of the end montage is, however, clear. Study war no more. Not in Los Angeles.

Conclusion

I hope to have demonstrated through this analysis that the television discussion, exemplified *par excellence* by *The Oprah Winfrey Show*, is much more than just an open forum for discussion and debate. I have been attempting to identify the ways in which a minor hegemonic crisis manifests itself in this fragment of television as Winfrey's presentation techniques and the overall structure of the show are strained to near breaking-point in order to maintain a universe of discourse which cannot be contained within the usual presentational strategies of the programme. Through Winfrey's linking comments, the programme offers a very selective version of history and an emotionally charged but weakly presented account of the sanctity of private property. Above all, the programme is unable to recognise or address the economic system of production and exchange in and through which it is made. The programme set out to address issues of racism in North American society. The discourses of free market capitalism, and the generic requirements of the television discussion/talk show ensured that it failed. The beating of Rodney King, which was mentioned at the beginning of the show, was hardly addressed. Nor was the ill-judged question about black people being angry. We only know that the truth shall set us free.

5

Popular cinema and anti-racism

This chapter will consider the ideological significance of three feature films which have the issue of 'race' as their central concern, and all of which are based upon historical fact (Carr, 1978). The films are *Cry Freedom* (1987), *Malcolm X* (1992) and *Schindler's List* (1993), and each has attracted praise and opprobrium from various quarters. The films are very different from each other in many ways, but they have one thing in common: they are each designed with a didactic as well as an 'entertainment' purpose. Their subject matter in each case has been and is of crucial historical and political significance in the latter half of the twentieth century. The re-presentation of the protagonists in the films, of the historical contexts of which they were a part, and of the outcomes of their respective lives are therefore most significant.

The directors of each of these films (Sir Richard Attenborough, Spike Lee and Steven Spielberg, respectively) have formidable track records in the industry. I will be discussing the films individually before attempting a comparative analysis. The readings I make will be based on the ideological implications of specific presences, absences and representational forms which the films offer, and some of the critical writing which has been produced about each film. The purpose in doing this is not to allocate praise or blame to the film makers for what they have put in or left out of their films, but rather to ask about the ideological implications of the films as texts, particularly in relation to their representation of issues of 'race'. I will also be discussing some of the contradictions and ideological tensions which each film generated and attempt to ascertain, from a consideration of the films, the nature of the political and historical conceptualisations upon which they are based.

Cry Freedom

Too many times have the Steven Bikos ended up minor characters in feature films that were supposed to be about them.

Spike Lee (1992, p. 11)

Cry Freedom was based upon the writings of the South African journalist Donald Woods about the life and death of the South African leader Steven Biko (Woods, 1987). The film was quite well received in Europe but grossed only 5.8 million dollars in the United States – where *Malcolm X* grossed 48.1 million and *Schindler's List* 96 million. Attenborough had shown a previous interest in biographic films of 'major' historical figures as long ago as 1972 with his *Young Winston*, but achieved his first major success and an Oscar for his direction of *Gandhi* (1972). In *Cry Freedom*, Donald Woods (Kevin Kline) is chief editor of the liberal newspaper *Daily Dispatch* in South Africa. Woods is shown to be critical, from a privileged white position, of the apartheid government. He is also very critical of Steven Biko (Denzel Washington), the leader of the 'Black Consciousness' movement, whom he sees as a black supremacist. When the two meet, Woods begins to change his mind about Biko and they become 'friends'. Eventually Biko is murdered in prison and Woods decides to write a book about Biko's life and death. By this time Woods is a banned person and confined to his home. He resolves to escape from South Africa with his family and the manuscript of the book. The last third of the film is taken up with the planning and execution of the escape.

The film *Cry Freedom* was made by an indignant white liberal, based upon the accounts by another white liberal of the life and work of Steven Biko. Neither of these white liberals had ever experienced, except as observers, anything of the suffering, oppression and physical brutality which Steven Biko endured before he was finally murdered by the South African Government. The film is also structured as an adventure story which takes place, so to speak, in a land with an evil regime and a few fine warriors engaged in the service of truth and justice. These warriors are shown to be mainly white and they demonstrate good humour and bravery on behalf of a largely silent mass of black South Africans. There is virtually no mention in the film of the Indian or 'Coloured' sectors of society under apartheid; nor is there any engagement with the economics of apartheid. The film is made up of several set piece crowd scenes, held together by narrative passages which provide the sometimes verbose thread of the adventure story.

There is a lush soundtrack, punctuated by loud bursts of South Africanesque choral singing. The real hero of the film is the middle-class, privileged Donald Woods, on his lone mission to carry the banner, or rather the plastic bag containing his manuscript, back to the 'free world' because the 'free world', like Mount Everest is *there*. Where Steven Biko is given any serious screen time, it is as a black 'buddy' and foil to the adventures of Donald Woods.

The above points, and a few others beside, have to be made and reappraised before any serious consideration of the film's ideological import can be offered. There are several reasons for this. The first is that, like so many films which combine politics, history and adventure, the film is open to cheap shots. I have just fired off a few, but the critics had a field day. They reminded us again and again, if we did not already know, that both Attenborough and Woods were white liberals. There was a finality in that correct judgement which hid a multitude of ideological problems, for it was often one made by both white and black *liberal* critics. There were also some conservatives among them and very few revolutionaries. The naïvety of their critical positions was often surprising. Representations of apartheid, it seems, facilitate rela-tively easy judgements about what constitutes worthwhile conduct on the part of the privileged classes in an exploitative society.

Lack of space does not permit a detailed engagement with the whole range of judgements passed upon the film, but I will identify a few in order to discuss the ideological issues which they raise. Writing in the *Washington Post* on 6 November 1987, Desson Howe made the follow-ing observation: '*Cry Freedom* is a pill movie. You take it with a glass of water and you feel better about your social consciousness in the morning.' Howe describes Woods' change of attitude towards Biko as follows: 'But after meeting Biko (Denzel Washington), he undergoes a radical change and makes Biko's Apartheid battles his own.' Howe suggests, as did many hostile critics, that the film disintegrated after representing the death of Biko:

> When Biko dies halfway through, so does the movie. The Woods family's subsequent flight from South Africa becomes the cinematic equivalent of a Gerald Ford presidency. Attenborough tries to rally with Biko flashbacks and a depiction of the Soweto massacre. But the 1976 slaughter of black schoolchildren . . . is chronologically and dramatically out of place.

Howe finally dismisses the movie with an interesting if crass cross-reference to Chile: 'In a country busier than Chile with oppression, violence and subjugation, the story of Woods' slow awakening is certainly not the most exciting, or revealing. But Attenborough's aims are more academic and political than dramatic.'

Roger Ebert, writing for *Cinemania* (1996) in an uncharacteristically vindictive mood, likens the representation of Donald Woods to the fictional character of Charles Tatum (Kirk Douglas) in the Billy Wilder film *Ace in the Hole* (1951):

> *Cry Freedom* is not really a story of today's South Africa, and it is not really the story of a black leader who tried to change it. Like *All the President's Men,* it's essentially the story of heroic, glamorous journalism. Remember *Ace in the Hole,* that Kirk Douglas movie where the man was trapped in the cave, and Douglas played the ambitious reporter who prolonged the man's imprisonment so he could make his reputation by covering the story? I'm not saying the Donald Woods story is a parallel. But somehow the comparison did arise in my mind.

What is so surprising about this ill-informed comment is that the fictional character played brilliantly by Douglas is without principle and driven only by the urge for journalistic fame. Woods (Kline), it seems, makes many people uncomfortable because he *does* have principles.

A more measured critique is mounted by Johnston (1991) where he observes that Woods' relationship with Biko is idealised 'beyond sentimentality', and 'perpetuates the myth that race relations are essentially personal relations, affairs of the heart, to be improved, not so much by accommodation of power to power, but through personal conversion' (1991, p. 90). This is a more valid criticism which has often been made in relation to liberal representations of oppressive regimes. The question which has to be asked, however, is whether *Cry Freedom* is a film which deals only with personal relations and interactions, or whether it demonstrates a broad political opposition to the apartheid regime, albeit from a liberal perspective. Detailed study of the film suggests that there are numerous occasions when Attenborough moves beyond a simplistic, emotional or individualist interpretation of his subject matter and into the realm of liberal political condemnation. The issue then becomes ideological. If one opposes *liberal* condemnation, it behoves one to offer alternative positions.

Cry Liberal!

The film has often been criticised for being made by white liberals. Much of this criticism has the sophistication of someone who suggests that the problem with musicals is that the people in them often sing. The questions which need to be addressed to a white liberal film should be based upon an identification of the characteristics of such films and the integrity with which they address their subject matter. Too often they are dismissed with judgements which are puerile. The first point to note is that films made by liberals (white in this case is incidental) are not likely to be critiques of capitalism, and *Cry Freedom* is no exception. Nor are such films likely to analyse power relations from a Marxist or Foucauldian position, and the main narrative of *Cry Freedom*, as Johnston rightly comments, concentrates on personal relationships. In terms of popular cinema, however, there is at least a case to be made for working towards the structural understanding of power relations through a recognition of the importance of the personal. This, of course, begins to rehearse those once crucial debates between realism and modernism (NLB, 1977) as to which mode of representation would bring about radical social change. It is a somewhat hollow rehearsal, however, as many of the critics of *Cry Freedom* would not campaign (let alone struggle) for radical social change, beyond their opposition to apartheid in another country.

This relates to the ideological significance of labelling Attenborough and Woods as liberals in such a way as to make further argument superfluous. I suggest that an alternative reading of *Cry Freedom* might consider that it is easier for a camel to go through the eye of a needle than for a privileged white middle-class male to give up his house, home, job and endanger his family. Unfortunately, many critics make their armchair judgements of representations of political action on an inflexible and restrictive scale which suggests that when the privileged fight oppression it is somehow less significant than the struggle of the oppressed. In ideological terms this is a questionable matter.

It is significant, ideologically, that it has been necessary to make the above points before coming to what I argue is the core of the film, despite its treatment by mainly liberal critics. This is the film's concern with the Black Struggle and the abomination that was apartheid.

Narrative Freedom

The narrative of *Cry Freedom* centres on a relatively small number of people, and particularly on Biko and Woods. It is also structured very much as a conventional adventure story where one protagonist learns from another, who is wrongfully killed, and 'vows' to make the views of the latter known to the rest of the world. These narrative constraints, and many more such as those which demand that the film is divided into 'chapters' and has a suitable end, are part and parcel of the realist film text. In literal terms the film does spend some time showing how Woods and his family escaped. But an analysis of the ways in which Attenborough has represented and structured the realities of apartheid and the ideas of Steven Biko might provide us with a different sense of the film's ideological importance.

The film opens with an extended and evocative representation of the destruction of the Crossroads Settlement in Cape Province by the forces of the apartheid state on 24 November 1975. The film's assault upon the eyes and ears demonstrates cinematically the callous metallic power of apartheid with a minimum of words. When Biko does speak in the film, he carries authority, though his words have often been simplified or rescripted to meet the needs of the realist text. There is an irony here. The demands of popular cinema mean that popular heroes are very often intellectually caricatured in order to comply with generic norms. Of course there may also be occasions when the 'hero' is carefully reinvented so that his political beliefs are more acceptable to a wider audience, or to fit with the predilections of the director or production company. Attenborough's representation of Biko was, perhaps, a little over-indulgent with its lighting, from the first meeting with Woods when Biko appears, Christ-like in the garden of the church in King Williams Town, to his time in court when the light from the 'window' provides Biko with a soft aura. Indeed, it might be said that Attenborough idealised Biko much more than he idealised Woods. But the film also had a didactic purpose which it carried relatively lightly. This was to inform the audience about the conditions under which black people lived in the apartheid state. Biko's death, however, was not idealised. The scene in the mortuary when Biko's body is photographed is harrowing in its restraint.

The portrayal of the Minister of Justice, James Kruger (played by John Thaw), also demonstrated the icy calculation of white apartheid thinking. Denzel Washington as Biko managed to impart something of the twinkling eye and verbal eloquence with which Steven Biko was able to oppose and infuriate his oppressors. The film draws to a conclusion with the successful escape of the Woods family, but it is the massacre at Soweto which is more powerfully represented and which hangs in the memory like drifting smoke. To point out, as Howe does, that the Soweto massacre is not chronologically accurate, is to miss the point. Ideologically, the film is indeed liberal, and its protagonists are idealised to varying degrees. Its point of focus, however, is the apartheid state. It finishes with a rolling list of those people who have died in detention in apartheid prisons. Many of the audiences who saw the film were stunned into silence. Some of them had improved their scant knowledge of the workings of apartheid, and in some cases discovered for the first time the location of South Africa. The film lacks political sophistication, but in representing issues of 'race' its liberalism carries a strong anti-racist message. It's ideological blind spot, which stands in flat contradiction to the film's universalising approach to matters of 'race', is the relationship between the apartheid state and international capital. Biko was not so blind.

Malcolm X

Two of my favourite touches in *Malcolm X* are the opening, a full-frame of the American flag, which then burns down to an American red-white-and-blue X; and near the end, when Denzel-as-Malcolm is taking that fateful drive from the New York Hilton to the Audubon Ballroom, on February 21, 1965. The music, behind him is of Sam Cooke singing 'A Change Is Gonna Come.' I love that song, love the way Sam Cooke interpreted it. I've always loved it, and knew one day the way to use it would make itself known to me.

(Lee, 1992, p. 160)

None of his (Malcolm X's) powerful critiques of capitalism and colonialism are dramatised in this film.

(hooks, 1994, p. 159)

If the general appraisal of *Cry Freedom* tended to label it as a white liberal film, *Malcolm X* was known from the beginning as a feature produced by whites with a black director. Ed Guerrero describes *Malcolm X* as 'the outstanding achievement of the 1990s black film wave' (Guerrero, 1993, p. 197). Much of Guerrero's praise is for the very fact that Lee managed to get the film on the screen, in the face of an overwhelmingly white Hollywood power bloc, and serious opposition from some African Americans. All the available evidence suggests that this is a wise judgement. It is possible, however, that Lee's struggle in the end produced a film which did not live up to the director's own high expectations. Todd Boyd attacks the film from a radical perspective:

> Having been subjected to several months of publicity about the filmmaker's struggle in getting the film made and having this discourse situate the viewer, we witness the redundant image of the Rodney King beating, which slowly dissolves into a burning X now visibly displaying the American flag. We are presented with Lee's objective from the outset: placing Malcolm X in the pantheon of important *American* political figures. Immediately following this graphic opening scene, we witness a close-up shot of Spike Lee himself, which is later revealed to be his character of Shorty, Malcolm's friend.
>
> (Boyd, 1997, pp. 26–7)

The question which needs to be posed, as with the other two films under discussion, is whether Lee took account of the possible ideological ramifications of the way in which he structured the life and work of Malcolm X. Such a question cannot be separated from the modes of signification which Lee adopted to achieve his ends. Lee chose a chronological approach to Malcolm X's life, and this is what might have been expected. What might not have been expected was the slickness with which jitterbug, fashion and social mores are combined in the opening sequences in such a way as to present an image of African-American people which might be thought, at the very least, to be generically inappropriate. The apparently radical montage with which Lee opens his film is undercut by the strutting, the choreography, the nostalgic glamorising. Guerrero has almost nothing but praise for the film, but bell hooks is nearer to Boyd in her appraisal.

> As sentimental, romanticised drama, *Malcolm X* seduces by encouraging us to forget the brutal reality that created black rage and militancy. The film does not compel viewers to confront, challenge and change. It embraces and rewards passive response – inaction.
>
> (Boyd, 1997, p. 64)

This comment by Boyd could well be related to the passage by Lee at the opening of this section. The burning American flag, which Lee describes as a 'favourite touch' has a limited semiotic force in an era when it has been burned or re-presented burning so many times and in so many places. Ideologically, the graphic quality of the X as a synecdochic reminder of the thought of Malcolm X, suggests rather something closer to the Bat symbol projected in the sky over Gotham City. The hope it offers is brief, selective and superficial. One is reminded, in the baseball caps and T shirts with the X on them, of Marcuse's comment that Che Guevara had been good for the poster business. The other passage in the film which Lee relishes is the playing of the Sam Cooke song when Malcolm X is riding to his tragic death. Lee's reading of the moment is, however, very personal. The melancholy and beauty of Cooke's rendering hardly relate to the fury one senses in Lee's own description of its significance in the film (Lee, 1992, p. 161).

Lee views the role of the artist in society as crucial. There is, however, a tension in his preface to *By Any Means Necessary*, where he describes *Malcolm X* as 'my artistic vision'. On the one hand, he identifies a (media) war situation which is concerned with the way people think. In this he adopts a straight determinist line – 'At stake is the way to control the way people think or [do] not think, act or be passive.' On the other hand, he looks to the artist/film maker to move people. If they succeed, it is because 'it's about the HUMAN SPIRIT' [*sic*]. Lee's concept of the human spirit has distinct universalist overtones, whereas his political analyses are much more narrowly focused. It may be the contradiction between what Lee sees as the role of the artist in representing Malcolm X ('my personal interpretation of the man') and the focus of his politics which weakens the potential of his film.

Malcolm X was an orator, an activist and a political strategist. There are so many of his astute political statements which Lee might have chosen as a part of the film, that almost every one which is left out raises questions about the ideological significance of the film text. It is, of course, Lee's right to choose as an artist, as an African American, as a citizen in a democracy. Speculative thinking requires, however, that we ask just a few 'what if?' questions. It is worth recalling bell hooks' comment that the film

> suggests Lee is primarily fascinated by Malcolm's fierce critique of white racism, and his early obsession with viewing racism as being solely about a masculinist phallocentric struggle for power between white and black men. It is this aspect of Malcolm's politics that most

resembles Lee's, not the critique of racism in conjunction with imperialism and colonialism, and certainly not the critique of capitalism.

(hooks, 1994, p. 161)

In his last years, Malcolm X made many political statements which are of fundamental importance – so fundamental that it could be argued they need to be re-presented by anyone who produces a text about Malcolm's life. These statements also have profound implications for an understanding of the issue of 'race', of racism and of politics today. If Malcolm X's judgements are wrong, there is a strong argument for demonstrating that he was capable, as are all humans, of error. If they are deemed to be right, they have important strategic and intellectual implications. The ideological significance of Lee's film, then, has to be gauged in terms of its structured absences.

First, we should note that Malcolm X made an unambiguous link between capitalism and racism:

It's impossible for a white person to believe in capitalism and not believe in racism. You can't have capitalism without racism. And if you find one and you happen to get a person into a conversation and they have a philosophy that makes you sure that they don't have this racism in their outlook, usually they're all socialists or their political philosophy is socialism.

(Breitman, 1965, p. 69)

Malcolm X also made a potentially profound statement on the relationship between oppressors and oppressed which has not escaped the attention of certain political organisations:

I believe that there will ultimately be a clash between the oppressed and those doing the oppressing. I believe that there will be a clash between those who want freedom, justice and equality for everyone and those who want to continue the systems of exploitation. I believe that there will be that kind of clash, but I don't think it will be based upon the colour of the skin.

(Breitman, 1965, p. 216)

Many other examples could be cited from the speeches and discussions of Malcolm X. Some of the things which Malcolm X said are controversial and would be likely to offend some group or another. Criticism of capitalism as a system is, however, too fundamental an issue to pass over without comment. It is certain that some selection has to be made by any director who makes a biopic, but given the intensity with which Lee argues his case on the printed page, it is disturbing that there is little evidence in the movie of the above dimensions of Malcolm X's politics. There is no doubt that J. Edgar Hoover and many others were keenly aware of the broad political and potentially revolutionary sweep of Malcolm X's ideas. This is hinted at when we see Malcolm being followed and photographed on his visit to the Arab world. My contention, however, is that the absence of any serious critique of either capitalism or imperialism in the film, apart from one or two rhetorical flourishes, makes it ideologically quietist. The rage at racism is there but, as hooks has argued, 'it is not the political revolutionary Malcolm X that Lee identifies with' (hooks, 1994, p. 161).

Malcolm X is a film which demonstrates Lee's undoubted cinematic talent and provides a personal view of Malcolm X, which was Lee's prime intention. Whatever one makes of the film as narrative, as performance, or as cinema, *ideologically* it is universal sadness which wins out over political indignation or even personal fury. The montages at the opening of the film and Malcolm X's lip-synch 'By any means necessary' at the end cannot disguise this.

Schindler's List

Schindler's List was released in 1993 and has generated considerable response from writers and researchers in fields as diverse as historiography, cinema studies, Holocaust studies and general education. It has also been reported on and discussed in a vast number of newspapers and magazines around the world. It was based upon the 1982 McConnell Prize-winning book *Schindler's Ark* by Thomas Keneally. The film tells a story of a limited number of key figures against a backdrop of racist state murder. These figures include Oskar Schindler (Liam Neeson), Amon Goeth (Ralph Fiennes) and Itzhak Stern (Ben Kingsley). Schindler is the *bon viveur* and entrepreneur who takes the opportunity to make a small fortune from the slave labour which the Nazi era offered through its persecution of the Jews. Schindler changes as the war proceeds (or the film progresses), and by the end of the film he has sacrificed his wealth and risked his own life in order to save as many of 'his' Jews as possible from almost certain death. The second key figure, Goeth (Fiennes) is a camp commandant who is shown to be a sadist, emotionally disabled and a dedicated Nazi. This might sound like the basis for an absurdly over-ambitious melodrama, were it not for the fact that the characters were not invented for the film, but actually existed. The historical Schindler was indeed a remarkable person and he did manage to save many Jews from extermination, whose descendants in Israel now number over 6000. There was an Amon Goeth, who was a commandant of the Plaszów concentration camp.

As with *Cry Freedom*, *Schindler's List* is a film which focuses upon a particular 'moment' in a period of gross and, for some, unimaginable institutionalised inhumanity, immorality and injustice. The question which has exercised many writers and researchers is whether it is possible or desirable to dramatise aspects of the life of Oskar Schindler and use these as a means of telling the world about the horrors of the Holocaust. The film is, of course, based upon a novel which, in turn is based upon accounts of what happened during the period. I do not mean by mentioning this to imply for one moment that I doubt the existence of the Holocaust. On the contrary, I wish to argue, with many others, that the horror of what happened is, perhaps unrepresentable. Spielberg went to great pains to create a sense of verisimilitude. The locations are often the actual places where events occurred, including the factory which Schindler owned. The attention to detail in costume is equally meticulous. The same cannot be said, however, for the characterisation of the main protagonists. I will return to these later in the chapter. First, I wish to suggest that Spielberg worked upon the misguided premise that if one comes nearer to demonstrating the levels of violence and sadism which were often practised by the Nazis, one would better understand the 'meaning' of the Holocaust. This is ideologically questionable for at least two reasons. The first is that the horrors which Spielberg did represent, including blood gushing from the skulls of those who were shot, came closer to recognised generic Hollywood forms than representing the 'unknown' that is the Holocaust. At the same time these representations were woefully inadequate. The infamous sequence where a group of women were taken to the showers in Auschwitz and shown naked to the audience while they waited to see whether they were to be washed or gassed demonstrates this well. These women did not look as though they had been undergoing months of slave labour. Their cropped hair was eerily fashionable. There was a sense in which the audience was invited to participate in a voyeuristic experience which simply took its licence from actual Nazi atrocities. It is even more worrying to note that the scene was inserted after the completion of the film at the insistence of the film's producer Carlo Ponti (Horowitz, 1997, p. 129). There is a misplaced faith in realism in such representations which does highlight the limits of a representational modality. It also demeans the subject of its representation through unintentional ghoulish fascination with what is obviously a dramatic recreation. Horowitz makes the point clearly when she argues that the shower scene at Auschwitz is

> a scene pornographic both for its depiction of terrified, naked Jewish women and for its use of the gas chamber to provoke the viewer's sense of suspense. In Resnais's *Night and Fog*, the camera probes this dark centre of genocide years after the final killing. Aware of the magnitude of horror and sheer human misery of the place, Resnais's narrator momentarily pauses. 'You have to know to look,' he says quietly, before explaining what the camera reveals; fingernail marks left on the gas chamber ceiling by the death struggles of its victims.
>
> (Horowitz, 1997, p. 128)

There are other occasions in the film when attempts at showing unspeakable cruelty are reduced to the language of the Hollywood adventure epic. The rescue of Itzhak Stern from the train journey which would lead to his certain death is another example. In terms of the drama, it is breathtakingly exciting to see Schindler shout 'Stop the train!' In terms of understanding the magnitude of the Holocaust it is vaguely obscene. Spielberg has, perhaps from generic necessity, seduced his audience into cheering for 'Schindler's Jews' while the Holocaust goes on in the background, as have the lives of American Indians or 'African natives' in so many other filmic catalogues of atrocity. The harsh judgement which has to be made is that if this is a fault of realism, then it is an inappropriate mode of representation. Otherwise it is simply an inadequate film. The use of black-and-white photography has been much vaunted as the means by which Spielberg chose to add a gritty realism to the film. In fact, the opening of the film is so polished that it adds an aesthetic charm to its gruesome subject matter. The lighting is not simply reminiscent of *film noir*. It supersedes *film noir* in its formally contrived 'naturalisation' of every feature, its polished chiaroscuro.

The fact that the realist text seems to require a limited number of key protagonists is not necessarily a weakness. It depends upon the subject matter. In *Schindler's List* there are two key protagonists who are

German and one who is a Jew. Schindler is, from the beginning, established as the Good German. It is true that he is shown as an opportunist entrepreneur at the beginning of the film, but he grows in moral stature as it progresses. At the end he breaks down and confesses that he could have done more and demonstrates his Christian ethics by making the sign of the cross. This is, for some, a distortion of what Schindler was, and his breakdown at the end of the film tends to reduce him as a credible historical figure. He is more convincing, by this time, as a Hollywood hero – the James Stewart of the Holocaust. This is in no way a reflection upon the quality of Neeson's acting which is always measured and utterly professional. It is the conception of the character which is at fault. Omer Bartov has suggested that the way in which Schindler is presented at the end of the film is a banal humanisation of a character who did not break down. It is also banalises the context of his actions.

> For only the kind of Schindler who precedes this scene, that do-gooder crook who gets a kick from helping Jews and fooling Nazis, that anarchist underworld character with a swastika badge who never ceases to enjoy his cognac and cigars even under the shadow of Auschwitz, that trickster who befriends one of the most sadistic of all concentration camp commanders, that incompetent failure of prewar and postwar normality who thoroughly relishes the mad universe of the SS where he is king, only that man could have saved the Jews in quite that manner. And this kind of man could not, and did not, break down. . . . Tears have no place in this tale, whether 'authentic' or not.
>
> (Bartov, 1997, p. 45)

The characterisation of Amon Goeth is equally problematic. He is seductively attractive in his evil doings. Ralph Fiennes tries to look as flabby and gross as the actual Goeth, but he cannot repress his own charms, even as a Nazi war criminal. The very sensitivity with which Fienes portrays Goeth's struggle with his Nazi beliefs and his attraction to Helen Hirsch dignifies something which has no dignity. Spielberg provides questionable erotic titillation, with Helen Hirsch shown inexplicably clad in wet, clinging underwear, followed by a vicious beating which the audience is invited to 'share' once more because it is perpetrated by a Nazi. Goeth becomes, in cinematic terms, an amiable murderous drunken slob. True, he is a wicked man, but he is a cinematic villain who gets his come-uppance at the end as part of the catharsis which Spielberg offers his predominantly non-Jewish audience.

The third main character in the film is, of course, Itzhak Stern (Ben Kingsley). It is an almost flawless performance. That is the problem. Stern is portrayed as the stoical, weary, intelligent, subservient Jew. He recognises, in the context of the Nazi onslaught, that to remain alive and in relative good health is as much as one can hope for. This requires, however, a practised invisibility unless one is needed. Stern can inhabit cinematic space without ever occupying it. He exudes a controlled fear and a reconciliation with the awfulness of his (and the Jews') plight. There is a sense of tranquillity in his behaviour and it has been linked by at least one writer to the feminisation of the Jew (Doneson, 1997). It is clear from a study of the film that there are many occasions when Jews are represented as pathetic or helpless. This should not be confused, however, with those representations which feed anti-Semitism. In the latter, the representation of the Jew becomes closely related to certain representations of the Arab as identified so meticulously by Said in his work on Orientalism. The coinage of the term 'feminisation' is used to suggest passive behaviour and meek compliance. It can be related back to such writers as Bruno Bettelheim who argued that 'A certain type of ghetto thinking has as its purpose the avoidance of taking action. It is a type of deadening of the senses and emotions, so that one can bow down to the mujik who pulls one's beard, laugh with the baron at his anti-Semitic stories, degrade oneself so that one will be permitted to survive' (Bettelheim, 1990, cited in Doneson, 1997). Ideologically, there is no awareness in the film that any Jew might have been moved to opposition to the Nazis, that there might have been a resistance. Nor is there any sense that Stern has any interest or even existence outside of his relation with Schindler.

Stern, as the main Jewish character in a film whose subject matter is ostensibly the annihilation of the Jewish people, is a likeable but tragic figure. Other Jews are not given such a sympathetic representation. There is much provided to confirm anyone's prejudices, whether or not these are recognised as virulent or 'naturalised' anti-Semitism. The Jews with whom Schindler bargains over investment have been descri- bed with razor-sharp indignation by one critic:

When Stern brings Jewish investors to meet with Schindler in the latter's limousine, the Jews huddling in the back seat could be straight out of a Nazi propaganda poster on eugenics and racial science. One appears apelike, with a large jaw covered in stubble. Dishevelled, large-nosed and unkempt, the Jews contrast negatively with Schindler's clean good looks, as the short stature of the Jews contrasts repeatedly with Schindler's towering height. Spielberg films the Jews through the rear-view mirror so that Schindler's gaze becomes the viewer's gaze. The Jews mutter in Yiddish, the 'secret' language of Eastern European Jews.

(Horowitz, 1997, p. 126)

Spielberg's cinematic conclusion to the Holocaust is the epic walk by Schindler's Jews, stretched across the horizon on the cinemascope screen, to their own Zionist state. The fact that this is not remotely problematised is perhaps not surprising in a film whose subject matter was to bring a version of the Holocaust to the screen. Nevertheless it has enormous implications for the understanding of representations of 'race'. The answer to systematised persecution and attempted annihilation is, it would seem, to separate from the world and to establish a racism-free zone, a promised land where persecution is no longer a possibility. The intensity of the emotion in this sequence is at once moving and Disneyesque. For those with any knowledge of post-war developments in the Middle East, it is depressingly ironic. For others it is simply a happy ending to a particularly depressing fairy tale.

The question of whether or not the Holocaust is susceptible to cinematic representation is one which will remain unresolved, and perhaps that is to the good. What I have attempted to demonstrate in this brief overview of *Schindler's List* is that there are serious ideological questions about the ways in which the narrative is structured and the Jews become a backdrop to as much as subject of the action.

This debate has taken a new turn with the release of Spielberg's film *Amistad* (1997), which deals with a shameful and little known episode in the period of slavery in the United States. Much more will be written about this film, but for my purposes, it is important to note once again the significance of the issue of historiography. One has to ask whether or not it is acceptable, in films which purport to be 'history', to manufacture composite characters and to romanticise the subject matter, however accomplished the cinematographer may be. Lurking behind these debates is the fundamental issue about whether or not it is acceptable to reproduce history as myth.

Conclusion

It is the fact that the three films I have discussed purport, in one way or another, to represent history, which makes them of such significance. As such, they are each examples of popular contemporary historiography. They are about writing a history of issues concerning 'race' and society as much as re-presenting it. There are many questions which may be asked of the history writer, whether he or she is an academic or, in this case, a film maker. These relate to the ways in which the films are structured, to the decision about who will be the key protagonists, and the precise modes of signification which will be utilised. The immense pull of narrative structure is clear in each movie. The very different political realities of Nazi-occupied Poland, of South Africa under apartheid and the United States of America are presented through tightly knit, carefully crafted narrative forms. This leads, unsurprisingly, to a concentration upon key characters and the exploration of their motives and the consequences of their actions. There is also in each film a tendency towards the creation of heroes and villains who sometimes serve the needs of narrative as much as the discipline of the historian. Each of the films moves towards a temporary narrative closure with a strong cathartic impulse.

It is important to devise questions which we need to address to these and similar feature films which are concerned with 'race' and racism and history. What are the strengths and limitations of such films? How much political enlightenment or anti-racist persuasion can we expect from a popular film designed for a cinema audience and often marketed with a whole range of other materials? I will attempt to address some of these questions by way of a conclusion. The main issues at stake in the films I have considered are the provision of information, the narrative and other discourses through which such information is structured, and the absences which have an impact upon such films and their potential.

Each of the films has a didactic purpose, and each is made by a director who operates on a spectrum of indignation which encompasses issues of identity and ranges in its signifying practices from rage to emotive rhetoric. Because this book is about representations of 'race', one might expect the researcher to concentrate on the representation of the oppressed – of the Jews, of South African Black people, of African Americans. This I have tried to do, but it becomes increasingly apparent that a key ideological issue is often the way in which the oppressors are represented. The extent to which the narrative offers the viewer a naturalised view of the 'good' and 'bad' German, or the 'good' and 'bad' white South African is important. Such representations could be seen as a way of absolving others linked with the oppressive group of potential or real culpability ('I am white but I'm not like him ... '). For the non-committed or uninvolved it may be a way of facilitating a 'feelgood' factor which places the viewer and the issues addressed in the film in a symbiotic relationship ('It's a good film and I feel glad that I have seen it.').

There is an interesting variation on this tendency in *Malcolm X* where Lee leaves virtually no space for a 'good' white person. This is encapsulated in the memorably depressing scene where the young white student comes to Malcolm X and says: 'Mr X, I've read some of your speeches and I honestly believe a lot of what you say has truth to it. I have a good heart. I'm a good person despite my whiteness. What can the good white people like myself, who are not prejudiced, or racist, what can we do to help the cause?' Malcolm's answer is brief: 'Nothing!' (Lee, 1992, p. 278). There would be a way of reading this sequence where one might question the precise phrasing of the question. Either the young student is more pompous than she knows, and Malcolm X's answer is not so surprising, or her question was written as a vehicle for the dramatic moment of Malcolm X's response. It would seem that the narrative which insists that there are no 'good' people in the camp of the oppressors is as ideologically suspect as that which suggests that there will always be a hero somewhere to save the day (or more often the 'race'). The power of the life (and the film) of Malcolm X comes precisely from the absence of such a hero in the ranks of the oppressors. It is also a tragedy. The ideological question which it raises is why Lee found it acceptable to include something like that in the film without any qualification or explanation, while he managed to exclude any mention of Malcolm X's critique of capitalism or imperialism, and his sympathy with the working class. Perhaps such a film would not have been blocked by the Hollywood financiers. What we are left with is a tale which is told about a world where racism, politics and economics are held as relatively discrete fields and never come together to offer the shock of understanding. There is only the tragedy of persecution and the salt in the wound of sectarian divisions among the oppressed.

The contradictions generated by *Schindler's List* are of a different order. In this case there is a hero to save the day. But in order for this to happen the film has to use the wider context of the Holocaust, in which virtually no one escaped and the horror was unremitting, as little more than a dramatic backdrop. What we have instead is the adventure of 'Schindler's Jews'. A small narrative victory is thus snatched from the jaws of cataclysmic disaster. It is highly selective in its choice of historical data, but it is easier to take than it might otherwise have been. It also operates on the central importance of a (Christian) saviour figure who helps the Jews to their freedom.

Finally, there is *Cry Freedom*. This is a film which is, as I have argued, undoubtedly liberal and geared towards the mass market. It does not, however, romanticise or distort apartheid, and takes a clear anti-apartheid stance. The irony here is that Attenborough did change one scene when Biko strikes the police officer who had struck him. There were actually more police in the room than those shown in the film, but Attenborough considered the inclusion of more figures would lessen the credibility of the scene. *Cry Freedom* is also a film with some kind of non-aligned hope embedded in its generic and narrative forms. It is undoubtedly a story told from the viewpoint of white middle-class privilege, but with an attempt to empathise with the oppressed. To condemn it for this means that one is likely to miss the strengths which the film demonstrates. It is a politically astute representation of Biko's thought and the conditions under which South African Blacks exist, with the notable absence of any critique of the economic foundations of apartheid.

But, then, all the films I have discussed consider this an irrelevance to their narrative drives. It is apparent from the films chosen for comment here that representing racism and oppression on a grand scale through conventional narrative forms and in the realist mode is not an easy task. The films as texts all fall short of providing depth and breadth of analysis or understanding of their subjects. It is also the case that moral indignation or the rightness of one's case is no guarantee that the film one makes will further the audience's understanding of the issues represented. It is in the narrative tensions and contra-dictions, intentional or unintentional, that one may discover nodal points which highlight the operations of racism and the dignity and courage of the oppressed. In the next chapter I will consider some rather more everyday examples of racism in the media, as I look at examples from the British press.

6

Tabloids and broadsheets

This chapter will consider some of the ways in which the newspapers, particularly those in the United Kingdom, address or re-present issues of 'race'. Consideration of such representation brings to the fore a diversity of topics or themes, and an apparent diversity of newspapers. In order to give some structure to the discussion, specific categories of representation will be identified, and readings offered of specific pieces of journalism or reportage. The main aim of these readings will be to identify arguably recurrent themes or discursive patterns in relation to issues of 'race'. It is certainly the case that newspapers present their regular readers with a packaged and relatively ordered view of the world, through their layout and daily running order. Readers know where to look to find the sports page, the Stock Exchange figures, the women's page, the television listings, the astrology page and many others. In this way there is also a kind of discursive order provided for long-term readers of any specific news-paper. Issues relating to 'race' may, of course, be written about on any page of a newspaper, though it could be argued that they are more likely to be found under a limited number of categories or genres. These would include sport and entertainment, social 'problems' and crime. The fact that a familiar newspaper offers a sense of identity and possibly security to its regular readers is an important contextualising factor when considering questions of 'race' and ideology. It is some-thing which is demonstrated very well when people who go abroad for a holiday make a considerable effort to obtain 'their' daily paper. It is also interesting to note that individuals from many minority groups may purchase their newspaper knowing very well that it is often racist. This does not, except in the most extreme circumstances, make them change to another paper. Women readers are also likely to recognise that the same paper is sexist, though once again this does not mean that

TABLE 6.1
Daily newspapers' circulation and readership

Title	Type	Circulation (000)	Readership (000)
The Times	broadsheet	791	2016
Guardian	broadsheet	397	1234
Daily Telegraph	broadsheet	1084	2658
Independent	broadsheet	265	903
Financial Times	broadsheet	297	663
Daily Mail	tabloid	2091	5283
Express	tabloid	1195	2784
Sun	tabloid	3981	10009
Mirror	tabloid	2408	6139
Daily Star	tabloid	671	2132

Source: *Express* Newspapers Research Department, September 1997

they will reject the paper outright – simply that they will, if asked, identify certain features of the style or content of their daily paper.

There are, of course, many different national newspapers in Britain, though most of them have traditionally supported the Conservative Party. British national newspapers can be separated into three relatively distinct groups known as quality, middle market and popular. The quality papers are broadsheets and the middle market and popular are tabloids. They are identified in Table 6.1 and their circulation figures for 1996 are shown. While there may or may not be a significant correlation between circulation figures and ideological significance, it is important to recognise the fact that popular tabloid circulation amounts to approximately 7 million of a total daily circulation of approximately 13 million. The middle market newspapers bring that total up to more than 10 million out of 13 million. If we then consider the readership figures, it is clear that the vast majority of readers buy the tabloids every day. These statistics are used by some critics and researchers, linked with an open hostility to the tabloids, as an *a priori* means of explaining every negative effect or potential of the press on the masses. It is significant that the term 'effect' creeps back into the argument when it is put in this way. It is, however, much more productive to consider the discursive boundaries and structures within which papers operate if one wishes to identify the relationship they are likely to build and attempt to sustain with their readers. In this way the bald statistics are of less significance than the discourses which inform the construction of a whole range of issues relating to 'race' in both the tabloids and the broadsheets.

Researching the press and representations of 'race'

Some of the most influential and important research on the press and issues of 'race' has been undertaken by Teun Van Dijk (Van Dijk, 1987; 1991; 1993a). His work has provided much needed empirical data about the employment of black people in the media, about the socialisation of journalists and about the predominance in their work of social cognitions that 'generally tend to favour their own group' (1993a, pp. 241– 82). Van Dijk's researchers have undertaken extensive content analyses of newspapers from the UK and the Netherlands. They have obtained data about the subjects and topics in the news and attempted to address questions such as 'What does the press write or not write about racial or ethnic affairs – and why?' and 'How does the press write about this issue – and why?' (1991, p. 71). Van Dijk describes the topics of discourse dealt with by the press as 'semantic macro structures':

> These global, overall meaning structures of a text consist of a hierarchically arranged set of macro-propositions, which are derived from the meanings (propositions) of the sentences by way of macro-rules. These rules reduce the complex information of the text to its essential gist. For instance, if we have a story with a sequence of propositions such as 'I went to the station', 'I bought a ticket', 'I walked to the platform', 'I waited for the train . . . '. We may reduce this sequence by 'summarising' it with a single macro-proposition, for instance, 'I took the train to . . . ' Newspapers do this all the time, and typically express such summarising propositions in their headlines and leads.
>
> (Van Dijk, 1991, p. 72)

Van Dijk uses the metaphor of the tip of a pyramid as a way of conceptualising how complex issues are constantly presented in short, evocative statements which manifest themselves as headlines or captions. Such summary versions of events are, of course, very often misleading. They may also be ideologically suspect. The importance of Van Dijk's work, from the point of view of this book, is that it provides a further way of identifying the 'mechanics' of signification, whereby discourses based upon complex events can be reduced to little more than slogans. Such slogans are, of course, constantly present for public perusal. It is not necessary to buy a newspaper to see its headlines. In public places or on public transport in the UK this is particularly the case. Many readers of the tabloids are very interested in the sports headlines printed on the back page of the papers. In order to read them they hold the paper in such a way that they display the front page to others. One has also to remember that the brevity of most press headlines means that one does not have to see them for very long for their content to come across clearly. In the 1980s in the UK it was the *Sun* newspaper which was noted for its particularly damaging head-lines such as 'Arab Pig Sneaks Back In' (23 January 1986) or 'Get Out You Syrian Swine' (25 October 1986) (cited in (Searle, 1989)). The insult to Arab people, and the obscenity of such headlines for those who are Moslems marks a particularly low moment in the development of the popular press in the UK. The *Sun* is the newspaper which was most often cited in the 1980s as being guilty of such grossness (Searle, 1989). Similar headlines found their way on to the front pages of many tabloids. Van Dijk analysed the most frequent words in the headlines of five British newspapers from August 1981 until January 1986. He found that the four most frequently used words in the headlines were 'police' (388 times), 'riot' (320 times), 'black' (244 times) and 'race' (200 times). The word 'racism' was found in only 31 headlines during the period. Without a detailed analysis of the context and precise semantic formulation in which such words were used, it is wrong to infer too much from their use. The predominance of such vocabulary suggests, however, that the discursive agenda of these newspapers during the period is rooted in concerns with law, order and 'race'. If it is the case that there is what I have called a 'discursive reserve' upon which audiences may draw in relation to media representations of issues of 'race', then newspaper headlines are one of the key cueing devices in order to call up such a reserve.

Van Dijk has pointed out that blatant racism has become less common in the press over the last decade or so. Minorities are, however, still treated as a potential threat or problem. I will be arguing in the next chapter that the absence of blatant racism in the media does not weaken the force of representations which draw upon concepts of 'normality' in order to give strength to negative representations. The extensive content analysis which was undertaken by Van Dijk also demonstrated that ethnic minorities and anti-racists are 'systemat-ically associated with conflict, crime, intolerance, [and] unreliability'

(Van Dijk, 1991, p. 246). Perhaps the key finding of Van Dijk's research was that the press manages to manufacture what he calls an 'ethnic consensus in which the very latitude of opinions and attitudes is quite strictly contained'. Once again, one is reminded of the significance of Marcuse and his work on the closing of the universe of discourse. Where Van Dijk's research on the press and racism is less convincing is in his adoption of a model of ideology which lacks analytical potential. He suggests that is a 'shared, socio-cognitive system of a group, culture, or society' (1991, p. 36). This definition offers little more than a reference point from which what I earlier referred to as the 'mechanics' of signification can be identified. The problem with such research is that it uses empirical data to build an understanding of representation which can become somewhat *mechanical*. There is little mention in Van Dijk's work of contradiction. Consequently, the analyses provided leave little room for semiotic tensions in the reading of the texts he discusses. The power of ideology in this model tends to reside in its cumulative effect, demonstrated through content analysis, of descriptive terms of one kind or another. This is then linked with various schemata through which the news is organised and by which definitions and descriptions of situations are seen to serve the interests of the political right.

The weakness in this mode of analysis is most apparent when Van Dijk explains, correctly, that ethnic prejudices and stereotypes are not innate but acquired. He argues that the acquisition process occurs largely through text and talk. He then makes a strange jump when he suggests that the media play a vital role in what he calls 'this reproduction process'. It would seem from this as though the media are engaged in an endless process of reproducing already existing prejudices and stereotypes. This is a very inadequate approach to a process in which changes do occur. Van Dijk suggests that there are 'many readers' searching for interpretative frameworks in the face of 'fundamental changes in the social and ethnic context'. The newspapers, particularly through their editorials, offer practical, common-sense frameworks. Van Dijk suggests that 'many' readers do reject such common-sense understandings, while 'even more' readers accept the editorials wholesale. There is a vagueness here which is unhelpful and points towards the lack of convincing data drawn from audience research. It is also based on a weak theorisation of the ideological process. I have argued throughout this book that ideology should be conceptualised as a relationship of power and subordination. For Van Dijk ideology is little more than a belief system or code which is either swallowed neat or decoded critically by those in the know.

The absence of any serious engagement with the pictorial dimensions of the press, and the types of advertising which they carry is also significant. It is difficult to engage in serious analysis of media representations of issues of 'race' in the press without engaging with a range of descriptive or generic categories of representation. It has yet to be proven that readers of newspapers actively seek interpretative frameworks, or that they will look to editorials for explanations of events. A more convincing hypothesis might be that readers negotiate socially their relationship with their newspaper and with a whole range of representations which it offers them. They do this in the context of a lived social existence which includes their gender, their age, where they work, if they work, what they buy, where they live, who their friends are, what worries them, what scares them and a whole host of other factors. Van Dijk seems to want to reduce the whole issue to the provision of occasions and information which will somehow 'lead' to anti-racist attitudes and (in his terminology) ideologies.

The relative strength of the newspaper editorial or the framing of a news story about some issue concerning 'race' may not be measurable through content analysis. It may be that the significance of the editorial resides in its relationship with recognisable discourses which can be found elsewhere in the newspaper or in previous newspapers, plus those discourses which are in circulation in other media and in daily talk. It would be too reductive to suppose that newspaper editorials provide the cognitive templates through which we all make sense of the world. Media discourses have to be conceptualised as fluid, often contradictory and as one contributory element in the ideological formation and/or sustenance of an audience or society. It is with this in mind that I will now consider a range of representational categories through which issues of race may be addressed, and provide selective examples for analysis.

Categories of representation

Discussion of individual categories of representation in a newspaper is a necessary convenience. In fact, a newspaper is a daily assemblage of inter-related texts and discourses, which often draw upon considerable cultural, political and historical reserves from its readership. Fairclough's concept of 'members' resources', mentioned in Chapter 3, is important here (Fairclough, 1989). For Fairclough, readers do not simply decode utterances, but arrive at an active interpretation through a process of matching features of the utterance (or in this case a newspaper article) at various levels with representations stored in their long-term memory. This enables readers of specific newspapers to recognise certain discourses, or certain modalities of representation. The range of representations concerned with 'race' within a single paper would include, for instance, different modes of address in advertisements from those in an editorial or a sports column. Some of the representations will be supported by images and some will be dependent upon images.

The issue of how to make sense of text, image, and page layout in relation to representations of 'race' is one much in need of investigation. Barthes' early work in *Mythologies* is still very valid here and has been overlooked by many researchers to the detriment of their work (Barthes, 1972). More recently, Theo Van Leeuwen and Gunther Kress have begun a lengthy exploration of the ways in which it may be possible to evolve a language of description allowing us to be as accurate as possible about the ways in which images are structured and offer up their meanings (Van Leeuwen and Kress, 1994). Theirs is a somewhat more formal, though very necessary approach to social semiotics, and complements the more lyrical interpretations of meaning offered by the early Barthes. Van Leeuwen and Kress argue that front pages of different newspapers are related to the cultures from which they emanate. They note that the *Sun* relies heavily upon the pictorial and upon screamer headlines, while a paper like the *Frankfurter Allgemeine* is still rooted very much in ordered uniformity utilising a smaller type face and regular columns. They further argue that the readers of these newspapers become habituated to a complex set of practices which they recognise and with which they identify. These representational practices are also linked by Van Leeuwen and Kress to the long-term formation of identity. They suggest that a paper such as the *Sun* operates on a Given–New axis. What this means is that each main story is offered as an example of one or another paradigm, linked then with an instance of that paradigm. This mode of representation is inherently bound up with the layout and design of the page. They also point out that the front page of the German newspaper *Bildzeitung* is quite different in design from that of the *Sun* and that it appears somewhat anarchic, both pictorially and typographically, compared to the former. The class readership of both papers is, however, roughly equivalent. From this it is possible to deduce that differences in modes of signification are more likely to be related to cultural (or national) characteristics rather than those linked with class. These issues can play a very important part in our understanding of the modalities and structures of messages (stories) concerning 'race' as they appear in different daily papers. At the same time, argue Van Leeuwen and Kress, all papers do share certain common communicational functions and elements. They are intended to present what are considered the most important and significant events of the day for the paper and its readers. The precise way in which this is done may vary from context to context and culture to culture. So with representations of issues relating to 'race', we may expect to find differences in emphasis and the degree of subtlety in the coverage. The question which has to be carefully investigated is whether there are some kinds of essential and generalisable discourses about issues of 'race' represented in the press, or whether culturally specific representations produce culturally specific discourses. At the moment, this is an open question. With this in mind, I now turn to some specific categories of representation.

Sport

I will begin my consideration of newspaper categories of representation of issues concerning 'race' with sport, because I wish to argue that such reportage is very significant in the formation and sustenance of personal and national identity. For those who, for whatever reason, are not fans of sport, it is necessary to assert one's identity in response to the chauvinist discursive constructions of the enthusiasts. The agenda is pre-set. It is more important than any newspaper editorial, excluding, possibly, those written in times of all-out war. Althusser noted that the role of sport in chauvinism is of the first importance as part of the 'cultural apparatus' (Althusser, 1971b, p. 154). I wish to argue here that the way in which 'national' issues are represented in relation to sport often bridges any gap that might exist between chauvinism and racism. At the same time, such representations are full of contradictions which are apparently irrelevant to or unnoticed by the producers of such messages. The case of journalistic writing about football is the one I choose for this example and the chauvinism bordering on racism is that of the *Daily Mirror* towards the Germans at the time of the European Championship in 1996. It will be apparent from the example that the use of the term 'race' in this book is one which encompasses more than the racism and power struggles which occur on the axis of 'white' versus 'others'. It includes those forms of racism which have also built and sustained the required environment to justify war, and genocide where 'racial purity' not colour is the prime issue. There can be found, in these broader uses of the term 'race', those same ideological dimensions of media messages which facilitate racist discourse across a wide range of representations, from the most clearly outrageous to the apparently mundane.

The context for the reportage is that of the England football team reaching the semi-final of the European Championship, in which they would be playing Germany. On 24 June 1996 the *Daily Mirror* ran a front page which proved to be a monumental error of judgement on the part of its editor. It was, he later said, only supposed to be a joke of some kind. The *Daily Mirror* was, at the time, the one popular paper which supported the Labour Party. It was not until 1997 that the *Sun*, traditionally a bastion of working-class Toryism, also became a supporter of the Labour Party.

Three-quarters of the front page of the *Mirror* showed a photo-montage of the shouting or smiling heads of two English football players, Stuart Pearce and Paul Gascoigne. They were both, apparently, wearing the steel helmets worn by British troops in the Second World War. The two main words of the headline read simply: ACHTUNG! SURRENDER. At the bottom of the page was the statement 'For you Fritz, ze Euro 96 Championship is over.' Most of the paper was then turned into what looked like a wartime issue, drawing heavily upon references to the beginning of the Second World War. The readers of the paper are urged to cut out the image and slogan and stick in their windows. The 'humour' here may also refer to the *Sun* newspaper's front page at the time of the Gulf War, which carried a image of the Union Jack with a soldier's head superimposed on it, urging support for 'our boys' and encouraged readers to display it. The *Sun* and the *Daily Mirror* have long been rivals for the bulk of the 'popular' newspaper readership.

The main text on the front page of the *Daily Mirror*, written by the editor, is a declaration of 'football war' and is written in sombre tone. It contains many stylistic similarities to the British declaration of war on Germany in 1939. As one reads on it becomes progressively more silly, or insulting, depending upon how it is construed. The question which is important here is not whether or not the *Mirror*'s humour is particularly funny. It is whether such humour introduces or sustains racist discourses as part of everyday understanding, and in an important sense helps to justify other racist discourses which relate to other ethnic groups and/or nations.

The insertion of selected phrases and vocabulary within the *Mirror*'s numerous references to the impending semi-final is calculated to remind its readership, many of whom are too young to remember the Second World War, of the mythical part which 'we' played in it. Set out below is a selection of the kind of language used:

> 'Ve haf vays', 'Filthy Hun', 'You haf been warned'
> England's old enemy, defeated in two World Wars and one World Cup.
> We have decided to teach the Hun a lesson.
> Herr we go again.
>
> The Germans hate being reminded of their failures. Like eating well-matured cheese for breakfast. Or nicking all the sunloungers in the Mediterranean. But what they hate most of all is being reminded of that glorious day in 1966 when England made them the sourest of sour-krauts.
>
> (Justin Dunn, p. 2)

> But mein gott, how close they came to catching the first jet back to Munich this morning. Croatia gave the Teutonic titans the fright of their lives with a scrapping performance that had the German hordes thinking more about putting towels down on the Costas instead of a seat at Wembley on Wednesday.
> We are not fooled, Fritz!
> Who do you think you're kidding Mister Hitman?
> GERMANY FALLING! Herr we go. We want your faxes on England v Germany, the biggest battle between the two countries for 30 years. Fax your messages – and your German jokes – to us.
>
> (Steve Millar, pp. 28 and 31)

Most of the above examples make unambiguous reference to the Second World War, and particularly to film and television dramatisations of the Nazis in England and North America. There is also reference to the popular British song from the Second World War, 'Who do you think you're kidding, Mister Hitler?', which is also well known as the theme song of a recent British television comedy series about the war. The humour, it would seem, is to be derived from the way in which Hitler, Hitman and Klinsmann are associated in the headline next to a picture or Jürgen Klinsmann apparently holding his nose. Buried at the end of this short piece by Richard Tanner on the back page of the paper is a sentence which highlights an apparent contradiction in the message of the paper. Klinsmann is referred to as the 'former Spurs star', for though he had become one of 'the enemy' Klinsmann was a favourite with many English football fans.

The recognition that Klinsmann has been a star player for a top British team may be taken an indicator that everything which has gone before is really just a joke, and this may well have been the case. Indeed, many of the football fans who had cheered and appreciated the football of Klinsmann while he played for Tottenham Hotspurs are now being asked to laugh at him as the German enemy. To accomplish such a feat, it is necessary for the ideological subject (that is, you and me) to adopt a kind of schizoid interpretative repertoire. We have to embrace contradiction and move in and out of various interpretative positions as the need arises. If I am a Spurs supporter, the contradictions might be even more pronounced. I must find a way to laugh at the German 'enemy' if I am to be part of the general ideological drift. Such ideological pressure is similar to that of the worker who laughs when her/his fellow worker is ridiculed, in order to avoid any ridicule of her/himself. Ideological pressure is not easy to resist. What is of more significance than the humour is the ideological import of this cluster of descriptive terms about 'the Germans'. It is, of course, premised upon an unproblematic conception that there is such a thing as 'the Germans'. It is also an insistent reminder that the Germans are synonymous with the Nazis, or that they are synonymous with the 'enemy' because 'we' fought them in two World Wars. History is not so much removed from these representations as contorted, disfigured, rewritten. In its place the readers are encouraged to draw upon a discursive reserve which viciously stereotypes 'Germans'. That means *all* Germans. The fact that it is all nothing more than a joke is emphasised by the appeal, in a small box on the back page, for readers to send in 'German jokes'. This means 'Anti-German' jokes, just as Irish jokes are told at the expense of the Irish, Romanian jokes at the expense of the Romanians, and Polish jokes at the expense of the Poles. Such jokes, if they are to be amusing, depend upon acceptance of the terms of reference upon which they are based and the discourses about their subject.

There was a small outcry against the issue of the *Daily Mirror* from which I have quoted. One or two people even said that they had ceased buying the paper after being regular readers for all of their adult lives. The editor reiterated that it was supposed to have been a joke and the matter was quickly laid to rest. The ideological 'work' had, however, been well accomplished (Hall, 1977). *All* Germans had been confirmed, discursively, as sharing entirely negative characteristics and the discursive reserve, carried in the memories of computers, editorials, readers and other members of the public, had been suitably replenished.

War

It seems appropriate to move from the simulation of war and its representation through sport to the reality of war through the practice of killing people and its contemporary representation as a kind of high-tech sport. The issue of 'race' is never far from the agenda, and in times of war the linguistic abasement, which has been drawn upon for high level sporting contests, is given free rein. One of the most recent examples of this would be the Gulf War of 1991. Here the media could move their attention from the Germans to the Arabs, or some Arabs, as the dilemma they faced was that the enemy was not supposed to include *all* Arabs. The immediate recipients of media vituperation were the Iraqis, though the Palestinians were also in the picture from time to time. The ideological significance of many of the media representations lay in the way in which stereotypical notions of the 'Arab' were interwoven with discourses about tactics of war and the ways in which 'we' apparently pursued the path of the just.

There were numerous examples of the way in which sometimes benign though never inoffensive stereotypes of Arabs were toughened and sharpened to describe Saddam Hussein and the Iraqi forces. This was particularly apparent in the different vocabulary used to describe both the Iraqis and the 'Allies'. It should also be noted that claims to normality and stereotyping of various groups require that the norm is established as 'us'. There is always a 'we' and a 'they' in any situation of (ethnic) conflict and the media work hard to demonstrate the characteristics of both. The *Guardian* newspaper in the UK published a list of the vocabulary used in the media in relation to the conflict which is most revealing (cited in Hodge and Kress, 1993), *see* Table 6.2.

It is interesting to consider whether or not there is any relationship between the 'normalised' stereotypes in daily use and the propaganda

TABLE 6.2
Comparison of vocabulary used in the media to describe the Gulf War

We	They
Army, Navy and Air Force	A war machine
Reporting guidelines	Censorship
Press briefings	Propaganda
We	**They**
Take out	Destroy
Suppress	Destroy
Neutralise or decapitate	Kill
Our boys are ...	**Theirs are ...**
Professional	Brainwashed
Lion-hearts	Paper Tigers
Cautious	Cowardly
Confident	Desperate
Heroes	Cornered
Young knights of the skies	Bastards of Baghdad
Loyal	Blindly obedient
Desert rats	Mad dogs
Resolute	Ruthless
Brave	Fanatical
Our missiles cause ...	**Their missiles cause ...**
Collateral damage	Civilian casualties
George Bush is ...	**Saddam Hussein is ...**
At peace with himself	Demented
Resolute	Defiant
Statesmanlike	An evil tyrant
Assured	A crackpot monster

produced in time of conflict. The next chapter will explore this question further. There is clearly a relationship between the choice of vocabulary and the discourse which it will be used to construct or sustain. But this does not mean that being able to spot stereotypes is, of itself, enough. Stereotypes do not exist in a vacuum. They are produced in specific social, economic and political contexts and they are invoked in specific social, economic and political contexts.

The press produced, during the Gulf War, a series of negative characteristics associated with Saddam Hussein and some associated with his soldiers. Ideologically, in this context, they were also linked with what might be called the 'Arabicity' of the Iraqis. I derive this term from the concept of 'Italianicity' mentioned by Barthes in his essay 'The Rhetoric of the Image' (Barthes, 1977). This 'Arabicity' was not necessarily signified through direct racial slurs, but rather through the use of descriptive adjectives with heavy ideological and racist connotations. Obvious examples would include 'mad dogs' and 'bastards of Baghdad'. The discursive reserve which supports these terms is provided through the production of a whole series of adventure stories and, more recently, feature films which represent those designated as 'Arab' in such a way as to suggest that they are likely to possess such characteristics. On many occasions when this occurs in the media, chauvinism and racism become normalised and virtually synonymous.

Cultural Otherness

There are times when the press represents issues of 'race' under the general category of cultural Otherness. A most notable example of this kind of representation is that of Japan. It is not common today for newspapers to be as forthright with their prejudices about the Japanese as we have observed them to be about the Germans. Indeed, when a BBC Radio Newcastle presenter named Kevin Rowntree referred to the Japanese as 'our little yellow friends', he provoked a refreshing degree of outrage in his listeners and it was reported by the *Newcastle Journal* (6 February 1995) as a 'race row' (cited in Hammond, 1997, p. 100). Hammond and Stirner (1997) argue that it is through the discourse of cultural difference that prejudices of racial thinking are given a more acceptable gloss. The examples cited by Hammond and Stirner are mainly from the quality or middle market newspapers. They discuss the way in which the British press reported the tragic Kobe earthquake in Japan in January of 1995. It was used as an occasion for the journalists to argue that Japan is fundamentally Asian (whatever that might mean), and that it is a country where things are seldom as they appear. Apart from being the target of endless cheap jokes about their pronunciation of English, the Japanese are also represented as a culture which has only a veneer of modernity, but is still quite primitive beneath the surface.

Hammond and Stirner note that the apparently stoical attitude of the Japanese is explained by William Dawkins in the *Financial Times* as linked with their Shinto religion: 'This keeps alive the traditions of an agricultural race, long accustomed to the feeling that their livelihoods, and even lives, are in the hands of the elements' (*Financial Times*, 22/23

January 1995). Their most telling point, however, is made in relation to a piece in the *Independent* by Peter Popham. With reference to the earthquake, Popham makes the extraordinary assumption that underneath the surface the Japanese (all of them presumably) possess the 'unchanged, Asian contours of the Japanese soul'. What might be considered extraordinary is that this piece of writing appears in one of the 'respected' broadsheets. How can anyone seriously explain what they mean by the Asian contours of the Japanese soul? It is a piece of rhetoric which is constructed in fine English prose and hence would seem to be above the kind of criticisms so often aimed at the tabloids. But Hammond and Stirner provide enough examples to show how the quality press can construct or sustain discourses with a veneer of sophistication which, if you scratch the surface, demonstrate an attempt to normalise and eternalise Eurocentrism at the same time as apparently analysing the 'timeless' characteristics of the Japanese.

Advertising: burglary, blackness and business

The next example to be discussed is an advertisement which is a full page from the *Guardian* newspaper on 27 December 1988. It is for a charity called 'The Prince's Youth Business Trust'. I must be absolutely clear that the comments I am offering are not intended as a critique of the work of the Trust. The brief descriptive analysis is intended to illustrate the way in which character traits may be attributed to people by forms of insidious, though apparently good-natured, presentation. The advertisement draws upon a discourse of fear and distrust. In this discourse, black people (or Jews or the Irish or some other chosen exemplar according to the historical moment) are seen as potential thieves.

The young man represented in Figure 6.1 is seen against a plain background and is looking directly at the reader. He is asked a question which might seem innocuous in another context: 'What sort of business do you want to go into, Sydney?' But Sydney's answer triggers a whole range of prejudicial judgements with which the reader is then entertained: 'How about burglary?' Burglary seems like a 'natural' choice for Sydney. This we are told in what is, for an advertisement, an extended narrative beneath the image. Sydney is part of the vicious circle of deprivation and law-breaking which results from inner-city living conditions. He is also, in the implicit discourse which provides the core content of the advertisement, simply a young black

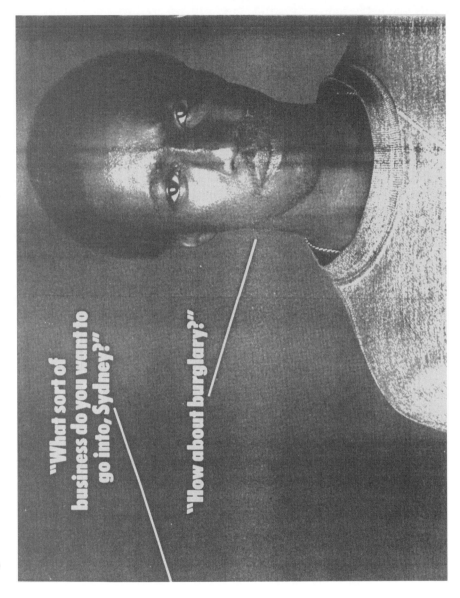

Figure 6.1

142

In the inner cities, it's all too easy for young people to drift into crime.

It's a vicious circle. Deprivation leads to law-breaking. Law-breaking leads to deprivation. Deprivation leads to law-breaking.

Sydney Campbell's a product of the inner city. He's had a hard time.

When he was made redundant from his job with the local council, he faced a tough decision.

Struck by the level of crime in his run-down neighbourhood, he decided to join in.

CRIME PAYS.

Sydney's the sort of bloke who sees every problem as an opportunity.

That's how he came to break into burglary.

Not committing it. Preventing it.

As Sydney says: "I was brought up in this area. It had more robberies and general crime than any other part of the city, so it made a lot of sense starting a security company here."

He worked out how much he'd need to start a one-man burglar alarm business and went to see his bank manager.

No go. Politely, the manager showed him the door. Other banks gave him the same treatment.

Who could blame them? Sydney had no idea of sales targets, overhead costs, or profit margins.

He was a 'bad risk'.

His fledgling company looked like a dead duck. Then someone told him about the Prince's Youth Business Trust.

WHERE BUSINESS MEETS CHARITY.

Our aim is to help the 18-25s set themselves up in business.

Not the sort of 18-25s with the right education and the right connections. They'll get on without a push from us.

We're especially interested in people like Sydney. People who have nowhere else to turn.

We gave Sydney a loan of £1,500 at a low rate of interest.

We also gave him Sabash Patel.

Sabash, a local accountant, became Sydney's Business Adviser. While Sydney installed the burglar alarms, Sabash installed the book-keeping system.

From being unemployed, Sydney has now become an employer. He has two people on the payroll, a secretary and an engineer.

His turnover in the first year will be over £25,000. Not bad for a 'bad risk'.

MONEY ISN'T EVERYTHING.

Early on, we realised that throwing money at would-be entrepreneurs isn't the answer. Keeping new business ventures going is as important as giving them the shove to start in the first place.

In Sydney's case, Sabash Patel helped him get over a difficult cash-flow problem. He found a factoring company to chase up the money on Sydney's behalf.

On a larger scale, someone else is now chasing up money on our behalf.

Our active President, the Prince of Wales, has just launched an Appeal for £40,000,000.

If you'd like to help, by giving money or time, please send the coupon.

And if you're looking for a burglar alarm, please call Sydney's 'Oaks Security Service' on 021-554 2214.

(A blatant plug, we admit, but we'll stop at nothing to help the 18-25s get on in business.)

THE PRINCE'S YOUTH BUSINESS TRUST.

man. This implicit discourse tells the reader what they are expected always already to know – that young black men are (potential) thieves.

The key part of the narrative is a deliberate attempt to retain the reader's attention by withholding information. It is important that we continue to believe that Sydney is going to become a thief:

> In the inner cities it's all too easy for young people to drift into crime.
>
> It's a vicious circle. Deprivation leads to law breaking. Law breaking leads to deprivation. Deprivation leads to law breaking.
>
> Sydney Campbell's a product of the inner city. He's had a hard time.
>
> When he was made redundant from his job with the local council, he faced a tough decision.
>
> Struck by the level of crime in his run down neighbourhood, he decided to join in.

By reading the whole text, it becomes clear that Sydney has gone into business, with the help of the 'Prince's Youth Business Trust', and that he is selling burglar alarms. The reader is offered the questionable pleasure of having been strung along by the narrative ploy of copy-writers. We are informed that Sydney was 'given' an accountant, whose name we are told is Sabash Patel. The only possible reason for naming the accountant would seem to be the desire to impress the reader with a name which accentuates the multiculturalism of the Trust. But whether the whole story with its 'happy ending' is read or not, the central motif of the narrative remains unchanged. It is one of a host of discourses about black people which are learned socially but very often perceived as 'natural', as common sense. Sydney ended up selling burglar alarms. Most of 'them' are likely to be thieves. Sydney is the exception. The overall purpose of the advertisement is to ask for donations. The aim is to avoid having more black thieves. It sounds crass when stated bluntly, but the discursive force of the message is unambiguous, phoney sociological analysis notwithstanding.

Back to politics

The 1997 Conservative Party Conference, which began on 6 October, had only been underway for one day when two of the party's senior figures caused a minor stir by making outrageous statements at fringe meetings. Whether the discursive force of their comments is directly related to their political positions is a matter for conjecture. Both the speeches drew, however, upon a discursive reserve in relation to questions of culture and identity, as well as arrogantly attempting to naturalise chauvinist thinking. I will first identify more precisely what the politicians concerned had to say, and then consider the way in which their comments were received by particular newspapers.

Dealing with the IRA

The first comment is brief and comes from the Tory MP for Kensington and Chelsea, Alan Clark, about whom more will be said in the next chapter. In a question and answer session during a fringe meeting he was asked what should be done about the Irish Republican Army. His response was: 'The only solution for dealing with the IRA is to kill 600 people in one night – and let the UN and Bill Clinton and everyone else make a scene – and it is over for 20 years.'

Alan Clark's comments work like an ideological rapier. They are so fast that it is not even clear that someone might have been wounded before the foil has been re-sheathed. The front page coverage of the incident in *The Times* refers to Mr Clark's 'gaffe'. It is interesting that this is the same word used by Clark himself in defence of another of his colleagues which is analysed in the next chapter. Clark prefaced his remark, according to *The Times*, by saying that everyone knew his view. This would seem to be an attempt by the paper to soften what might otherwise sound too crass a pronouncement. It suggests that we, the readers all know about old Alan. *The Times* suggests that Mr Hague, the Conservative Party leader, has taken a 'no-nonsense' line against both Mr Clark and Lord Tebbit. Once again the choice of phrase is telling. It is rather like the reprimand of a school teacher to a couple of cheeky pupils, but hardly signifies indignation or outrage.

The *Daily Mail*, in its editorial, makes the following comment: 'As the peace talks move towards a critical phase in Belfast, the former minister Alan Clark – notorious diarist, military historian and political cavalier – airily suggested that the answer to the Irish problem is to kill 600 of the IRA in one night.' The editorial does not condemn, but rather joins with Clark's modes of address: 'If only Mr Hague could suggest, with equal insouciance, taking out the people knee-capping his own party!' The choice of the word 'insouciance' and its companion 'airily' are attempts to euphemise the ideological impact of the reactionary 'cavalier'. To 'take out' opponents is not the usual language of the *Daily Mail*, unless of course it is making light of its subject matter. Knee-capping is a practice which in other contexts would rightfully receive the most severe condemnation from the paper. The overall impact of the two sentences devoted to Clark's words provide a delicate and dangerous balance between self-righteous remonstrance and the proud embarrassment of a parent with an intelligent but wayward child. It is a discourse of legitimation.

It does not matter that Clark was not serious in his suggestion, and I am willing for the moment to give him the benefit of the doubt. He said in a television interview the same evening that anyone who took his comments seriously had 'a mental problem'. This kind of comment has all the force of the practised lawyer who withdraws a statement which will be stricken from the record, knowing full well that the persuasive legal (or in this case ideological) work has been done. Clark's words may seem to have no immediate connection with issues of 'race', other than a clear implication that there are some Irish people with whom one should not attempt to talk. His words, however, help to sustain unspoken negative judgements about the Irish, particularly when associated with Lord Tebbit's speech about the alleged perils of a multicultural society. There is here a discursive symbiosis which offers readers the potential to 'put things together' rather like a jigsaw puzzle. This working out of how things fit together has been noted by Hall in relation to concepts of common sense (Hall, 1977, p. 325). Hall perceptively noted that 'You cannot learn, through common sense *how things are*: you can only discover *where they fit* into the existing scheme of things' (emphasis in original). A good indicator of the way in which the *Daily Mail* attempts to make things 'fit' is its use of the phrase 'Irish problem'. It requires a considerable load of naturalised intellectual and discursive baggage to facilitate such a formulation: one based on what is known as common sense. Otherwise it could be described as the 'English problem', or 'the Problem of Ulster', or one of several other possibilities.

Multi-cultural racism

The second set of inflammatory remarks was offered by former Cabinet Minister Lord Tebbit in an address delivered to a meeting 'Conservatives against a Federal Europe', Blackpool, 7 October 1997.

They were part of a carefully structured speech which included several veiled or open attacks on other Conservative politicians. The precise content of these attacks need not concern us here. What is significant, however, is the fact the Lord Tebbit's comments about multicultural society were part of a discursive flow rather than free-standing remarks. It could be argued that the power of media discourses concerning issues of 'race' often comes from the way in which they are integrated with other strands of thought and action: hence the significance of Clark's comments alongside those of Tebbit. In order to identify the speech as an example of the ways in which issues of 'race' are represented in the media, it is important to quote the relevant parts of the text. Tebbit, of course, knew very well that his speech would be reported in the media. The extract given comes after he has roundly condemned senior Tories for the downfall of the previous government, and generally indicated that the United Kingdom is disintegrating both morally and politically. The paragraphs have been numbered for ease of reference:

1. New Labour is also committed to multiculturalism. But unless we share standards, moral values, language and our national heritage we will constitute neither a society nor a nation, but just a population living under the same jurisdiction.
2. Humans cannot relate directly to each other beyond fairly restricted groups such as family, club, or gang without holding some over-riding beliefs or standards in common. Christians understand this – or did – very well. Christ repeatedly made the point that it was through Him that His disciples were joined. He spelled it out 'in so much as you do this to the least of them, you do it unto me'.
3. Monarchs understood this too. Allegiance to each other was by allegiance to the crown. Even field commanders promoted allegiance to the flag of the unit to ensure allegiance of each soldier to the next man in line.
4. It was our common inheritance, not conscription, which brought men to lay down their lives for each other and their country. Unless there is a shared commitment to the common values on which law is based, the friends of a transgressor will support him rather than the forces of law. Without shared values the law is ineffective against crime.
5. Multiculturalism is a divisive force. One cannot uphold two sets

of ethics, or be loyal to two nations, any more than a man can have two masters.

6. It perpetuates ethnic divisions because nationality is in the long term more about culture than ethics.

7. Youngsters of all races born here should be taught that British history is their history, or they will forever be foreigners holding British passports – and this kingdom will become a Yugoslavia.

8. I find it extraordinary that these sentiments should provoke outrage in some quarters. Especially since it is from those same quarters that we hear denunciations of the 'cultural imperialism' of the British Empire.

9. We are denounced because we took Christianity, parliamentary government, honest administration, fair judicial process, Milton, Shakespeare and the morning suit to our Empire and in so doing all but obliterated old, much loved cultures.

10. I have a good deal of sympathy with those whose world we changed. In many cases our imported value system was not appropriate to the people.

11. I accept that Moslem countries have every right to uphold Moslem law. We have no right to force multiculturalism upon them – nor they upon us. The British people are entitled to their culture too – respecting, valuing, but not adopting that of others.

12. Because the Church – especially the established Church – is now so weak and disoriented we are becoming a pagan society, worshipping Mother Earth with the Greens as a new priesthood. None the less, we need common values, a common culture and single language.

13. The British are not happy in our violent, ill-mannered, crime-ridden polyglot cities in which families live on welfare from generation to generation. They have no wish to be ruled from abroad.

14. But unless they discover a sense of nationhood they surely will be.

15. With no sense of nationhood, New Labour cannot defend our right to be an independent nation. Committed to multiculturalism, it is unable to foster a one-nation society. A Tory party which rejected multiculturalism, embraced integration, linked benefit to work, disciplined yobs, effectively punished criminals, supported the orthodox family and promoted our shared

values through school and home could gain support from all classes in every region ...

16. The issue on which to fight is the Balkanisation of our society and our nation.

I will offer some observations about the arguments put forward, though the main issue is how these points were mediated in the press. It is clear from paragraph 1 that, for Lord Tebbit, multiculturalism means an absence of shared values and standards. The opacity of the reference to Christ in paragraph 2 leaves the reader with little more than a divine reference point devoid of other significance. A common inheritance and allegiance to the Crown are, argues Tebbit, the foundations of a stable society, with multiculturalism incapable of providing this stability. For Tebbit, multiculturalism is divisive and perpetuates ethnic divisions. In paragraph 13 Tebbit lapses into the rhetoric of chauvinism based upon ethnic purity, counterposing the 'British' against the families living on welfare in 'our polyglot cities'. His claims are emotionally evocative and rationally bereft of structure. It is interesting to note that, where the text of the speech was reported, there was seldom any reference to the bad argument and logical inanities which it contains. Instead there was a tendency, especially in the Conservative press, to accept Lord Tebbit's general frame of reference. I will now consider the two main Conservative papers and their response to the speech.

The *Daily Mail* carried the complete text of the speech on page 6 under the caption 'Bombshell speech from Tebbit the Maverick'. Next to a photographic image of Tebbit speaking, from which the background had been erased, are the words 'Lord Tebbit last night: His comments were being seen as inflammatory.' I think two points are worth noting here. The first is the use of the word 'maverick' as a signifier of someone with unorthodox and independent views. In the context of the news such a signifier is often linked with grudging or open admiration. The caption next to the photograph ensures that the readers are distanced from any possibility of immediate condemnation. 'His comments were being seen as inflammatory' conveniently removes any agency from this act of perception. Of course there is the possibility that readers might read into the caption a solidarity with this agentless condemnation. More likely, however, is the possibility that the 'members' resources' called up in this case would sense that the 'inflammatory' comments were timely and brave.

A further indication of what the readers might be expected to make of the speech can be found in the *Mail*'s editorial. Tebbit is introduced here as someone coming 'like a bat out of an unforgiving political hell'. His speech is described as a 'formidable tirade', and with a recognition of the importance of free speech, the editorial accepts Tebbit's 'withering scorn, perfectly acceptable in the shot and shell of battle'. Of course there is a qualifier to follow this, but it is not designed to distance the paper from what Tebbit said, and it is preceded by the *Mail*'s own support for parts of Tebbit's speech: 'While this paper deplores the fact that English history, culture and religion are no longer properly taught in schools . . . '. I will not comment further here on the question of history, as Chapter 8 will address the issue in some detail. The *Mail*, having made its assertive point about education and history, is actually more concerned with Tebbit's sense of timing. The comment was 'about as suitable . . . as a stink bomb at a wake'. The editorial then suggests that Tebbit's secondary target here was the Conservative leader William Hague. Hague is not mentioned in Tebbit's speech, but the *Mail knows* that it was a response to Hague's comments about the Notting Hill Carnival. Hague, according to the *Mail* 'gushingly lauded' the carnival as 'the greatest cultural event' in the national calendar. The second quote is from Mr Hague, but the first phrase is that of the editor. In this way the *Mail* establishes a second order of discourse which is condemnatory – of the hot-headedness of Mr Hague ('a young leader in a hurry to establish his identity'), and of the possibility that the Notting Hill Carnival could be considered as the greatest cultural event in the national calendar. The final comment on Tebbit is as follows:

> Although Tebbit's *visceral views will have a resonance* for many Tories, the last thing the party needs in its desperately weakened state is *the debilitating spectacle of this old populist* in a fury threatening to upstage a young leader in a hurry to establish himself.
>
> (emphasis added)

Although the discursive and ideological significance of such media representations require more than straightforward 'comprehension' analysis, it is sometimes not a bad place to start. 'Visceral' views are gut feelings. They may be condemned, but here they are identified and dignified by the reference to the 'resonance' they will have for many Tories. Resonance suggests a sympathetic reading, and the 'old populist' is gently reprimanded for threatening to upstage the party leader (the last thing the party needs). In other circumstances the *Mail* can be much more forthcoming with its condemnation of events or persons.

It is interesting to compare the *Mail*'s editorial with that of the *Daily Telegraph*. The *Telegraph* gives the matter less coverage and responds briefly in its editorial, in relation to Mr Hague's performance at the conference:

> The most striking aspect of the conference to date is his determination to reach out beyond habitual supporters to young people, ethnic minority voters and younger women. Although he is unwise to have entangled himself with Lord Tebbit in a needless row about multi-culturalism, and must beware of any hint of political correctness, this bold approach is surely right.

Hague is credited with a wish to contact ethnic minority voters, but warned of the extreme dangers of political correctness, hence ensuring that the readers recognise the *Telegraph*'s perception of the close ties between the two. This also allows the *Telegraph*'s editor to restate a position of unqualified hostility to anything linked to the concept of political correctness. There is an impatience in the suggestion that Hague is unwise to tangle with Tebbit, the implication perhaps being that it could result in Hague being damaged by the encounter. The further suggestion that it is about a 'needless' row, is fecund with ambiguity. Is it 'needless' because Lord Tebbit is the dinosaur which some less sympathetic newspapers labelled him? Is it because he is a reactionary fool who should be ignored? Or is it because he is quite correct in his judgements but ... not now? Hodge and Kress write of what they call an 'ideological complex', whereby contradictory versions of reality have to coexist, because contradiction is intrinsic to their function (Hodge and Kress, 1993, p. 37). So readers of the *Telegraph* are encouraged, with Hague, to approach ethnic minority voters, but to avoid needless rows about multiculturalism as a divisive force. Is this because the *Telegraph* has such a strong view that Tebbit is wrong that there is little point in pursuing the matter? Or is it because Tebbit is right and it would be better to keep quiet about it at this sensitive moment? It is clear that the contradictory messages in the editorial, when linked with a comment on political correctness, are inflected towards a less than progressive reading.

Other papers were forthright in expressing their distaste for Tebbit's words. The Scottish *Daily Record* referred to Tebbit's 'ugly rant, [which] with its elements of racism displayed the rabid extremism that still lurks below the surface' (editorial, 8 October 1997). The *Daily Star*, somewhat more sensationally, carried a short piece on page 2 under the heading 'Whizkid's race shock'. A 15-year-old Asian Tory named Munish Chopra had made a speech to the conference in which he said that Enoch Powell 'was misunderstood by a lot of people'. As an afterthought to this minuscule coverage, there is a two-sentence reference to Lord Tebbit. It is reported as not of great consequence. The 'shock' is that the young man who, it is reported, hopes to become Britain's first Asian Prime Minister, admires 'outspoken immigration opponent' Powell. A descriptive phrase is used which places Powell's racism in the respectable category of outspoken opposition. Powell had made his racist speeches in April 1968, and his prognostications have proven to be ill-founded, as have many of his statistical projections. The *Daily Star* uses the name Powell here as a visible way of drawing upon a fear-bound and reactionary discursive reserve. It is inviting those who wish to reiterate such a formulation to enjoy this young man's realisation of that which 'we' all know – Powell was right. The *Express*, another Conservative paper, does not mention either Clark or Tebbit in its editorial. It does report on their speeches, but quotes Hague as saying 'I assume Norman Tebbit's views have been misinterpreted. There is no place for bigotry in my Conservative Party' (p. 2). The article, by Patrick O'Flynn and Roland Watson, goes on to quote comments made by Tebbit after the speech: 'Last night Lord Tebbit insisted that he had not been talking about immigration or racism and said he was concerned "more about culture than ethnics".' No comment is offered upon Tebbit's choice of the term 'ethnics' in a way which is closer to apartheid than multicultural Britain. There is a sense in the article that Clark and Tebbit had done no more, in the words of the front-page headline, than threaten to 'spoil the party'. The two high circulation tabloids which both support the Labour Party, the *Mirror* and the *Sun*, did not mention either Clark or Tebbit in their editorials. Overall, despite the indignation of one or two papers, the ideological impact of Clark and Tebbit went unchallenged.

Conclusion

I have tried in this chapter to provide a range of examples of the ways in which issues of 'race' have been covered by the press. There are many, many more examples which could have been selected. It would be possible to consider the more vicious forms of racism which have been identified by Gordon and Rosenberg (1989) or by Searle (1989). It would also be possible to trawl through a vast number of advertisements and find numerous examples of questionable or openly racist representations. All these activities are and will be essential for the media researcher. It is also important to consider the ways in which specific forms of discourse are structured in relation to these issues, and the rhetorical skill with which such matters are often handled in the press. The recurrent patterns certainly occur at the level of choice of vocabulary. They also occur through the way in which discursive reserves are simply invoked, or enriched with fresh ideological inflexions, or exploited for their contradictory potential in order to encourage conservative readings of issues relating to 'race'.

There is another significant feature of press reportage of issues of 'race' and this is the extent to which it is involved in, reflects or generates change. Many more longitudinal studies are needed of the way in which specific newspapers deal with specific issues. It is clear that some of the excesses of the 1970s' and 1980s' reportage of issues concerning 'race' have been tempered over the decades. This does not, however, mean that such representations have simply become so innocuous as to be of little consequence. What has to be studied is the extent to which underlying media discourses have moved or changed over time. It is my contention that we are indeed in a period of change, but that there is little evidence to suggest that it is more than a surface transition. The discourses of nationalism, chauvinism, patriotism and racism are still there and sometimes bubble to the surface or appear in sanitised or reformist guise. The examples I have been considering cover a range of representations and discursive practices. In the next chapter I will be focusing more specifically on the ways in which the concept of 'normality' is invoked in relation to reportage of issues of 'race'.

7

Racism and normality

In the previous chapter emphasis was given to discussion of the different approaches of the broadsheet and tabloid newspapers as they represent issues of 'race'. It was also suggested that such newspapers can and often do change the modality of their judgements over time. In other words, the crassness of some racist reportage is superseded by a more measured approach to the reportage of 'race'. This does not necessarily mean that the representations are more progressive, although this may sometimes be the case. What is more likely, however, is that the ideological import of specific messages is embedded in implicit as much as explicit discourses. This is never more the case than when the media are dealing with what is considered to be normal, common sense, the 'way things are'. The invocation of normality and the establishment of culturally and politically acceptable behavioural patterns often form the keystone for ideological arguments made at the expense of individuals, groups or nations deemed to be 'other'. In this chapter I will consider two different media examples where normality is either used as a defensive gauge in order to bolster pride in being British, or where a criticism of normality results in responses which are revelatory in relation to particular media audiences and their attitude to 'race'. In both cases it will be apparent that racist discourse comes quickly to the fore. I will be arguing here that there is a close relationship between those media discourses which feed on concepts of normality and those discourses which are overtly racist. One feeds the other in a symbiotic relationship.

The horror of racist violence is, of course, ever present as the primary material correlate of specific signifying practices. But correlation may or may not be related to causality. It may be that we need to analyse issues of 'race' and normality as represented in the media, in order to explore the ways in which that which is normal acts as a foundation upon which more extreme behaviour is sustained. It may be that the analysis of representations of deviant or violent behaviour in relation to issues of race will tell us less than a careful scrutiny of that which is represented as the bedrock of normality.

The excesses of mindless nationalism, the resentment and fear of outsiders, the persecution, intimidation, and sometimes murder of ethnic minorities, all take their place in a catalogue of human misery which is part of late twentieth-century life. The crucial difference between this and earlier times may or may not be that things are worse now than they have ever been. In the past there have been pogroms, massacres, chauvinistic excursions which sought to colonise and exploit vast areas of the globe. And there has been the chilling reminder of the depths to which the project of Modernity can sink with the Holocaust (Bauman, 1989). It is not surprising, then, that concerned individuals, organisations or academic and research communities wish to concentrate upon such abominations in order to try to understand what is happening now at the local, regional, national and global levels.

What distinguishes the present from the past most significantly is that today the media, most notably television, bring reports of events to what is virtually a global audience within a very short amount of time. There is not the literal or metaphorical space for the messenger to travel over land and sea with the news of a fresh disaster or atrocity. Today the audience may be there as it happens. In the press in most parts of the world it is possible to read of these same (televisual) happenings less than 24 hours later. Wars, murders, racist attacks are part of the seemingly endless flow of media representations (Williams, 1974). It is clear from what has already been argued that the events of which we hear or read are mediated accounts of what has happened, and that these mediations need to be carefully studied in order to clarify their formal organisation, the principles upon which they are based, and the interests likely to be served by the way in which such messages offer up their meanings.

On the one hand, the messages of which I am writing may be sensationalised accounts in the tabloid press or treated with a version of intellectual and analytical rigour in the broadsheets; on the other, they may be sent out in soundbites and image clusters like bursts from an electronic machine gun along the television and radio airwaves. The result of this media deluge, this perpetual discourse of violence, often integrally linked with issues of 'race', is that these representations may become normalised. This does not have to mean that such messages are uncritically accepted by media audiences (although they may be), but they have become part of everyday experience. As such, they are a late twentieth-century material and psychological hazard, to be avoided if possible and tolerated with some stress. As hazards, they are also representations of issues which are usually dealt with by experts or professionals.

There is now an extended tapestry of cruelty and violence which has been woven into popular memory. We may have seen media representations of Israeli soldiers attempting to break the arms of Palestinian men using large rocks. We may have seen the beating of Rodney King (Hunt, 1997, p. 407; Gooding-Williams, 1993). We may have watched as one or another scene of intense and horrific violence is played out before us. Recurrent images of brutality and violence, often linked with issues of 'race', do not, however, guarantee that any insight into the underlying causes or range of possible explanations for such occurrences will be forthcoming. They fall upon us like water on a wet rag placed over our faces to stop us breathing. There is no respite, no pause in the flow. The only immediate relief to be had is to turn off or to risk changing channels.

Given the predominance of violence and violent acts reported in the media, the temptation is to concentrate one's attention as a media researcher mainly on such phenomena. Such research is, of course, very necessary. The visible acts of violence which occur in our societies, particularly when linked with issues of 'race', could also be conceptualised as no more than the tip of an iceberg. If we use this metaphor to explore certain ideological and discursive possibilities, then the bulk of this iceberg will remain under the water and not immediately visible. It is not, however, buried in our unconscious or a 'false consciousness'; it is merely out of sight. In this chapter I wish to argue that the vast bulk of our metaphorical iceberg, upon which racism, nationalism and xenophobia can be sustained, may be designated as the state of *normality*.

The concepts of normality and the 'natural' are of considerable significance in relation to the construction and sustenance of various ideological positions. Following Barthes (1972), I will argue that naturalisation is the process whereby specific social relationships, often of power and subordination, are constructed and presented as natural rather than being the result of complex historical interactions between individuals, ethnic or other groups, genders, classes and power blocs.

Representations of normality, or the invocation of a discursive structure of normality, are used again and again in the media in order to provide ballast for views and representations which are, upon further consideration, highly questionable. Normal life is that which can be summed up in the phrase 'it's only natural'. The construction of 'otherness' is, unsurprisingly, something which stands in symbiotic relationship to the discourses of normality. There is clearly an important connection to be explored between this symbiotic relationship and the contradictions which it smooths over. Chauvinistic and xenophobic behaviour towards the stranger, or representations rooted in racist discourse are, in this way, made to seem natural. From these relatively simple beginnings, a whole range of popular discourses can arise and flourish. Such discourses, at least from the viewpoint of the 'Natural Englishman', justify the retention of the crassest racist stereotypes in the name of 'our' normality.

There is little about normality in the literature about the media and issues of 'race'. The emphasis tends to be on concepts of deviance and the treatment (or construction) of deviance in the media. Just as a newspaper editor might argue that a good story does not come from reporting that 30,000 anti-racists went on a demonstration where there was no violence and a great deal of good will generated, so the media researcher and theorist might decide that researching the normal would be unbelievably boring and possibly intellectually and academically unrewarding. As noted in Chapter 2, debates about the nature of ideological domination have tended to centre on discussion of whether or not audiences are being manipulated or are 'making use' of media messages for their own ends. The former position has found a large number of sympathisers in what has become known as the 'effects' tradition in media research, and with the Frankfurt School (Mcleod *et al.*, 1991; Bronner and Kellner, 1989). The latter position has become more significant in recent years, and has been argued with some persuasiveness by de Certeau, who writes of the 'silent, transgressive, ironic or poetic activities of readers [including media readers for our purposes] who maintain their reserve in private and without the knowledge of the "masters" ' (de Certeau, 1988, p. 172). This is a sophisticated and generous account of the activities of some audiences in some socio-cultural settings. Another, and parallel, theorisation might also be considered. This would conceptualise media audiences as amorphous bodies that somehow seek social and psychological stability (homeostasis) in the messages they receive. It would also be possible to conceptualise communicators as professionals who seek to maintain social stability in the messages which they construct. Such stability would be premised upon the maintenance of established relations of power and subordination in society, so messages which undermined that stability would be curtailed or rejected. Both audience and communicators could then be conceptualised as, unsurprisingly, in search of the security which a strong sense of the normal provides. In the case of the communicator, that sense of normality can be used as the dramatic and discursive platform from which various representational forays into the realms of ideology can be made.

In this chapter I wish to argue for the detailed and patient engagement with representations which serve to confirm ideological positions, mainly through appeals to common sense and a notion of normality. The first example which will be discussed here relates to an occasion when a government minister in the United Kingdom publicly voiced racist sentiments which are more usually confined to the relative privacy of the bar or the meal table. The voicing of such discourses of racism and power have a critical role to play in what I will call the 'discursive reserve'. By this I mean that there is available in social and cultural formations a range of rhetorical and linguistic reference points which are constructed over time and which can be identified and passed from individual to individual and group to group. I would wish to stress that they are reference points rather than scripts. The media producer, the reader or audiences thus have, within identifiable discursive parameters, the freedom to utilise selected reference points in order to sustain particular discourses. This range of reference points does not necessarily require subtlety of argument or clarity of exposition and is usually invoked by means of implicature. This concept is derived from the work of the philosopher H. P. Grice.

> An implicature is a proposition emerging from something that is said, but not actually stated by the words uttered, nor logically derivable from them. It must therefore be a product of the relationship between utterance and context; and a vital part of context would be the knowledge and motives of the speaker and addressee.
>
> (Fowler, 1986, p. 172)

The concept of implicature will be related analytically to the construction of 'normality'.

Telling the truth about foreigners

The source of this example is speech made on 4 February 1994 by the then Conservative minister Michael Portillo, and a newspaper column written by a fellow Conservative, Alan Clark, some days later. Mr Portillo had been speaking to a gathering of students at Southampton University when he launched a virulent attack on the corruption of (unnamed) foreigners. His speech was widely reported in the British media and elicited, amongst other things, a response from Mr Clark which will be analysed below. The core of Portillo's argument was that Britain was the most honest country in the world. Foreigners did not rate so highly in his estimation:

> Outside of this country the standards of public life are way below what goes on in this country. If any of you in this room have got an A Level it is because you have worked to get it. Go to any other country and when you have got an A level you have bought it or because you were a friend of a minister [sic].

> (*Guardian*, 5 February 1994)

The construction of Portillo's argument is based on gross and unproblematic generalisation. The students to whom he was speaking may or may not have accepted his statement as a serious commentary on 'other' countries. Portillo's speech was widely reported, and some newspapers suggested that his political credibility was under severe strain as a result of his ill-judged remarks. For others, as I will show, Portillo was seen as a man of integrity. Through utilising the concept of implicature, it is possible to understand Portillo's comments as redolent with the discourse of British middle-class white racism. Understanding implicature is about understanding how to fill in blank spaces, whether they are literal or metaphorical.

The piece which will now be analysed was written by Alan Clark in his weekly column in the Conservative *Mail on Sunday*. It is probably more significant in ideological terms than was the original speech by Portillo. On 6 February Clark devoted the whole of his column to a discussion of Portillo's speech. In so doing he provided a paradigmatic instance of what might be described as soft or 'normal' white British racism. He structured an argument built on an upper middle class-based judgement of 'foreigners', and one which serves to sustain deeper and more worrying judgements about Otherness.

Under the photograph of Clark and his name – there to signify that it is his personal column – the piece is headed 'A sorry "gaffe" blown out of all proportion'. This title establishes the general modality of the article. It is based on invocations of what 'we' all know to be the case. The unpleasant inferences scattered throughout are offered up with an air of bonhomie and bravura. Indeed, words from 'other' languages seem appropriate here. The use of the word 'gaffe' in inverted commas is itself either ironic or grossly misjudged, coming as it does from the French. But the phrase 'sorry gaffe' is very much a piece of upper middle-class English vernacular. To speak of a 'sorry mess', a 'sorry gaffe' or a sorry anything is to place the situation described in a world of public school education and after dinner chat. This is confirmed by the remainder of the title – 'blown out of all proportion', for which, from a position inside the ideological and discursive framework of the *Mail on Sunday*, one might read 'made into something much more significant than it should have been to anyone with half a grain of (British) common sense'.

Clark thanks God that Portillo is around. This is not an act of religious devotion. It is another piece of class rhetoric, inviting silent discourses of reactionary fervour in the preferred reader. Thank God that Portillo is around so that somebody at least can tell the truth about these bloody foreigners! He praises Portillo for two other speeches made earlier in the month. Clark uses very English descriptive terms, such as 'shower', to describe the British Establishment. The connotation of the term 'shower' is generally that of a disorganised and disreputable group of people, and was famously used by the British comedian Terry Thomas. It is also used, as with the adjective 'sorry', as a means of colloquialising and euphemising unpleasant or potentially offensive judgements. By demonstrating that Portillo has been critical of the Establishment, Clark seeks to vindicate the former's judgement of 'foreigners'. In this way the discourses of racism and chauvinism can be offered as no more or less than common-sense arguments by reasonable men.

Clark, however, is in no mood to compromise with the critics of Portillo. 'Since when has it been a gaffe,' he asks, 'to say what everyone knows to be true?' Portillo had suggested that outside the sanctity of the United Kingdom, people were corrupt and bought their qualifications. No country was named where this occurs, though he might have mentioned the great tradition of Oxford and Cambridge in England where it is normal to purchase one's MA qualification. Instead, Clark rounds on alleged bureaucratic procedures and the corruption of officials in France, Italy and Greece. He equates this alleged corruption, somehow, with xenophobia – probably of the corrupt officials, but that is not made clear. By this stage of the argument it does not really matter. Clark then turns his venom on those 'closet liberals or worse' who are suspicious of nationalism. He has moved away from Portillo's accusations and into the discursive modality which allows for the (re)construction of Great Britain and those who dare criticise her. In order to accomplish this move he has to introduce some fifth columnists in the form of liberals and high-minded commentators. These unidentified persons are then linked to the humiliation of Britain. Clark has by now moved into a new and more vicious discursive mode. He is, metaphorically at least, foaming at the mouth: 'So it does not matter to what humiliation Britain is subjected, the recommended response is always the same – roll about on the ground and wave your paws in the air.' One can only assume that the reference to 'paws' is intended to evoke an image of a humiliated British Lion. The reader has by this time been taken a long way from the speech of Portillo. Clark roams with ease from the visit of Gerry Adams to the USA, to unintelligible but sombre warnings about North American society and its 'urban concentrations of power on Eastern and Pacific seaboards which are violent, rootless, and prone to hysteria'. A brief diversion into Conservative politics and Clark has come just about full circle.

Portillo, according to Clark, is someone who can articulate his ideas and who should be listened to in the name of Tory unity. It is now time to administer to the reader the final rhetorical blow. Clark admits that 'what Michael Portillo said might have seemed, from the lips of the Foreign Secretary indecorous. But he is a junior member of the Cabinet and he was talking to a student meeting.' The choice of the word 'indecorous' is important here. Once again it is a word with a good middle-class or upper middle-class pedigree. It carries with it connotations of lacking propriety or good taste. It is from the same discursive repertoire as terms such as 'sorry gaffe'. Such terms are a cover for vindictive thought and malicious discourse. They also serve to impart a sense of normality to what might otherwise appear jingoistic and racist claptrap.

Clark's logic has not yet reached the point of exhaustion. From reminding his readers that what might have seemed 'indecorous' from the lips of the Foreign Secretary can hardly be deemed so when it comes from the lips of a mere junior member of the Cabinet, Clark notes that Portillo was talking to an audience of students. Presumably this gives licence to a junior Cabinet minister to let his thoughts run riot. What's wrong with a little xenophobia, racism and chauvinism when talking to a group of students?, cries Clark's discourse from between the lines. Any sympathetic reader of Clark's column, and it is for such that it is written, might now be wondering if the column will move towards reconciliation with Portillo's critics. It is not to be. Clark continues: 'Now we have been told he is sorry. So am I. There are few spectacles so distasteful as that of one who has *told the truth* being compelled to apologise' (italics added). In the final comment there is the self-righteous indignation of the reactionary who reserves the right to spread his views as the norm against which all other discourse should be measured. We have, finally, moved from implicature to invective; normality has been reasserted.

The above example has been chosen because it illustrates the fact that racism may be manifested in many different ways in the media. In the second part of this chapter I will provide an example of the way in which discourses that are usually suppressed can come to the surface if certain members of the media audience feel they have been provoked beyond endurance. Before doing so, however, I wish to comment on the ways in which the 'normal' and invocations of normality, with their feigned intimacy and discursive closeness, facilitate the nurture and practice of racism and xenophobia. It is my contention that, behind the invocation of normality, there lurks the potential of violence from those who wish to preserve 'normality' at all costs. These invocations may sometimes come from the relative anonymity of newspaper editorials, or from the mediation of the speeches and comments of public figures. Media messages address their audiences in the language of the everyday and require a theorisation which recognises that the everyday has become the apolitical centre of the 'mediasation' of culture (Thompson, 1990). Making media sense of outsiders is often accomplished through appeals to that (usually national) lifestyle which allegedly existed and is now potentially under threat. The 'past' for the xenophobe is sacred and to be guarded as a precious memory. Normality must invent the 'good old days', whether these take the form of street parties or reminders of the Empire and its 'civilising' mission.

Racist and xenophobic discourse operates frequently on what might be called the 'wink-and-nod' approach to the issue of 'race'. Clark is an expert at such inferential argument. His technique of bemoaning the fact that one can no longer speak the truth about issues and (Other) people is one which recurs on occasion in bus queues, in right-wing newspaper editorials and some bars when alcohol loosens the tongue. The precise ways in which the discursive reserve is drawn upon for this and similar purposes are difficult to research. Sometimes it has become necessary to turn to the dramatist or novelist in order to recognise that for which the researcher cannot collect appropriate data. The reason for this is simple enough. Most overt racist discourse is likely to take place behind closed doors or in the company of sympathetic listeners. There are exceptions, but the discreet face of racism is not responsive to established research methodologies. A researcher who wishes to document the operations of racist discourse is likely to become more like a spy and informer than a conventional academic. There will always be problems associated with the reliability of such data in qualitative audience research. Everyday life and the 'normal' are two of the most inaccessible facets of social existence. It is often easier to research our rituals and our celebrations than the mundane behaviour of quotidian existence. Yet it is often within the latter that the ideological foundations of racism and xenophobia are sustained.

The next example of the relationship between normality and discourses of 'race', racism and the media is offered with all the above difficulties very much in mind. The fact that it was not designed as a piece of research does not, I believe, detract from the importance of the data which it provided. It is a miniature case study which demonstrates how media reportage can lead to defensive racist responses from admirers of a popular and 'normal' children's television programme. More so than with Alan Clark's defence of Michael Portillo, the responses which will be identified here give voice to discourses which are usually reserved for private communication. The data used here has never been published before because I decided that it was necessary for some time to pass in order to avoid sensationalising what I consider to be important research material.

The friends of *Blue Peter*

Blue Peter, named after the flag which ships raise as a signal that they are leaving port, began on BBC television in 1958 and it is still flourishing. There have been many presenters over the years as well as a variety of *Blue Peter* pets which have been popular with its audience. The programme offers young children the chance to take part in a range of practical activities and was famous in its early days for making maximum use of plastic bottles and cardboard tubes to construct various toys. It was also intensely respectable and was what is known in the United Kingdom as 'Middle England'. The programme celebrated matters royal and was often involved with the military in one or another form. It mounted campaigns designed to benefit various charities, and was famous in its early years for asking children to collect metal milk bottle tops. These could then be sold to raise money for guide dogs for the blind. *Blue Peter* became, over the years, something of a British television institution. This section will consider some responses to criticism of *Blue Peter* and will suggest that these, ranging as they do from the indignant to the obscene, are rooted in ideological concepts of normality which are largely unacknowledged.

The context

In 1982, Sir Keith Joseph, then Secretary for Education and Science, asked Her Majesty's Inspectorate to bring together a group of teachers to report on the values and images of adult life presented in a series of popular evening television programmes. The resulting report, entitled *Popular TV and Schoolchildren*, was published in 1983. One suggestion which the report made was that all teachers should be 'involved in examining and discussing television programmes with children'. The British Film Institute and the Institute of Education of the University of London organised a conference in 1983 under the title of Television and Schooling. A book was published as a result of the conference with the same title (Lusted and Drummond, 1985). In the book was a short, over-zealous and under-theorised polemical piece which I wrote and which offered some criticisms of *Blue Peter* (Ferguson, 1985, pp. 47–52). I noted that the programme was royalist and pro-capitalist, and that it was often racist and sexist, as well as being 'ostensibly Christian'. I then suggested that it might be a good idea, in a move towards genuine plurality in children's programming, if there was another programme shown every other week entitled *Red Peter*. This programme would be

> presented, possibly, by two women and one man. It would campaign against any government that could tolerate poverty, degradation, poor housing or health care. It would be openly anti-royalist, anti-racist and anti-sexist. It would deplore the need for charity when millions of pounds are spent each minute to defend us

from a future. If funds were raised, they would be for publicity campaigns against nuclear arms and against pusillanimity in the face of privilege.

The book was published in March 1985. On 18 March the *Daily Telegraph*, a stalwart Conservative paper, published a short piece on page 2 entitled 'Red rival urged for "racist" *Blue Peter*.' The article was relatively measured in tone and made it clear that my proposal was that it might be possible to broaden children's horizons by broadcasting a *Red Peter* programme as well as the existing *Blue Peter*. The story was quickly picked up by the British tabloids and several tried to interview me. I agreed to one interview later that same day, with Corinna Honan, television correspondent of the *Daily Mail*. It is important to trace the way in which at least part of this was conducted for two reasons. The first is that it demonstrates how difficult it is to make an alternative argument when the 'discursive reserve' is crowding in with full ideological force. The second is that it was the misrepresentation by the *Daily Mail* which acted as a spur to those who gave voice to their racism in defence of *Blue Peter*.

Honan came to my office at lunchtime, as I declined the offer of lunch. She carried with her a copy of the piece from the *Daily Telegraph* which she had clearly read and marked. Throughout the interview she took notes. I will provide three examples of her interviewing approach. She first commented upon my attitude to charity, particularly in relation to *Blue Peter*. I made it clear to her immediately and again at the end of the interview that I was not against charity, but that I thought it was not and could never be a substitute for direct government action on an international scale.

Honan then picked up on a single reference in my article to the trades union movement. The actual sentence reads:

> Hence the emphasis on raising money through charity for usually worthy causes without questioning why charity has to be invoked instead of direct government action, and the preference for connecting worthy causes to royal patrons rather than to figures in the trades union movement who are struggling against injustice.
>
> (Ferguson, 1985, p. 48)

Honan asked if I would like to see Arthur Scargill, a militant miner involved in major industrial action at the time, presenting charity appeals. I said that I thought that would not be a good idea. She asked me if I thought there was something wrong with Arthur Scargill. I said no, but he did not seem to be an appropriate person to cite in the middle of a bitter industrial dispute. I said that my argument rested upon principle rather than personalities. If one had to give an example one could as well choose Michael McGahey (another militant miners' leader) as Arthur Scargill, though this was not important in relation to our discussion. Honan had what she wanted.

The next issue we discussed was the appearance of the presenters on *Blue Peter*. Honan asked me what was wrong with them, and I said that they did seem rather clean-living 'goody-goody' types. She made a comment to the effect that they were not so clean-living when they were not on television from what she had heard. I explained that I felt they were obviously chosen for their appearance and that, over the years, an identifiable *Blue Peter* image had evolved. Honan asked whether I wanted very different presenters. Should they *not* be good-looking? Could they be fat or ugly? I ventured to suggest that what constituted 'good looks' might have as much to do with personality as physiognomy. Honan did not pursue the matter further.

After the interview I telephoned home to find that another *Daily Mail* journalist had been speaking with my wife and children. My wife had invited her into the house thinking that she was doing some kind of market research. She knew nothing of the piece in the *Daily Telegraph*. Honan rang me back a few minutes later asking for more biographical details. I asked her whether she was going to 'let me down'. She seemed to understand me immediately and assured me that she was giving the article very careful attention. The next day (19 March) the article appeared in the *Daily Mail* under the headline 'RED PETER . . . Lecturer's dream TV show for children . . . anti-royal, anti-sexist, with fat, ugly hosts'. *Red Peter*, it said, 'would consider presenters who were fat, ugly, or from an ethnic minority'. I will not go into further detail here, except to note that it mentioned that my wife was from Israel. The editorial of the *Daily Mail* also mentioned me by name with the clear suggestion that I was indoctrinating my students.

On 22 March the letters column of the *Daily Mail* carried three letters relating to the *Red Peter* story. One was from the Public Relations Officer of the Royal National Lifeboat Institution. The piece extracted in the paper read as follows: 'More than 400 people have reason to be very grateful to *Blue Peter*. Their lives have been saved by *Blue Peter* Lifeboats provided by charity appeals which Bob Ferguson does not like.' On the same day I received a letter from Corinna Honan which included the following:

Dear Bob,

Alas, you were right. I wrote the story very carefully but the sub-editors had other ideas that evening. I was particularly upset that it made you sound as though you were against *Blue Peter* charity appeals – not what you said and not what I wrote. So, many apologies.

A second letter in the *Daily Mail* moved a little closer than the first to articulating discourses which are less often spoken. It was from a reader in Aldershot and read as follows:

... What is so wrong with being clean living, sport-loving, fun-loving white middle or any other class, and British? For heaven's sake, most of us are still just that, and this is Britain after all.

(*Daily Mail*, 22 March 1985, p. 18)

The point of my narrative so far has been to demonstrate the way in which the tabloids, with the help of the sub-editors, are able to manufacture stories which have more to do with their own discursive reserve than with anything as restrictive as the facts. I hope I have also shown how it is possible for a journalist to wash her hands of any responsibility for a story which appears under her own name. This is, however, a preface to the discourses simmering under the surface of normality and which were articulated in letters sent to the university in the coming weeks. My purpose in quoting from some of these letters is to identify specific characteristics of racist discourse which are usually handled with more tact but which nevertheless use as their reference point a state of 'normality'.

I have selected two types of letter for consideration. The first demonstrates open racism, and tends not to mention anything about what I might have written. The second type is more conventionally eloquent and hurt. I have retained the original spelling and punctuation throughout.

Letter 1. No name or address. Posted in Manchester.
Mr Ferguson.

It is people like you who brain washing children and pupils to turn to Scarghill & McGahey, you ought to be deported. You would like to see Red Peter, Black peter. There are too many coloured people feeding on the English & sods like you, to give to £17,000 a year is an insult to our country. Blue Peter does a good job to our children so keep your dirty hands and thoughts off. Too many blacks on our television screens already. You ought to know by now that mining is good job now, no dust, that there are things worse than mining & when they turn out Scarghills and McGaheys, it is something an honest miner does not want. So keep your trap shut.

Letter 2. No name or address. Posted in Hendon, North London.
You must be a very unhappy familie having to live here und criticize innocent programmes like Blue Peter and That's Life, at least all these charities are for good causes, unlike all the thousands and thousands of pounds going to Iserael from English Jews every year, just to kill innocent people.

We think we know the kind of presenters you would like to see Men with big black hats & beards & curls hanging from their ears wives with tight scarfs round their heads pushing prams with three and four children hardly speaking English of which we see to many in N & NW London

The quicker you & your clever know-all children make an exit to Iserael the better for everyone.

Letter 3. No name or address. Posted in Ipswich, Suffolk.
To Fergusson and his obvious black bastard wife if you don't like our blue Peter or our Royal Family or our culture then clear off to Russia where you belong and take your dirty little bastard of a daughter with you I and my family are working class but we dont need you and your crap to tell us what we should do we love our Royal Family and you can stick your red flag right up your ass you are just a communist nigger lover as for your daughter I bet she is a four eyed half caste creep as for sexist as far as we are concerned a man is a man a woman a woman I dont expect your little creep are either

Letter 4. No address. Posted in Leeds, Yorkshire.
Dear Mr Ferguson
Re your ideas about Blue Peter, what a load of rubbish. I am an ex soldier, ex dustman, and ex miner now retired and living on O.A. Pension *with satisfaction*. To many OAPs spend their money on Bingo Beer etc., instead of food. I'm also disabled through work but don't grumble. My Children, Grandchildren and Greatgrandchildren don't want see or listen to the people you mention. They and you are revolutionists and we should end up like Iran and Iraq. If

your good lady doesn't like our English ways she knows where to go. My father worked 50 years down the pit and he didn't grumble. His O.A. Pension was only 10 shillings a week but no grumbles.

Don't talk as if I was a racist, I lived in India for six years. I went to the trouble of mixing with them and learning their language. They all fought for us. The Irish didn't nor middle east people. £17,000 a year and not satisfied. You're greedy.

Excuse the scribble as I am crippled with arthritis, BUT I still do voluntary work.

As for the Royal Family, How much work have you done for the Children in need. It is the likes of you that will, given the chance bring this country to its knees.

Yours sincerely

Letter 5. No address. Signed from an 'OAP'.
R, Ferguson.

Red Peter

Racism is very much in evidence in our country today.

White people are attacked and robbed by Blacks and rape by these thugs is also on the increase. Significantly, there are no reports of this violence by Whites against Blacks. [*sic*] The illicit drugs trade too by coloured immigrants is growing. Another reason why Race mixing should not be tolerated as it was contrary to public opinion.

The sooner these overseas people are persuaded to leave the better, Otherwise in time by superior numbers, they will take over when racism will really mean something as it does where they govern in other countries. I am sure the public would definitely prefer royalty to scum like Scargill, McGahey etc. With them holding the reins, there would be riots and permanent political unrest. Is this what you want?

Letter 6. Name and address supplied, Walton on Thames.
[Passages here have been edited for the purposes of highlighting the key points concerning issues of 'race'.]
Dear Mr Ferguson
... As I am not sure what you mean by racist, I am unable to understand what you mean by anti-racist. We had to accept, by law, a multi-racial society, although I am not aware that we were consulted at the time. I, and millions like me, accept the situation, but we are not yet forced to love it ... I would much prefer my country

England to be occupied by the English, but I obey the law and will continue to do so. Does that make me a racist? ... I only hope that your comments have not appeared in the so-called popular press. The 'lower orders' have a tendency to believe what they read in the newspapers, and I am sure you would not want to corrupt the masses.

Please do reassure me that you were only joking.

Yours sincerely

Ideology and social psychology

The selection of letters quoted above offers a range of linked positions on the issue of 'race'. The positions taken are, in fact, much closer than their apparent disparity in choice of vocabulary and expression might suggest. I will now use reference to the piece written in the *Daily Mail* and the responses by readers to try to assemble a tentative schematic outline of the discursive reserve which serves both rabid racists and those who uphold the cherished norms of their society with apparent decorum (*see* Figure 7.1). In doing so I will be suggesting that the discursive reserve is something drawn upon by both the media and the audience. It is not inflicted by one upon the other, it is shared. How the various discursive categories are drawn upon will depend upon the context and purpose of their usage. What is suggested, however, is that they will tend to cluster around concepts of normality which, in turn, will be used to attempt a justification of racist positions. Such positions may display more or less sophistication, but their underlying structures are likely to be the same. This should not, however, be mistaken for some kind of essentialist claim about the nature of racist discourse. The discursive categories may change and on occasion be replaced by others. They will also interrelate in a multitude of ways, but they will always centre on appeals to the normal, normality, or an idealisation of normality. This tendency towards homeostasis is likely to impact upon the constitution of a whole range of discursive reserves which employ a whole range of discursive categories.

In Figure 7.1 a cluster of discursive categories is shown, although these are not linked by arrows or dotted lines. This is because the type of relationship we are dealing with is, like the question of ideology, not easily susceptible to diagrammatic representation. It is a relationship in a state of fluctuation and tension, and it is quite common for the way

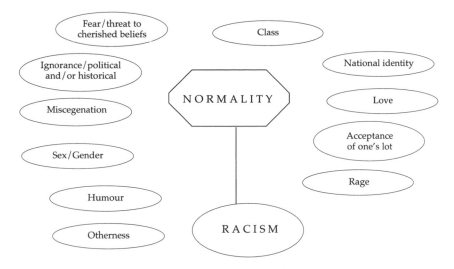

FIGURE 7.1 Racism, normality and discursive categorisation

the different discursive categories are utilised to throw up contra-dictions within specific discourses. I will now offer a brief commentary on some of the categories by making reference to the letters quoted above. I will then attempt to draw together certain discursive and representational threads which link the two newspaper articles and the letters. It should be noted, however, that the various categories are separated here for discussion purposes. In practice they constantly overlap, interact and impact upon each other.

Normality: a fragile concept

It is in the defence of the normal that the discourses of racism become their most erratic and prone to dissimulation. For the *Daily Mail*, in this context, normality centres on the enthusiastic acceptance of royalism. It has already been noted that the *Mail* attacked the 'Lecturer's dream' of an 'anti-royal' programme, apparently refusing the distinction between anti-royal and anti-royalist, though 'anti-sexist' was not changed to 'anti-sex'. The *Daily Mail* unashamedly structures normal-ity around royalism. It may be acceptable, if the occasion necessitates, to criticise members of the royal family. To suggest that a royal family may be an anachronism is perverse. The letter from a reader cited on page 18 of the *Daily Mail* uses a form of euphemisation to describe the 'normal' British person, suggesting that 'most of us' have laudable characteristics, particularly that of whiteness. Stripped to its bare essentials, the letter asks what is wrong with being white and British. The rhetorical flourish with which it ends indicates a slight trace of petulance with strong class overtones: 'For heaven's sake ... This is Britain after all.' It is clear from such discourse that normal British people are, naturally, white. Letter 6 also contains a stuffy middle-class appeal for the importance of being 'Anglo-centric'. In relation to *Blue Peter* we are reminded that 'this is England, most of us are English and some of us are still proud to be so'. The normality of whiteness is reinforced in the same letter by recognising that we are now 'a multi-racial society' but noting that the writer would have preferred to see England 'occupied by the English'. There is reinforcement here of the implicit claim that to be English is to be part of a mono-racial community. There is snobbish and leaden humour at the end of the letter with reference to the 'lower orders', where the argument used is of the 'You can't fool me but I wouldn't want lesser minds to be corrupted' type.

Normality and purity

The two letters cited above hint at the importance of 'racial purity'. This argument has its more direct application in the rage with which racist beliefs are expressed in Letter 3. The references to being a 'nigger lover' and to a child being a 'half-caste creep' are more forthright articulations of the assertions put forward in the earlier letters. They are not incompatible with the gentility of 'I would much prefer my country England to be occupied by the English.' The latter position is righteously indignant, while the former boils with rage. The viability of both positions depends upon the conceptualisation of a 'normal' or nominal English person. If there is a continuum of racism which operates across the positions put forward here, it is certainly not based on vocabulary. It is, rather, discursive and hence not dependent upon individual words or even phrases. Discursive structures are reliant upon narrative and/or rational constructions. This is why 'political correctness' which depends upon watching one's choice of words will never be able to bring about more than superficial change. I am not arguing here that vicious racist insults do not hurt, but rather pointing out that the longer-term damage of racist discourse can just as well be sustained with a velvet tongue. The forthright racism which displays a horror of miscegenation is complemented by the genteel nationalism which offers 'love' of one's country as a foundation stone of ('racial') purity. The purveyors of such discourses may not keep the same company, but they champion the same cause.

Identifying the 'Others'

The interplay between notions of self-identity and Otherness is apparent in the letters and in the column by Alan Clark. At its most basic level, notions of the self centre on being English which (regrettably for the writers) so many inhabitants of the UK are alleged not to be. Otherness is signified in a variety of ways, such as Portillo's gross allegation about the inhabitants of 'any other country', or 'these overseas people' (Letter 5), or 'them' (Letter 4), or 'too many coloured people' (Letter 1), or 'middle east people' [sic] (Letter 4). There is little sophistication in any of the arguments. They seem more concerned with establishing a necessary Other which will, in the long run, validate their concept of normality. Perhaps the most eloquent and sinister is from the anti-Semitic writer who envisages television presenters of children's programmes as 'Men with big black hats & beards & curls hanging from their ears wives with tight scarfs round their heads pushing prams with three and four children hardly speaking English of which we see to many in N & NW London' (Letter 2).

Identity is also implicitly defended as various writers voice their fears, whether it be about the family size of those who are 'others', or fears of permanent unrest and riots, or trade unionists. Here we can see that concepts of Otherness can transcend barriers of 'race' and ethnicity and include under the same category those who are deemed to be 'revolutionists' or just plain 'scum'. There is also reference to 'our English ways' and the need to accept them as the most desirable ways to live. If 'others' do not like them , they should 'know what to do'. Again and again the discourses of racism are associated with negative discourses about socialism, trade unionism, general ingratitude and social unrest. Conversely, racist discourses can become the implicit or explicit illustrative material for those whose primary interest is ostensibly the negative appraisal of another issue. The only racism which is enunciated with relative 'purity' is that which takes the form of the racist obscenity. Otherwise it will be linked in one way or another to the various categories set out in Figure 7.1. A more detailed analysis of the letters and the newspaper articles would demonstrate the ways in which racism is interwoven with a wide range of other discourses. These range from contemporary political matters, to deep-seated fears and fantasies of a sexual nature. It is significant, for instance, that the letters were written at a time of industrial unrest in the UK. This suggests that media representations cannot be changed by simply expunging overtly racist references, although that might be a start. Media representations of issues of race are a structured part of evolving, socially based epistemologies. They also relate to material relations and lived existence. Media discourses about 'race' and normality are shared and circulate amongst the media producers, public figures and members of the public constituted as audiences. It is less productive to ask where such discourses originate than it is to ask how they are sustained.

By way of conclusion

This chapter has tried to argue that there is a connection between the voiced discourses about 'race' in the media and the usually unvoiced discourses of those who write to the perceived source of their aggravation or injury rather than sending a letter to the editor of the newspaper or programme. I have argued that there is an important and complex relationship between the virulent racist denunciations found in some such correspondence and the media representations which purport to operate at the level of normality. The relationship is not necessarily manifested at the level of vocabulary, but is more likely to be at the level of discursive structures. It is these structures which need to be studied and researched if we are to identify with more clarity the operations of media racism in the context of 'normal' discourse.

In the next chapter I will look more specifically at media representations which purport to represent issues of 'race' in the material world: in news, current affairs and documentary. In doing so, I will be arguing that we should not forget the importance of those discourses of normality which are still part of the discursive reserve upon which both producers and audiences will draw to structure a meaningful response to events in the material world.

8

Television news, current affairs and documentary

I'm afraid you're going to see more on the rescue efforts accorded an injured
canine than you are on race relations.

(Campbell, 1995, p. 36)

In a book concerned with representations of issues concerning 'race', it is clearly important to give some consideration to the news, documentary and current affairs on television. There is a very large amount of writing and research in this field, though less which specifically concerns itself with issues of 'race'. An important sourcebook of examples from British television is John Twitchen's *The Black and White Media Book* (1990). On the one hand, it is possible to look for examples of positive representations which demonstrate the ways in which multicultural societies are becoming recognised and positively represented in the media. On the other hand, it is possible to spend time identifying the numerous occasions when forms of racism, whether overt or covert, find their way into the news, or current affairs broadcasting, or documentaries. Both activities are necessary, although neither by themselves are likely to render the full complexity of the contexts in which such media messages are produced and received. Nevertheless, it is always helpful to commence with a consideration of specific texts which can then be analysed and debated with specific contexts and potential readerships in mind. I will be considering each of the three generic forms, and some key questions for media researchers in relation to the genres. I will also discuss in more detail a current affairs programme which dealt with the far right in European politics. In the final section I will discuss the documentary genre and make some observations about the ways in which it represents issues of 'race' on television.

The news

The reality of news takes precedence over the news of reality.
(Nichols, 1991, p. 128)

The news is part of the daily flow of television. In some cases, such as that of CNN, it is the main reason why a television channel exists. Researchers have demonstrated how television news is carefully produced and structured according to routines, and that it is more likely to be reactive than proactive. In other words, the news teams react to the stories put out by the news agencies (Schlesinger, 1987; Elliott and Golding, 1979). This means that there is seldom any chance, even if it were felt desirable, for the news teams to offer analysis or even any detailed contextualisation of their stories. The news is about immediacy, especially in the age of satellite broadcasting. Immediacy is also linked with an almost frenetic concern with the minutiae of change. Hence the emphasis on the latest headlines, on news 'updates' and 'on the spot' reportage.

How events become part of the news depends upon news values. Once they have become news, and while they remain news, their reportage depends upon codes of representation and journalistic practice. There have been several researchers who have outlined the reasons why occurrences and events may become news. One of the most important was by Galtung and Ruge (1965). They attempted to identify categories related to newsworthiness which were generalisable, and ranged from the importance of continuity, to reference to elite nations and simple 'bad' news. Set out below is a more contemporary list from the Ron Whittaker's Television Production Course, which suggests twelve factors in newsworthiness (Whittaker, 1997, p. 449). They are significant for my purposes because they are aimed at the *practice* of the broadcast journalist, and they are described *transparently*. By this I mean that they are not problematised, but simply stated as 'what we do and why we do it'.

Twelve Factors in Newsworthiness

Timeliness: News is what's new. An afternoon raid on a rock cocaine house may warrant a live ENG report during the 6 p.m. news. However, tomorrow, unless there are major new developments, the same story will probably not be important enough to mention.
Proximity: If 15 people are killed in your hometown, your local TV station will undoubtedly consider it news. But if 15 people are killed

in Manzanillo, Montserrat, Moyobambaor, or some other distant place you've never heard of, it will probably pass unnoted. But there are exceptions.

Exceptional quality: One exception centres on how the people died. If the people in Manzanillo were killed because of a bus accident, this would not be nearly so newsworthy as if they died because of stings from 'killer bees', feared insects that have now invaded the United States. Exceptional quality refers to how uncommon an event is. A man getting a job as a music conductor is not news – unless that man is blind.

Possible future impact: The killer bee example illustrates another news element: possible future impact. The fact that the killer bees are now in the United States and may eventually be a threat to people watching the news, or to their relatives living in another state, makes the story much more newsworthy. A mundane burglary of an office in the Watergate Hotel in Washington, D.C., was hardly news until two reporters named Woodward and Bernstein saw the implications and the possible future impact. Eventually, the story behind this seemingly common burglary brought down a presidency.

Prominence: The 15 deaths in Manzanillo might also go by unnoticed by the local media unless someone prominent was on the bus – possibly a movie star or a well-known politician. If a US Supreme Court Justice or your local mayor gets married, it's news; if John Smith, your next-door neighbour, gets married, it probably isn't.

Conflict: Conflict in its many forms has long held the interest of observers. The conflict may be physical or emotional. It can be open, overt conflict, such as a civil uprising against police authority, or it may be ideological conflict between political candidates. The conflict could be as simple as a person standing on their principles and spending a year 'fighting city hall' over a parking citation. In addition to 'people against people' conflict, there can be conflict with wild animals, nature, the environment or even the frontier of space.

The number of people involved or affected: The more people involved in a news event, be it a demonstration or a tragic accident, the more newsworthy the story is. Likewise, the number of people affected by the event, whether it's a new health threat or a new ruling by the IRS, the more newsworthy the story is.

Consequence: The fact that a car hit a utility pole isn't news, unless, as a consequence, power is lost throughout a city for several hours. The fact that a computer virus found its way into a computer system may not become major news until it bankrupts a business, shuts down a telephone system, or destroys important medical data at a major hospital.

Human interest: Human interest stories are generally soft news. Examples would be a baby beauty contest, a person whose pet happens to be a nine-foot boa constrictor, or a man who makes a cart so that his two-legged dog can move around again. On a slow news day even a story of fire fighters getting a cat out of a tree might make a suitable story. Human interest angles can be found in most hard news stories. A flood in Tennessee will undoubtedly have many human interest angles: a child reunited with its parents after two days; a boy who lost his dog; or families returning to their mud-filled homes.

Pathos: The fact that people like to hear about the misfortunes of others can't be denied. Seeing or hearing about such things commonly elicits feelings of pity, sorrow, sympathy and compassion. Some would call such stories 'tear jerkers'. Examples are the child who is now all alone after his parents were killed in a fire; the elderly woman who just lost her life savings to a con artist; the blind man whose seeing-eye dog was poisoned. This category isn't just limited to people. How about the horses that were found neglected and starving, or the dog that sits at the curb expectantly waiting for its master to return from work each day even though the man was killed in an accident weeks ago.

Shock value: An explosion in a factory has less shock value if it was caused by gas leak than if it was caused by a terrorist. The story of a six-year-old boy who shot his mother with a revolver found in a bedside drawer has more shock (and therefore news) value than if same woman died in an automobile accident. Both shock value and the titillation factor are well known to the tabloid press. The lure of these two factors is also related to some stories getting inordinate attention such as the sordid details of a politician's or evangelist's affair – which brings us to the final point.

Titillation component: This factor primarily involves sex and is commonly featured – some would say exploited – during rating periods. This category includes everything from the new fashions in men and women's swim wear to an in-depth series on legal prostitution in Nevada.

(Reproduced with the author's permission)

Many questions come to mind. How do these factors impinge upon the representation of issues concerning 'race'? Are the values implicit in these factors shared internationally, or is this a national or regional code of practice? Rather than attempt to answer these questions directly, I will consider some of the points made in the twelve factors and discuss their implications for those studying the representation of 'race'. The merit of the list provided by Whittaker is that it is unapologetic. News is what is new, and that is that. An event is also likely to be given more coverage if it is local. This does not explain, however, how it is that 'local' news does not spend as much time considering social deprivation and racism in the locality as it does the threat to property, well-being and lifestyles of the better off. It is also interesting that many factors determining newsworthiness relate to the unusual, to the bizarre and to shock value. What these factors do not spell out, but is of considerable significance, is that they must all be measured against some kind of norms. It is these norms which are the key issue, and it is norms which can and do change. For the news broadcaster, for most of the time, such norms are taken for granted. Apart from anything else, television news has to keep on going and that means that it has to have an unshakeable faith in its own ability to re-present the world. Once again we are reminded of the importance of a discursive reserve. In order for the news to be structured in a specific way, the people who produce it have to have an agreed set of practices which constitute what Hall has called 'good television'. This operates at the level of signifying practice, but it is reliant upon discursive repertoires. The way in which this operates in relation to issues of 'race' has been considered in some detail by Christopher Campbell (1995).

Campbell studied the newscasts from 29 cities in North America, and noted above all how similar they were in structure. His main interest, however, was the sameness of what he calls the 'racial mythology' which is embedded in the these similarly structured programmes. There are positive stereotypes in the news which show African Americans as successful athletes or musicians, and there are negative stereotypes which portray them as criminals, mothers who leave their children home alone and in a whole range of antisocial or criminal roles. Campbell notes that this is not as damaging, however, as the way in which the positive stereotypes feed the myth that success is equally accessible to all. What this suggests, according to Campbell, is that those who are not successful have decided not to accept and embrace the American Dream, and have chosen 'a life of savagery and/or destitution instead' (Campbell, 1995, p. 133).

Regional television news presentation in the United Kingdom has many similarities in its programme structures to those found in the United States. There has, however, been a marked change in the last two decades in the specific modes of addressing issues of 'race' by many broadcasters. This does not mean that there are no longer any questionable representations, but it does mean that both broadcasters and, I hypothesise, audiences have modified their relationship to specific signifying practices. The news in the UK has become much more careful about the surface of its discourse. Whether the deeper structures of meaning have changed is still very much open to question. Social and political change in other parts of the world has undoubtedly had an impact upon the situation, particularly the coming of post-apartheid South Africa. It is most interesting to compare the vocabulary of the news reporter today with those of ten or fifteen years ago. When Independent Television News broadcast from what was then Salisbury, Rhodesia, on 4 March 1980, it adopted a very dramatic and 'race'-oriented approach. It was the day of the victory of the ZANU(PF) Party led by Robert Mugabe. The newscaster was Alastair Burnett and he spoke his opening words with authority as he declared: 'Rhodesia's Black Master is taking over. He may have a white man in his cabinet.' The obvious has now to be stated. Mugabe was elected leader with a wider franchise base than his predecessor Ian Smith. Ian Smith was never, to my knowledge, referred to as Rhodesia's White Master in television news broadcasts. It is not common practice to call any leader 'master' or indeed 'mistress' of their country. The connotations of such words would be deemed too problematic or blatantly offensive. The unusual authority which Burnett's words carried were accentuated by the fact that it was the very first item on a *News at Ten Special* and it was being broadcast live from London and Salisbury. The ideological significance of the announcement lay in the fact that it did not cause a general outrage, but was accepted virtually without notice. The addition of 'He may have a white man in his cabinet' invites the response (from white people) of 'Oh, thank God for that!' Fear for the loss of white power had dominated news and discussion programmes about what would soon be Zimbabwe. It seemed that, for the broadcasters, whiteness was a prerequisite for civilisation to exist. The scenario was to be re-enacted as the end of apartheid approached in South Africa. Whiteness, and the power that goes with it, have been represented as so utterly normal that any other possibility seems like an aberration. Dyer has astutely noted that most people do not believe in myths of 'total' whiteness, where everything that is white is automatically good and pure. Nevertheless, it is a useful myth if it can justify a slightly more soft-edged version of white 'normality':

> Most white people, and even most representations of white people, are not virginal women glowing in the light, hyper-muscular men sorting out other people's problems or privileged marginals transfixed by the dilemma of doing. ... Yet the extreme, very white white image is functional in relation to the ordinary, is even perhaps a condition of establishing whiteness as ordinary.
>
> (Dyer, 1997, p. 222)

Current affairs

> The discursive status of the television reporter as a source of truth, for instance, is authenticated by the unproblematic relation of what he or she says with the viewer's near transparent perception of its topic.
>
> (Wilson, 1993, p. 115)

> An event becomes a media event not at the whim of the media alone but also to the extent that it gives presence to abstract cultural currents that long precede it and will long outlast it.
>
> (Fiske, 1994, p. xxi)

Current affairs programming is not a flourishing genre, and it is likely to be watched by relatively small audiences. Unlike the news, it promises the possibility of a more extended engagement with its subject matter. Immediacy need not be the central goal. It is usually presented by a link-person who will offer pieces to camera and supply an amount of voice-over commentary on the more 'documentary' passages of the programme. With the help of a limited range of cutting and framing techniques, the presenter will construct a discursive framework with which the viewer is encouraged to identify. The discursive framework may address a range of views of the matter being discussed, some of which may be diametrically opposed to each other. What must retain a steady path through all this is the credibility of the presenter's own discourse. The presenter is, for most of the audience for most of the time, closer to a true knowledge of the subject than any other participant in the programme. This can have particularly powerful implications in relation to representations of 'race'. I will explore some of these questions in more detail in relation to a specific programme. It is one which directly addressed the whole issue of 'race' and engaged in some verbal interplay with prominent neo-Nazis.

On 6 November 1993, Channel 4 television in the UK broadcast a 90-minute programme with the title *Bloody Foreigners*. It was presented by Jon Snow, who is a well-known and respected Channel 4 newsreader and interviewer. It was introduced as a major debate on 'racism and the right'. Channel 4 is highly regarded for its serious documentary and current affairs programming, as well as its one-hour news broadcasts at seven every weekday evening. I have no reason to doubt the sincerity of the motives of the programme makers. They *were* trying to tackle, through a current affairs debate format, an issue which they felt demanded full attention. The programme which followed was an interesting *mélange* of very different points of view and attempts at serious investigative television reporting. It centred around discussion in the studio, interspersed with some documentary footage. The purpose of my short analysis is to highlight the premises upon which the programme seems to be based. I will argue that it presumes an inherent and shared 'goodness' in its viewers which is never clearly articulated. The reason this presumption is particularly important is because of the way in which the concept of identity is handled. I will return to this in a moment.

The title sequence is an interesting and increasingly questionable presentation, if we accept the serious intent of the programme makers. Along with the necessary written information, the main impact of the titles comes from close-up shots of a skinhead (actor) adjusting his dress and eventually standing with his feet across a map of Europe, on which his boot has left a white swastika footprint over Germany. It is not an idle comparison to recall here Lee Marvin in *Cat Ballou* (Silverstein, 1965) as he prepared himself for a gunfight. In this case it is the *Doc Martin* boots and the tattoos, the leather and the sinew, which provide much of the visual interest. While one would not want to make too much of a semiotic meal of this sequence, a plausible reading seems to be that the issue of the far right and 'foreigners' is intimately linked with young thugs and their fascination with Hitler's Nazi beliefs and practices. The programme does attempt to confirm this reading on more than one occasion. Sometimes, as we will see, this is done in flat contradiction to its own content.

Following the title sequence, there is a documentary montage of racist violence and neo-Nazi meetings. It is harrowing but not at all sensational in the manner of the title sequence. Jon Snow then opens the programme with a piece to camera. This is reproduced below with my emphasis added to highlight what I consider to be the key questions which the programme says it will address:

> Shocking symbolism and shocking reality. People killed for their race. People burned out of their homes because of their colour. Tonight we're going to explore racism and the rise of the extreme right across Europe. *Should we worry about it? How many people are involved? Who runs with race? Who votes for those who do? What fuels racism and what should we do about it?*
>
> We shall be debating with elements of Europe's extreme right, with some less far to the right and with a cross-section who are trying to combat racism. We've been to Austria, Germany, France and Romania and to London's East End to look at the reality on the ground. Some of what you will see and hear will offend you. *Our ambition tonight is to try to understand what is happening and see what can be learned from it.* First, a guide to the increase in racial violence across Europe, at a time when reported incidents in Britain reached nearly 8,000, but where the true number of racial incidents is estimated to be anything up to twice that.

I will state once more that I believe the programme was made in good faith and that it does offer some insights into the ways in which racism and racist violence can operate. Having said this, however, a reconsideration of the way in which issues are presented might lead to a certain cynicism on the part of those who are the subjects of racist violence. Who, for instance, is the 'we' being addressed by Snow when he asks: 'Should we worry about it?' Given that those who have been attacked are hardly likely to need to have this question put to them, it might be rephrased as: 'Should those of us who have not been subject to racist attack worry about such attacks?' Perhaps an even more thorough formulation would be 'Should we worry about any ethnic minorities who have been attacked?' By this time it is becoming very clear that the identity of the 'we' addressed is based on whiteness and membership of what could be called the 'ethnic majority'. It is important to note here that even whiteness is not an all-embracing term:

Whiteness can determine who is to be included and excluded from the category and also discriminate amongst those deemed to be within it. Some people – the Irish, Latins, Jews – are white sometimes, and some white people are whiter than others.

(Dyer, 1997, p. 51)

So the first problem for a current affairs programme addressing issues of 'race' is to be very careful about how it uses the term 'we'. *Bloody Foreigners* then moves on to show three short pieces of video shot in London, Germany and Austria. Two comments are made by German neo-Nazis which would have been worthy of careful analysis, mainly on the basis of weak logic, but also because of the ways in which the sentiments expressed relate to the beliefs and practices of the Nazis and the white supporters of apartheid South Africa. A male member of *Deutsche Nationalisten* who is young and polite says: 'We are white. It's got nothing to do with racism. It's just common sense.' The leader of the party, Mikhael Petri, also in his twenties adds:

What we must aim for is that this mixing of all different cultures doesn't continue any more. It's absolutely clear – you can see it in animals. It's the simplest, most natural truth. Any dog that is pure bred is valuable. You can buy it for a lot of money. [*sic*] When it's been inter-bred, you can't give it away.

Both these comments are made, we must remember, as part of the flow of video reports from different countries. They will not be returned to or commented upon. One has to presume that the programme makers expect the audience to pick up on these arguments and reject them without further comment. While I do not believe that all people can be rationally argued out of the racist views they may hold, I do believe that some are susceptible to the influence of considered argument. To abandon this small hope is to give way, at the very least, to confusion. *Bloody Foreigners* makes no comment at all. It is important, I suggest, to note that the contributions above make reference to 'common sense' and 'natural truth'. The relationship between representations of 'race' and the issue of ideology are seldom more critically relevant. With breathtaking euphemisation, Petri moves from the mixing of cultures (multiculturalism, one might presume) to miscegenation. The choice of breeding as an example is one which demonstrates a 'natural' truth which is a core racist argument, and allows the discursive reserve to keep 'the mongrelisation of the race' as another 'natural truth' to be called upon when needed.

My purpose in highlighting these factors is that they are introduced before the 'debate' in the programme commences and they move along as part of a flow which will not be halted or questioned. By this time we are almost at the end of Part One (on Channel 4 there are advertisements). Snow rounds off with another comment to camera: 'After the break we hear directly from the leaders of the right. *How do they see themselves – racists or patriots?* Join us again.' I am reminded here of the kind of questions posed by Oprah Winfrey in Chapter 5, such as 'Why are black people so angry?' Of all the questions that might be posed to the leaders of the far right, one might wish to know why this one is the one to ask. But one need not worry because it is never directly posed. It does, however, work as a useful discursive marker for the programme, placing the dubious binary of racist/patriot at the core of its thinking. Before we have chance to reflect on Snow's question and before we are shown a number of advertisements, we see a big close-up of the young thug actor who says, quietly and belligerently 'End of Part One'. By this time the genre, as happened with Winfrey, is under considerable stress for any viewer trying to hold on to the possibility of rational thought. The alternative, in the words of the Oasis song, is that 'You gotta roll with it'. The fact that the first advertisement in the commercial break is for a feature in a coming edition of the *Sun* newspaper on 'Singles Sex' only adds to the discursive miasma. The young couple seen stripping down to their underwear and attempting an erotic embrace, are very white indeed. It is, I am sure, a coincidence that the advertisement is shown twice in that one break, but it is also a fact.

Snow begins Part Two with another statement to camera, which includes the following comments:

> For this second section of the programme we are joined by some of the people on the far right of the political spectrum ... They are going to be confronted by a group of our audience who have agreed to challenge them.

The sad truth is that, during the rest of the programme, the leaders of the far right are neither confronted nor challenged in any meaningful way, although some fundamentally important points are made by some members of the audience. It is to some of these points that I will turn as they relate to my arguments elsewhere in this book. When the members of far right groups from France, Belgium, Germany, Holland and England are questioned, they put much effort into appearing to be reasonable democrats. The French National Front, represented by Captain Jacques Dore, makes the very valid point that 'the actual [French] government is doing what we have been asking since 1973 concerning immigration'.

An academic and researcher, Dr Roger Eatwell, is asked to comment on whether the French National Front can barely be distinguished from the French government. He answers as follows:

> It's certainly the case if we look across Europe that mainstream parties have tended to borrow from the programmes of these insurgent groups. One can see this in France where politicians of both the right and the left have almost fallen over themselves to talk of things like the smell of immigrants – or a socialist Prime Minister talked of the need to deport by military plane illegal immigrants. So in that sense I think it is true that the mainstream parties have picked up part of their programme.

Snow does not comment on this but moves straight on to an ex-member of the British National Party who is now a member of the British Conservative Party and who speaks with mellifluous charm about immigration control. The linear string of comments which follow turn one way and the other without any sense of debate. A German neo-Nazi points out that the young Germans who have been called 'Nazi kids' are in fact the children of democrats. He says, with a rhetorical flourish that contains no perceptible logical structure, but disturbing hints of fields for possible exploration: 'They have seen He Man and Rambo as heroes, and they are following the theories of education of today.'

The first person invited to speak from the audience is the writer Dilip Hiro, with Snow trying to find a way to bring him in following on from the German neo-Nazi's comments. Hiro tries to make a complex point by showing an image of a bronze standard from the Turkey in the third millennium BC. It is covered in swastikas and Hiro argues that the swastika is a Turkish symbol which is now being used against the Turks. It is certainly possible that an interesting and potentially profound argument might have been developed from Hiro's introduction, but this is current affairs television. The neo-Nazi from the Netherlands makes another plea for the moderation of his party by taking a lead from Hiro, and pointing out that they do not tolerate swastikas at their rallies. The person from the BNP then adds that swastikas are 'not worn with our approval'. He comments with some strategic sophistication that the question we should be asking is 'what it is that has driven these youngsters to adopt this kind of symbol which we do not favour'.

For the opposition, the journalist and writer Kenan Malik then speaks and makes several points which deserve careful consideration and debate. They echo the points made by Dr Eatwell and take them a little further. Kenan comments as follows:

> I don't think it's very helpful to constantly associate the problems of the far right with those of Hitler or the swastika because it misses the real dangers that we face. There are two reasons for the rise of the far right in recent years. The first is people's general disenchantment with mainstream political organisations, policies, parties, and so on. There is what you might call a crisis of political legitimacy throughout the Western world, where governments don't have any answers to the problems we face and people have lost faith in the ability of government to carry out – to find solutions to our problems. This has often taken a racist form, this disenchantment, because mainstream politicians have used race as a political weapon. They have constantly blamed problems within our society on outsiders, they've blamed it on immigrants, on refugees, and so on. And when you have a former French Prime Minister talking about immigrants as smelly, when you have German Chancellor saying the boat is full in Germany, when you have a Tory Cabinet Minister making a speech at Tory Party conference who blames foreigners as scroungers, it's inevitable, is it not, that the kind of ideas that the far right promote become acceptable.

This is the second major effort by an audience member to place on the agenda the fact that racism is founded in one or another kind of 'normality'. There will be a third occasion which I will discuss in a moment. For now, it should be noted that this appeal to consider the assimilation of racist ideas by mainstream politics goes by unnoticed, though I cannot help feeling that it is the members of the far right groups who would be encouraged by the suggestion. The liberal discursive framework of the programme, however, remains with swastikas and violent attacks. It would be insane and inhuman to deny the importance of racist violence, but it is naïvety or wilful neglect to turn one's back on the political implications of racist beliefs and practices becoming part of mainstream politics.

In this second part of the programme the far right representatives are allowed to develop their racist arguments. The BNP representative manages to make several doctrinal points whilst Jon Snow is stressing the fact that 'the violence suits you, though, doesn't it?' The German neo-Nazi makes a plea to be understood. He has suffered a great deal, he says, from years of attacks by communists and anarchists, and suggests that it is the anti-Nazis who have kept the name of Hitler alive. We are shown another montage of events from Romania, France and England. We see victims of racist attacks in England. We see an Asian woman, Sajida Malik, who has suffered racial abuse and attacks in her home, insisting that she is British. We see a Syrian woman, Sala Kodman, in Paris. She speaks of how times have changed, and how France is no longer a welcoming country. In Romania we see a small village where three gypsies were killed and their homes burned to the ground.

When we return to the studio the BNP representative insists that all his party wants is the 'long-term policy of phased, orderly, humane repatriation'. Gerald Hartup of the Freedom Association asks if there is a future 'for black and brown people within your political movements'. The BNP representative and the Revolutionary Conservative answer at the same time. The BNP answer is chillingly short: 'We do not believe so.'

The Conservative gives a longer and more sophisticatedly racist response:

> I would say very clearly to you Mr Hartup that there is a case for immigrant people from Afro-Caribbean and Indian backgrounds participating in British life. The problem of colour and race would not have arisen in this country if immigration had been at a lower level. What we've seen is an overwhelming, intrusive immigration that has alienated the indigenous people of this country.

Another BNP representative points out that:

> the fact of the matter is [a favourite phrase of the BNP it would seem] that our cause is an emotional one. There's a great deal at stake, which is the future of this nation and the future of European nations and indeed world-wide to protect, if you like, their heritage, their racial and genetic identity, and to protect the traditions of countries which have made them what they are.

The attempt to soften vicious racist propaganda by utilising the terms associated with soft and heart-warming patriotism, and the qualifier 'if you like', is another example of the euphemisation through which a great deal of racist propaganda works when politeness is unavoidable. And so the programme grinds along to the next commercial break. Jon Snow cuts in on the BNP representative at one point with the comment that there are people who fought and died for this country 'and you want to deport their children'. The emotional thrust of the question does not deter the BNP person, who says 'Well, the fact of the matter is we believe that multiculturalism is a non-viable ordering of society which must be brought to an end.' Snow, as I said, cuts in on him, but only to say, 'We should come back to many of the points here.' It is time for another commercial break. After the break the far right representatives are no longer there, so the points they make are never challenged in their presence.

The third part of the programme is full of interesting comments from a range of participants. They include a telling point by the MEP Glyn Ford, who points out that J. M. Le Pen, leader of the French National Front has suggested that it was the Americans who built the gas chambers at Dachau after the Second World War. Kenan Malik speaks once more about the ways in which racism is becoming respectable. It is noted that the law in Europe generally is ineffective in combating racism. (I am conscious as I write this that in 1997 we have in the UK a New Labour Government with a massive majority which is at pains to assure the people that it will be fair but very firm with immigrants.) The third part of the programme concludes with a mention of the potential significance of education as a means of opposing racism.

In the final part or act of this longish and well-intentioned drama, entitled 'Possible Solutions', we hear on more than one occasion from the audience the oft-repeated suggestion that the problem is related to everyday life and to economics. Tete Kofi from the *Weekly Journal* comments as follows:

> There are three issues here which are very important. One is denial, the other is human values and thirdly is the function of the media in relation to the situation. As to denial, people tend to deny their basic attitudes, inherent within themselves, and are always happy to point at the far right, certain politicians, as people who are the bad guys of the piece. But in actual fact, the far right movements and the

politicians can only possibly exploit attitudes which are held very very deeply by perfectly ordinary members of society.

An unnamed black man then eloquently points out that the resources of the world have been disproportionately distributed to the white minority nations of the world and that the IMF and the World Bank and others need to be involved in a necessary redistribution process. This point is taken up by Steve Burman from the University of Sussex, who points out that black citizens are becoming worse off in the USA as capital is relocated. Many other points are made, but the pace is unremitting and the chance for reflection or the development of understanding is relatively small. There is simply no time. The poet Benjamin Zephania is asked to finish the programme with a recitation, which does with a gentle but nevertheless telling irony which shines out above the stream of unfocused debate which has preceded him. The poem includes the following memorable lines:

I am not the problem, but I bear the brunt
Of silly playground taunts and racist stunts.
I am not the problem, I am a born academic
But they got me on the run – now I'm branded athletic.

Finally, Jon Snow stands, literally wringing his hands, and says, 'I hope we learned a lot together.' The end titles come up on the screen. They scroll past the same skinhead/actor we have seen at every break as he scornfully watches them. He finally takes a flying kick at the title bearing the name of the editor and turns and strolls away. What did we learn?

The programme came with its own agenda. It was an agenda based on racist violence and the possible threat which far right parties might pose beyond the immediate one to their chosen subjects of repression and violence. Many of the most articulate and qualified members of the audience made points which went far beyond those which were on the agenda for the programme makers. Channel 4 had, however, already made their documentary footage, and it is significant that in none of that footage from any of the countries represented was there any mention of economic issues. Nor did the programme raise the question of the unjust distribution of the world's resources. There are several possible reasons for this. One is that it was not thought to be important. Another is that it was thought that the questions of economics and social development are not related to racism. Yet another matter avoided by the programme producers is the question of everyday racism and the assimilation or appropriation of racist policies by mainstream politicians and their parties. All of this passed by them as they prepared for what was a major time slot for such a discussion. The programme could have been other than it was. It would have required, however, a challenging of the established universe of discourse and action. Such a challenge could still be made, although the media studies researcher may note the depressing regularity with which programmes skirt major issues and operate to a pre-set agenda of a drama of phenomenal forms.

Documentary

Every spectator is a coward or a traitor.

(Franz Fanon)

The television documentary is a form based on questions of identity. Whether the film is about a local or global topic, about a person or a process, it involves an engagement with other people and the construction of a relationship between those others and the audience. The same might be said for many genres, but it is in the documentary that the issue of identity is most significant. Bill Nichols identifies four specific modes of representation in the documentary form. These are: expository, observational, interactive, and reflexive (Nichols, 1991). The expository documentary usually incorporates a commentary, often known as the Voice of God commentary because of the (unseen) authority it carries. It is based upon a belief that it is important to offer information about the world and to see the world afresh. Sometimes such a form can become romantic or over-didactic. Observational documentary is associated with the coming of lighter-weight and portable film and sound-recording equipment. This made it possible for the film maker to 'be around' the action and to let it somehow speak for itself, rather than offering moralising or other judgements through the use of commentary. This mode raised important questions about whether and how a documentary film maker could be inconspicuous to the point of invisibility. There was also the question of whether or not the presence of the film maker altered the nature of the 'reality' being represented, or possibly influenced and structured that reality. The interactive mode was one where the film makers wanted to become more involved with what was happening. It led to the development of interventionist interviewing styles and sometimes the intervention of the camera into a happening. The fourth mode, the reflexive, was willing to incorporate features of the other three modes, but always attempted to highlight its own techniques and mode of production as much as the topic of the film.

It is seldom that we find a pure documentary mode of representation. In recent years the television documentary has often combined the observational mode with the Voice of God commentary. This has become very apparent in those documentaries which follow the police around the city at night as they go about their duties. The 'reality' of the documentary which is shot to portray immediacy, is given added credibility by a voice-over commentary. We may also add to the modes of representation a more recent one which has been made possible by the development of light and cheap video recording equipment. This is the 'video diary', where any person may combine footage which they shoot on location with their own to-camera comments, or where the video camera becomes a confidant to which the video maker speaks 'in confidence'. Contemporary documentary practice is often a mixture of all these modes, though what all documentaries share in common is a concern with and perception of the world 'out there' and with a few exceptions, with the people who inhabit it. The documentary form thus becomes the measure of the relationship to reality for the vast majority of its audience. How does this relate to representations of 'race'?

I will consider two examples with over 30 years separating them in order to comment on some of the disturbing potential of some representations of 'race'. The two examples I have chosen demonstrate the strengths of television as a medium which can implicate its audience in the events of which it speaks. There is one reading of television which interprets it as a medium of endless superficiality with an inability to deal with serious or demanding matters (Postman, 1986). It is, of course a correct reading, but a partial one. For television *can* sometimes be read as a medium which questions our status as viewers or 'spectators'.

The first example I will cite comes from a documentary series entitled *Eyes on the Prize*, which was produced by Blackside Production in 1987. The series covers the period of the major civil rights struggles in the United States in the 1950s and 1960s. It is comprised of six programmes, and the one to which I will refer is programme five, entitled *Mississippi: Is This America? 1963–1964*. The mode of representation adopted by the documentary is that of exposition with some footage which is observational. The documentary was first released in 1987, although some of the footage, mainly in black and white, was shot in the 1950s and 1960s. The period with which the documentary deals is the one which was so brilliantly shot and acted and so professionally and competently distorted in the film *Mississippi Burning* (Parker, 1988). *Mississippi: Is This America?* begins with Unita Blackwell, shot in colour, speaking quietly about her love for the Mississippi Delta as a place for which she and other African Americans had given blood, sweat and tears. It is their home. The single shot is relaxed and restrained. The second sequence is in black and white and shows two white men sitting on a river bank. It was clearly shot in the 1950s or 1960s. One of them speaks and describes his links with the land and his perception that there are two cultures in Mississippi which exist side by side – the white and the 'coloured'. He realises that change is coming, and faster than he would like. His suggestion that change is occurring because of allegations that they (the whites) had not treated black citizens fairly, is delivered in a southern, disbelieving drawl. The third person we see in the film is William Simmons and he is a member of a Citizen's Council. These councils were set up as an unashamed attempt to ensure that the white population of Mississippi retained control of the state in the face of democratic change. He speaks to the interviewer who is off camera and he speaks slowly and quietly:

> I was born in Mississippi in the United States and I am a product of my heredity and education and the society in which I was raised. And I, along with a million other white Mississippians will do everything in our power to protect that vested interest. It's just as simple as that.

A few scenes later, Simmons is cut in once more and this time he adds: 'It's primarily a struggle for power and I think we would be stupid indeed if we failed to see where the consequences of a supine surrender on our part would lead.' This identification of a power struggle, by both film maker and the subject, offers a textbook example of hegemony in crisis. There is a chilling, matter-of-fact politeness in the way in which Simmons speaks. It demonstrates the power of the simple interview to represent the threat of deeply held racist views through the etiquette of interviewing style. On several occasions the veiled hatred of white racists tells the viewer more than the demoralising news footage of locations where racist attacks had taken place. It demonstrates, in fact, that the speaking human face is still the source of multiple and subtle modes of signification which are often overlooked in the making of 'good television'. One is reminded here of the comment of the documentarist Richard Leacock that his camera could often observe more about human interaction than he himself had spotted. *Eyes on the Prize* is a remarkable documentary, which allows us to look in on or observe the coldness of racism and the dignity and courage of the oppressed. It is, however, primarily an experience of looking in.

The second example I wish to discuss is more concerned with its main protagonists *looking out* at us, the viewers. This change in the mode of representation is brought about by the video diary technique previously mentioned. The programme was broadcast by BBC2 on 24 April 1993 and is entitled *LA Stories: From the Eye of the Storm*. Ten inhabitants of Los Angeles were given video cameras for the year following the social unrest. They included a South Central school teacher, two police officers and a journalist among their number. I will concentrate on the recordings produced by a 12-year-old African-American boy named Ennis Beley. He lives in South Central Los Angeles and his recordings tell the viewer something of his main concerns in life. He tends to hold the small external microphone in his cupped hand as he speaks to the camera, leaving his left hand free to express non-verbally what his voice does not say. The first time we see him he introduces himself with a few short statements which are devastating in their directness and unpretentiousness:

> My name is Ennis and I hope to live to the end of 92 and 93. And I hope to make it through these years cuz, you know, niggers killin' little people cuz they didn't do nothin', and I hope I live to 25 years or more. I hope I live 'til God says I gotta go right then.

Beley's speech is not 'good television'. The shot is composed more by chance than plan and he speaks with his hands up to his mouth holding the microphone. In the second shot he is in close up, but still holding the microphone with one hand. The quality of the communication is, of course, influenced by the recording technique. This does not amount to much more than a recognition, however, that one is watching a piece of a video diary. The power of the communication comes through because of the intensity of the delivery, and the resulting signification of a young person with more feelings than the single shots can contain. This is not easily susceptible to textual analysis. In a later statement to camera, made in the evening while he is reclining on his bed, we feel even more powerfully the depth of Beley's feelings:

> I don't like to go to school cuz I don't know how to read. I don't know how to do language and I don't know how to spell too good. They say they gonna tutor me. But they don't ... I have my problems with school and at home and – see you later.

At this point he turns off the camera and he seems near to tears. The main strength of documentary is that it can lead the viewer to contemplate a reality beyond the representation. There is a world of difference between the testimony of Ennis Beley and the footage of the violence in Los Angeles which was discussed in Chapter 5. This may be because there is humanity in Beley's statements to camera, and it may be that showing violence seldom offers any insight or understanding into its causes or consequences. Of course we can observe if someone is shown to be wounded or mutilated, but this is not the same modality as Ennis Beley saying 'see you later'. Both are, of course, representations, but the former comes from a stockpile of violent images which are neither truth nor fiction. They operate from within what I have called a semiotics of horror, and leave us in a state of voyeuristic, suspended animation. The statements of Beley are in another semiotic sphere. They tell of experience deeply felt and speak with a humanity which is always absent from images of violence. He speaks of a friend of his called Goofy who was shot dead in front of him. His description, the evocative movement of his left hand, and his facial expression offer the viewer more insights about questions of identity than many programmes devoted entirely to the subject:

> And I was like – fuck – what to do – I was like – ... This never happened to me before. I'm shocked. Somebody just got shot in my face. I don't know what the fuck is going on. Goofy tellin' me to help him. An' I'm like – damn, I don't know what to do, man. Wow. What do you want me to do? Fuck that. Call the paramedics man. I ain't touchin' him, you know. I ain't touchin' no dead body. And then I fainted when we went to see him.

This is a statement made, one assumes, with no-one else present. It is tempting to pursue a lengthy socio-political analysis of the reasons why a 12-year-old boy is in the position of recounting such events in a country not supposed to be at war. Much more could and should be said. The key point for now, however, is that this representation of an issue relating to 'race' has a power which transcends the specificity of the mode of representation. It does not depend upon the signifying practices associated with news and current affairs. Its force lies in the fact that it does not evade any issues but states them forthrightly. It is, also, a very rare and untypical piece of television.

I have tried, in this chapter, to consider just a few of the important ways in which television news, current affairs and documentary may represent issues of 'race'. I have not been concerned to impugn the sincerity or professionalism of the media producers. It is their discursive foundations I hope to rock a little. It is clear that there is a wide range of signifying practice used in their business. These include the general codes of professional practice which dictate what is newsworthy, the authoritative newsreader, the heated studio debate, the various documentary modes. It would seem that only the video diarist can speak clearly, although many of the others speak grammatically. It would also seem that the discourses which inform news and current affairs programmes are usually pre-set and never radical in their thinking. Their investigations are more likely to work to an agenda which is liberally tormented but shy of overt anti-racist positioning. The media, it seems, measure the real world using a scale of values based upon hue, with the norm firmly fixed around the lighter varieties. The only way this can be tested is by tireless empirical investigation, though there is sufficient data already in existence to substantiate the above conjecture – until a powerful enough refutation comes along.

9

Representations of history:
case studies in children's television

A great deal of time, energy and argument has been devoted to analysing the relationship between children and the media. It usually involves debate founded upon fears about the effects which television, and occasionally other media, are having upon young people. The focal point for this worry is usually violence. This usually means the re-presentation of violence which has been staged specifically for the cameras, though it is often conflated or confused with violence in the material world. There is seldom any indignation in this literature when the violence is a media representation of 'our' troops doing what has to be done, or when the violence shown is of the kind which bolsters chauvinistic pride. The literature in this field is primarily aimed at Hollywood movies, and constantly bemoans the kind of violence to be found in the films of Tarantino, Stone and others. The reason I begin this chapter with reference to such debates is that they are often very close to debates about history and representations of 'race'. I can best illustrate this by quoting from Michael Medved in his blistering and seriously flawed attack on Hollywood, which he sees as pitched in battle with 'America'. I am not concerned here with the merits or otherwise of Medved's arguments about violence and obscenity in the media and popular culture. I do wish to comment on his approach to aspects of history as they are represented in Hollywood films. His comments are indicative of the way in which so much history has been taught, directly or indirectly, by those formal or informal educators who do not see their own historiography as in need of critical attention. Historical re-presentation in film and television, especially when it involves the dramatisation of its subject matter, is seldom over-concerned about empirical back-up for its narrative and discursive structure. The ideological import of this is highlighted by the tolerance for distortion shown by those who write histories which, unsurprisingly, do not weaken or challenge their own world-view. Hence, Medved adopts a mode of writing when discussing his kind of historical movie which is chatty and full of old-world charm. Medved knows, as do so many who represent history in the media, that they are permitted there much artistic licence. He justifies such films, where he admires them, on the basis that they were fun to watch as a child, missing the point that most of the films of which he speaks were in fact aimed at an adult audience.

It is relevant to quote his argument in full as a preface to the consideration of specific representations of history made for children's television in the UK. Medved's conceptualisation of history is very similar to that of many educators, particularly those concerned with the education of younger children. Medved insists that he was not taken in by any of the films he saw as a child, and then proceeds to undermine his argument by demonstrating his ideologically reactionary position. First, he scoffs at those who wish to identify the questionable or reactionary character of so many historical representations:

> I still recall every one of these long-ago entertainments with enormous affection, though I would never go so far as to offer them my blanket critical endorsement. It's easy to spot the artistic and historical shortcomings in such projects, to decry their jingoistic simplicity and to lament the way that America's enemies are callously reduced to two-dimensional bad guys.
>
> (Medved, 1992, p. 232)

There is little public evidence that what Medved finds 'easy' has been the general educational experience of citizens of the United States. Medved's approach to history is certainly not an unusual one. It has been shared by many of those who have been responsible for establishing curricula over generations and for different nations. It is based on the development of pride in one's national identity and celebration of one's national prowess, whether in war or sport or science or literature. There is little recognition by Medved that his approach to history might not carry the same message of hope and pride for those about whom he speaks little – the African-American population of the United States:

> Nevertheless, I miss the energetic, flag-waving films of my boyhood and regret that comparable projects have found no place in today's movie mix. Whatever their flaws, such stories served to fire my

imagination with visions of a glorious past that I somehow shared with my classmates and neighbours. It didn't matter that my mother had immigrated from Germany in 1934, or that my father's family arrived here from Russia after World War I; Hollywood's historical spectaculars helped me to identify with Andy Jackson and Abe Lincoln and encouraged the idea that I had every right to claim their legacy as my own. By emphasising the selflessness of previous generations in the cause of liberty, these stirring sagas fostered both a feeling of pride and a sense of obligation. They also spurred an interest in the more serious study of history that gloomy guilt-inducers like *Dances with Wolves* or *Come See the Paradise* never could. Even the violent scenes in the old patriotic pictures, with their emphasis on the discipline and sacrifice of the battlefield, conveyed a far less damaging message than the random urban brutality and individualised killing of contemporary kiddie fare.

(Medved, 1992, pp. 232–3)

There are many important points to note here:

1. Medved's pleasure in *belonging*, and the unstated but ever-present fear of rejection. Hence his reference to the fact that 'it didn't matter' where his parents came from. He is a generous interpreter of the rights of white Americans.
2. The false chumminess of associating oneself with 'Andy' and 'Abe'. ('Andy' was a slave owner and the 7th President of the United States and virtually destroyed the Creek people, confiscating 8 million hectares of their land as part of what Medved could claim as his heritage.)
3. The emphasis on the alleged selflessness of 'previous generations', a category with as heavy an ideological import as the 'national interest', or 'family values'.
4. The emphasis on pride and obligation.
5. The suggestion that critical thinking, rethinking, or possibly any thinking about history might induce guilt.
6. The suggestion that the way to a 'serious' study of history may be opened up by 'stirring sagas'.
7. The admiration for the discipline of the battlefield.
8. The justification of brutality and violence which is 'disciplined' in opposition to that which is urban and random. It seems that it better to kill people you do not know when following orders than it is to kill those from your own community for other reasons.

Medved does not pretend to be an historian and he is not known as a teacher. Nevertheless, his views articulate in concentrated form, some of the most questionable characteristics of educators who attempt to put into practice what Medved admires. These educators, it must be stressed, are not confined to any one nation. The examples I will be discussing do not come from the United States but from the United Kingdom. There are, however, numerous examples of histories from around the world which have been built upon virtually the same set of assertions and justifications, almost always at the expense of some or all of the indigenous peoples of specific nations or regions, and almost always resulting in one or another form of racism. With regard to the cinema and television, the fact that the original, very material events happened centuries ago is not as significant ideologically as the impor-tance of the ways in which such histories are reconstructed today, whether as narrative dramatisation or documentary. These histories often accomplish important ideological work in representing issues of 'race'. Marc Ferro (1984) has provided numerous examples of such histories constructed, published and circulated in a wide range of countries and contexts. Textbooks for children are of particular sig-nificance. Rob Gilbert (1984) has analysed in detail a wide range of history textbooks for children. Among other things, he notes how the 'historian' feels at liberty to construct quite fantastic images of people. He gives as an example a character sketch of William Pitt:

> His tall figure, his great hooked nose and his eye that, as it was said, 'could cut a diamond': his withering sarcasm and superb gift of phrase: his power of tearing an opponent's argument to shreds, and his sustained eloquence – all combined to overwhelm the Commons ... In some way that is hard to explain ... he managed to commu-nicate to the country a sense of his greatness, winning popularity and confidence among every class in the community.
>
> (Stuart, 1996, cited in Gilbert, 1984)

Such gross characterisation is not uncommon and one more example will illustrate how it is sometimes taken to excess. This comes from a small school book on the Peasants' Revolt of 1381 which took place in England (Price, 1980). It is significant because of its ideological pos-itioning. Mary Price begins with a frank admission that not much is known about Wat Tyler, one of the leaders of the revolt: 'The strange thing is that, though his name is famous, we really know very little about Wat Tyler and he remains a mystery to this day' (Price, 1980, pp.

32–3). This does not stop Price from immediately making the most extraordinary claims about Tyler: 'He was cunning, bold, insolent and merciless . . . He had such power over his followers that he could stop them from stealing from each other' (1980, p. 33). This is a superb example of damning both a leader and his followers with faint praise.

We can see from the above how the historiography of Price is both basic and ideologically imaginative. The question I now wish to ask is whether or not this same approach is taken when the medium of communication is television and when issues of 'race' are directly at stake. Once again, I am arguing that there is a strong ideological dimension to media messages which focuses on issues of 'race', and that this is very much the case in the way in which educational materials for young children are structured. As with concepts of normality, the understanding of issues of 'race' is intertwined with general understandings about the world. They are represented as a cluster and 'race' is seldom separated out for special consideration. What happens is that the educator, whether as teacher or as television producer, offers the young child a socially structured repertoire of meanings and discourses. These discourses are not taught as individual or discrete lessons, but are part of the warp and weft of discursive formations.

Educational television and 'race'

I will illustrate how this happens by reference to three examples. The first is from a popular educational television series produced in the UK by Yorkshire Television, first broadcast in 1992 and entitled *How We Used to Live*. The series is still very popular in primary schools. There have been several series of *How We Used to Live*, each of which concentrated on a specific period and each of which combined some form of dramatisation with reference to actual events, documentation, objects, or in more recent times, archive footage. The programmes are made with a professionalism not always found in educational television in the UK. The sets are better built, the research more thorough, the acting often better rehearsed, the pedagogy progressive in intent. It is for these reasons that they are highly regarded. They also carry with them their own historiography, which is seldom if ever acknowledged. The particular set of programmes from which my chosen example comes is entitled *Expansion, Trade and Industry*, and the specific programme is *Trading Places*. It deals with the period around the abolition of the slave trade. The ideological significance of the programme relates to issues of power and economics as well as historiography. The way in which black people are described or observed is, supposedly, sympathetic. I say 'described' because no black person appears in the programme, except as an illustration, a painting or a three-dimensional model.

The programme is presented by a sympathetic teenage girl called Gemma. She speaks directly to the camera in the opening minutes of the programme and discusses the awful working conditions facing working people in England at the beginning of the Industrial Revolution. Working people, in this context, means white people. She then tells us that, if the conditions of working people were bad, there were 'others whose lives were unthinkable today – the slaves'. It is, of course, of considerable ideological significance that the word 'others' is used in this context. Gemma speaks conversationally, but her words are scripted. The script from which she speaks relates to a larger script in which Otherness is a measure of one's normality and the characteristics of the stranger. In order to find out more about these 'others', Gemma decides (or rather the scriptwriter decides) that she will visit Wilberforce House in Hull to see a man called Peter Adamson. He shows Gemma around the museum and together they have a scripted discussion of some of the details of the slave trade and the conditions under which slaves had to exist. The programme seeks to be informative. It is clearly intended to encourage the pupils aged about 11 to 13 to reflect on the awfulness of slavery.

The re-presentation of history is, as we shall see, sometimes unclear in the way in which it addresses major issues. Above all, it is presented by two people who happen to be white. The programmes would be shown in large urban areas where the children come from a wide variety of ethnic and cultural backgrounds. Many of those children would be black. In the rural areas where the class might be all white, the whiteness of the presenters merely serves to emphasise the Otherness of its subject matter. Slaves, it seems, are to be pitied. Gemma's meeting with Peter is unsuccessfully scripted to look as though it has not been scripted. She has gone to the museum because she has seen a picture of a small tobacco box on the cover of which is a relief of a kneeling slave. Peter says he will be able to explain the origin of such boxes to Gemma. They begin, however, with an examination of some of the accoutrements associated with slaves. Peter shows Gemma some manacles designed to restrain large numbers of slaves at the same time by making them place their feet through metal hoops which are all held in place by a single straight metal rod. He tells her that they were designed to stop the slaves from 'running away'. It is likely that Peter thought the choice of phrase was more appealing for the younger audience. The connotation of 'running away', however, is that it is something which is associated with misbehaviour. Words like freedom, liberty, escape and injustice do not figure prominently in their conversation. Peter moves on to show Gemma a punishment collar with its four horizontal prongs to ensure that its wearer can neither relax nor recline. Such collars are illustrated in most of the educational or other books concerned with slavery. Peter suggests that perhaps Gemma would like to try the collar on. This she does, though she is clearly a little embarrassed by the way the collar ruffles her hair. Both she and Peter agree that the collar must have been dreadful to wear – being so heavy and almost certain to chafe the skin. White children and teachers watch this sequence with a sense of – of what? – perhaps of embarrassment such as that felt by the actor called Gemma; perhaps with a sense of unease about the whiteness of all this discussion of 'other' people, especially if they are seated in an inner city classroom with pupils from a variety of cultures and ethnic groups. And what about those pupils who are not white and who are, in a very real sense, being discussed as though they were absent? What does this form of representation accomplish ideologically in terms of understandings of issues of 'race'?

The programme does not allow for much reflection on this matter, because Gemma is scripted to ask an interesting and rather central question: 'So why did people have slaves?' This crucial question is answered by Peter as he engages in a complex series of manoeuvres. He has to help Gemma remove the collar which both have agreed is heavy and horrible. He lifts it over her head and, with his back to the camera, places it down on the floor. In consequence, Peter's answer to the question is delivered with his backside towards the camera for part of the time. He tells Gemma that people 'made an awful lot of money out of them. They came from Africa. They took them to the West Indian plantations to grow sugar cane, and then they brought the sugar back to England.'

This brief explanation is, it must be noted, inadequate. Bearing in mind that virtually everything said in the programme has been discussed carefully beforehand or formally scripted, some questions arise. Peter does not tell Gemma that not every (white) person had slaves, though this is something she might have intuited. Nor does he point out that those who made the money initially were called slave traders. He does point out that it involved 'the biggest movement of humanity in the history of the world', and there is more than one reference to a 'they' who did these things. More precise information about agency is, however, not on offer. Gemma is not scripted to ask with the same open manner which she has so far demonstrated: 'So, are you saying, Peter, that slavery and the racism that went with it were all about some white people getting rich? Are you telling me that at least some of the racism in the world today is the result of gross economic exploitation and the barbaric treatment of fellow human beings? Isn't that awful, Peter?' Instead, Peter simply tells Gemma that some people 'made an awful lot of money'. This choice of phrase is important ideologically. When someone makes an 'awful lot' of money, it suggests that one might be impressed with their luck or persistence, even if the means by which they did it are questionable. You do not say that someone murdered an awful lot of people. You do not say that Stalin and Hitler caused an awful lot of suffering. You do say 'you have eaten an awful lot of chocolate, Tommy'. The status and modality of such a phrase are important. It is, with one exception, the closest the programme will come to acknowledging the possibility of economic exploitation. The discourse thus established is one which is without anger at injustice. It is designed to elicit an 'ooh' or an 'ah' from white viewers. What are 'others' to make of it? There will be no cross-comparison with exploitation in the contemporary world, such as the use of child labour or the way in which miners in Colombia are treated. Instead, the young audience is encouraged, implicitly, to feel some gratitude that civilisation has moved forward since those awful days.

The next sequence in the programme is deeply disturbing, as much for the way it is handled as for the matters with which it deals. Peter and Gemma go together to a life-size model of the appalling conditions under which the African people were transported from their homes, with life-size replicas of African people stacked in the boats to save space. These two concerned white people stand and look at dark brown models of human suffering. Peter's reference to the 'biggest movement of humanity in the history of the world' becomes now somewhat euphemistic. They continue with their discussion of the terrifying conditions which the African people had to endure and Peter informs Gemma that 'The one bit of this display that you will have to imagine is the smell', to which she answers sympathetically 'Yeh'.

Peter goes on: 'They could smell these slave ships miles downwind of them.' There is a pause while this information sinks in and we are shown the three-dimensional life-size models of the ghosts at the feast. If you are a black child sitting in the classroom I wonder whether you would be reassured by the concern of Peter and Gemma.

The camera cuts to a shot of various rather quaint old posters advertising a slave auction and Peter walks into the frame with Gemma. 'And so to market', he says. We can see that one of the posters advertises the sale of a horse for more than the cost of a human.

The sequence in Wilberforce House finishes when Peter and Gemma go into another room where they look at a small tobacco box on which the word 'Humanity' is modelled in low relief under a crouching figure. They discuss the efforts of William Wilberforce to end the slave trade. Peter points out that Wilberforce did not actually succeed in his mission, that slavery was ended in 1806, that British slaves were freed in 1833, but that it did not really mean the end of exploitation. Peter did not actually use the word exploitation. It is for the viewer to discover that concept, another time perhaps. Instead, Peter says, 'but if you free somebody on a plantation and they've nowhere to go, they tend to stay there – so – slavery didn't finish then'. Here we are getting to some important issues. Peter has made a statement which could rock Gemma and the children viewing the programme. He seems to be saying something about unemployment and about wage-slavery. But no matter. Gemma has found out about the tobacco box, which showed there were some nice (white) people who wanted to remember that slavery was inhuman as they had a smoke. This version of history can be productively juxtaposed with the comments of Pieterse on abolitionism and emancipation:

> Abolitionism itself, no matter how well intended, was not the same as victory over racism. The abolition of slavery was not the same as black emancipation. Abolitionism produced new stereotypes of blacks – the movement humanised the image of blacks but also popularised the image of blacks as victims. The Christian tenor of abolitionist imagery underlined this. The central icon of abolitionism, the figure of a black kneeling, hands folded and eyes cast upward, clearly carried a message. It made emancipation conditional – on condition of conversion, on condition of docility and meekness, on condition of being on one's knees.
>
> (Pieterse, 1992, p. 60)

As a representation of the conditions, implications and consequences of slavery the programme is seriously deficient, possibly harmful and certainly hurtful. It contains just a sample of inhumanity but pulls back from analysis or comment beyond wonder at someone making an awful lot of money. Clare Pajakowska and Lola Young have noted that this strategy of constructing a discourse around filtered information is not new:

> Some of the unimaginably terrible conditions during the 'middle passage' of the triangular slave trade are illustrated in various school texts and isolated vicious incidents are described. However, this does not invalidate my main contention. The semiotician Roland Barthes describes a process of 'inoculation' whereby a limited number of inhumane actions are admitted by the perpetrators: this 'immunises' the contents of the collective imagination by means of a small inoculation of acknowledged evil: one thus protects its against the risk of a generalised subversion.
>
> (Pajakowska and Young, 1992, p. 217)

Exploring explorers

The second example I wish to discuss is from a programme for young children produced for the BBC and called *Watch*. It was made in 1988. The fact that it is now more than a decade old means that those children who watched it are now young adults. The justification for considering such programmes rests on the belief that they contribute to a discursive reserve upon which these young adults may draw. The mode of address of the programme would be less acceptable today, because it is so very middle class. The question of whether the historiography upon which it is based has fundamentally changed is a matter for debate. Once again it is part of a series of programmes whose central concern is not with issues of 'race.' They are designed to broaden the vistas of young children by showing them different and often distant features of the world in which we live. The choice of Captain Cook as an explorer who 'sailed the seven seas' thus seems, in a nationalistic sense, plausible. The programme is the last in a series on the voyages of Cook. It is presented in the studio from a simple set, designed to look like a sailing ship with poop deck and imitation cannon, by Louise Hall-Taylor and James Earl Adair. The director, Helen Murry, has obviously attempted to make the best use of archive footage of marine life and combine it with short studio sequences.

The programme traces Cook's last voyage with the help of a simple globe on the studio 'deck' and short clips of film of a sailing ship. Reference is made, at the beginning of the programme, to the fact that Cook took artists along with him who provided visual information about what the places and people seen actually looked like. While there is little doubt that much of the illustrative material they produced has been useful to those studying the period, their portrayal of the 'natives' at the end of the programme is less trustworthy. We learn that Cook pulled in to the North West coast of America in order to trade with the Indians who 'came paddling out to meet him'. Cook, it seems, spent more than a month 'with the Indians', learning about their lifestyle and culture. The programme then shows clips of archive footage of unidentified Indian families at home and involved in various ritual dancing, none of which is identified except by reference to the 'snapping birds' which they used in some of their dances.

Cook then sailed further north and this provides the opportunity for the programme to use archive footage of polar bears, seals and walruses. We are also shown groups of young (white) children working on murals which incorporate paintings of the various animals and marine life shown in the series. The tone of the programme then becomes increasingly sombre as Cook turns south on his last voyage. The two presenters take turns to tell us the story, with still illustrations provided by the artists who accompanied Cook on his travels:

Hall-Taylor: As he sailed down the North Pacific, he came to the island of Hawaii. Cook and some of his sailors went ashore to talk to the islanders. Suddenly fighting broke out. Nobody really knows quite why. But once again we have the ship's artists to show us what happened.

As Cook and his men retreated to the boats, the islanders rushed at them with clubs and knives. Within seconds, Cook was struck down and it was all over. The greatest sailor in the world had come to the end of his travels.

Adair: When the king of England heard the news of Cook's death he broke down in tears. And the islanders themselves were very upset when they realised what had happened. It was very sad. But mind you, now that Cook had been to the Arctic, he'd done what he set out to do. He had voyaged further than any other man, and had sailed the seven seas. And what more could a sailor ask for?

Hall-Taylor: (Standing in front of a portrait of Cook painted for the programme) And in some ways you could say that a part of him has never really died, for his memory is still very much alive. And for anyone who loves the sea, they will never forget the name of Captain Cook. I think that's what he would have wanted.

The programme finishes with a short piece of verse designed to imprint the memory of Cook on the minds of young children, recited intimately over shots of a sailing ship on the sea. What has all this to do with representations of 'race'? How successful is such a programme in its aims? There is considerable informal opinion that young children treat all these kinds of programmes as a bit of a joke. They quickly become somewhat cynical about such comments as 'And what more could a sailor ask for?' They learn to resist the narrative schmaltz. This may be true is some cases, but there is just as much informal opinion which suggests that children accept the general frameworks of such programmes without serious question and get on with their lives. What we do not have is any reputable research from which to draw meaningful conclusions.

I wish to suggest that, whether or not the seeds of chauvinism are being sown along with the epic adventures of Cook, there is a strong implicit discourse about 'others', about natives. These 'natives' are not presented as part of a culture with responsible rulers, and moreover as people with names. They are constructed as (a bunch of) natives. They are the human backdrop against which the adventures of white heroes are played out. For some of the time they form an acquiescent back-drop and occasionally they become aggressive. In this case they act 'inexplicably' to kill the 'world's greatest sailor'. This narrative con-struction, with natives as the supporting roles in the drama of white exploration may have a much more lasting impact upon the modes of discourse which children will employ than any of the cant about the greatest sailor in the world.

It is to the short passage on the death of Cook that I now wish to turn. We are told that Cook and some of his sailors went ashore to talk with the islanders. All historical records suggest that this was the case. What we are not told is why Cook went ashore to talk with the islanders, and what is known about the ensuing events. The producers of the pro-gramme may well have wished to offer young children a story which would allow them to recognise the dangers associated with being an explorer. Such a representation would also have to be partially restrai-ned so that it would not prove to be too upsetting. All this is perfectly understandable. What is not understandable is why the story then has to be told at the expense of the 'natives' and with a disregard for what *is* known about the incidents leading up to Cook's death. It is interesting that the programme makes an attempt to forgive the natives for what they have done by suggesting that they were very upset when they realised what had happened. Perhaps they were upset, but it would have been at more than the death of Cook.

According to most sources, Cook went ashore that day to investigate the disappearance and possible theft of a small boat which was an important part of his expedition equipment. He wanted to make sure that the islanders took him seriously, so he planned to take the King, Terreeoboo, hostage until the matter was resolved. He had also ordered the bay to be sealed off in order to prevent any canoes escaping. Canoes were very important to the Hawaiians and Cook had assumed that they could bargain with the Hawaiians to return their own cutter which, unbeknownst to him had already been destroyed. But when he went ashore, Cook was more interested in taking one or more hostages, a practice he had engaged in before in order to reach a successful conclusion when there had been a theft. According to Gavin Kennedy, from whose well-documented work much of this information is taken:

> Cook's behaviour on this Third Voyage was more aggressive and punitive than on previous voyages. The taking of hostages in the past had almost been a gentlemanly affair, with the chiefs concerned invariably co-operating. At Tahiti on this voyage Cook had gone much further to recover stolen property than he had ever done on the First and Second Voyages: he had seized canoes and burnt them or broken them up. He had also marched across the countryside burning and destroying Tahitian houses and other property until the object that had been stolen – a goat – was returned. Thus taking Terreeoboo hostage with an armed party of marines was ... consistent with the picture of Cook as a tired and impatient man on this, his last voyage.
>
> (Kennedy, 1978, pp. 50–1)

There are some interesting and troubling presumptions behind the actions of Cook. The first is that he and his expedition assumed the right to invent stern punitive measures against those whose land they were exploring. Burning down houses over the loss of a goat is the act of a power which is arrogant and self-righteous, convinced of its (God-given?) superiority. Kidnapping a king over the loss of a boat, however important it was to the expedition, is an act of extreme provocation.

The other point of significance was that when Cook was attacked the small number of marines with him fired their single musket shots, then dropped them and splashed into the water, attempting to escape. In doing so they left behind Captain Cook, a lieutenant, a sergeant and those marines who could not swim. It was an act of either cowardice or gross unprofessionalism – or both. These unhappy events could (and should) be read in a way which tells us much about the psychology and strategies of a famous British explorer. It is a messy and unpleasant end and it undermines the simple, sanitised heroism of the mythical Cook portrayed in the programme. How the Hawaiians, Tahitians and many others including native Americans felt when these explorers came to their lands is something which needs careful attention in the late twentieth century. Using the 'natives' as a backdrop to cheap mythologising is just one more example of the ways in which 'others' have been the measure of 'our' normality, bravery, heroism, scientific prowess, Christian faith and many more sanitised ideological constructions. Those who complain about the manipulation of innocent minds by the media would do well to consider such programmes.

My third and final example in this chapter is taken from another series of Schools Broadcasts, this time dealing with the voyages of Christopher Columbus and the Spanish *Conquistadors*. I have chosen these programmes because they represent an attempt at changing the pedagogy which informs the media representation of 'race'. The programmes do attempt to ask some crucially important questions and to highlight some important political and historical issues. They are a mixture of dramatisation and expository documentary. There is, however, a contradiction between the arguments which may be pieced together from the commentary in the documentary sections and the dramatic representation of Columbus. They are part of a series called *Landmarks* which is produced by the BBC for 9–12 year olds. The first two programmes deal specifically with Columbus, and the third is called *The Spanish Conquest*.

The Man Who Dared

The above title is in fact that of the first programme on Columbus. It is uncomfortably close to the motto of the SAS: Who Dares Wins. The two programmes begin in a contemporary American airport where a young girl called Jodie is waiting to be picked up by her mother, having just returned to the United States. Jodie is absent-mindedly staring at some books, on the cover of which is an image of Christopher Columbus. Columbus begins to speak, comes forward to Jodie and she remains in conversation with his ghostly presence for the two programmes. Columbus's journey's are dramatised with a model ship and a small cast and one or two visits to a dramatised Spanish Court. There are also a few studio scenes on the 'beach' at Santo Domingo. Columbus is portrayed as a pleasant enough chap. His appearance seems to be based upon the 'portrait' painted by Mariano Maella, probably in the late 1700s. In fact, no-one knows what Columbus looked like. He speaks with a gentleness and conviction and seems to use his authority with reluctance when the Indians need to be taught a lesson for one reason or another. It seems as though the only person willing to challenge him is Jodie. This she does in one of their infrequent interchanges about the events of Columbus's life and voyages. Columbus tells her about arriving in Spain in 1492 and she responds with limited enthusiasm.

> *Columbus*: I took possession of it for Spain.
> *Jodie*: What about the people who lived there?
> *Columbus*: They were a simple people. They thought we'd come from the sky.
> *Jodie*: So? Why should they become Spanish property? Or Christians for that matter?
> *Columbus*: They seemed to have no religion of their own.
> *Jodie*: Are you sure?
> *Columbus*: I was sure that they would make good servants of God and Spain.

Columbus is so quiet and reasonable that Jodie's question seem to verge on rudeness. Jodie is American and speaks with an American accent. Columbus is Italian/Portuguese/Spanish and speaks with a fine English accent. Jodie tends to treat Columbus as someone who was, himself, a little simple. He does not respond to the question about why Spain had the right to colonise Hispaniola, just because the Indians were a 'simple' people. Of course, this is a fictional encounter between two actors, one playing a ghost. This does not, however, detract from the significance of the scripted dialogue, just as it does not in the previous example in Wilberforce House. The scriptwriter did not require Jodie to ask what right Columbus had to 'convert' the Indians, even if they did not have a religion. Nor was she scripted to ask him just exactly what he meant by 'conversion', and how he went about it. Such questions would have changed the narrative of the programmes very much.

The second programme is more provocatively titled *For God and Gold*. Columbus, with the help of some dramatisation, tells Jodie how the *Santa Maria* was wrecked and how a settlement was established. Jodie seems worried about Columbus leaving some of his men behind, so far from Spain. Columbus explains that they were self-selecting, that they wanted to stay. Jodie is not scripted to ask whether it was because of the climate, or the friendliness of the Indians, or the fact that it was better to stay on these beautiful islands than to make a dangerous journey back to Spain. Columbus is, once again, quietly persuasive: 'They wanted to stay – to look for gold.' Jodie is not scripted to say 'Oh, that is disgusting!', or 'How would they get the gold from the Indians, assuming they could find any?' or 'What right did you think you had to plunder places like that?' Based upon available documentation, she might also have asked Colombus: 'Is it right that you asked for 10 per cent of all the wealth that you could get your hands on – not just now but for all your heirs, forever?' But she does not say anything. We are left with Columbus telling us through his general demeanour and restraint that he only did what he thought was right.

Later in the programme he says to Jodie that he had three aims on his voyages which he prioritises in line with documented historical record: 'Find gold, spread God's Word, explore.' Some of the Spaniards are represented as greedy for gold and some of the priests are represented as cruel towards the Indians. When Columbus first agrees that the Indians should be punished for resisting colonisation he is in a hammock and is feverish. It is with great reluctance that he gives the order. The carnage which followed is represented through a mixture of tableaux-like scenes and details from engravings. The programme does not shirk from showing images of mutilation, though it does not dwell on them. Bearing in mind the age group for which it is intended, this seems quite justified.

At the end of the programme, Jodie actually tries to comfort Columbus's ghost by telling him that he was on the right lines with his explorations, even though he thought he had discovered Asia. She also pointed out that many of the people who came after him found a lot of gold and became very rich indeed. There is, in fact, no questioning at all of the centrality of gold to the economy in the time of Columbus, and at the time of the making of the programme. Nor is the word 'found' problematised. Her final comment is one which resonates – or which would resonate in the classroom if the teacher so decided: 'I wonder if the Indians were ever sorry you found them.'

It is likely that any children who saw these two programmes would also go on to watch the third, entitled *The Spanish Conquest*, although this is not certain. I will first comment, however, on the two Columbus programmes. Once again, although there is some sympathy for the plight of the Indians, they simply form a backdrop against which the drama of Columbus and the Spanish Court is played out. They are the extras of history, the walk-on parts. One would no more be upset by their problems or deaths than those of the countless Indians, Arabs, Gypsies, Mexicans and a host of others who have provided the human fodder for the dramatisation of history. Unless, of course, you happen to belong to one of those groups. It is a pity that all those Arawaks had to die, but meanwhile let's see what was going on in the Spanish Court, or ask about whether Columbus had a troubled psyche.

The television representation of history for children demands that the scriptwriter and any researchers make choices and interpretations. This means that what is left out of their programmes is just as interesting for the media researcher as what goes in. When it relates to issues of 'race', presences and absences are significant because they demonstrate the ways in which discourses of 'race' and racism are structured and sustained. I will consider just one example of an absence from the Columbus programmes and consider what might have happened if it had been used as part of the dramatisation. The programmes did, in fact, draw upon part of the following extract from Columbus's log in which he is speaking about the Indians.

Some brought us water, others food, and still others jumped in the sea and swam out to us. We thought they were asking if we came from the heavens. One old man got into the boat, and the others, both men and women, cried, 'Come and see the men who have come from heaven, and bring them food and water.' Many men and women came, each bringing a gift and offering thanks to God. They threw themselves on the ground and pointing at the sky, called us ashore ... I went to view all this in the morning, to give an account to your Majesties and to see where a fort could be built. I saw a kind of peninsula with six huts. It could be made into an island in two days, though I feel no need to do this, for these people are totally unskilled in arms, as your Majesties will learn from seven whom I had captured and taken aboard, to learn our language and to take them to Spain. But, should your Majesties command it, all the inhabitants could be taken away to Castile, or made slaves on the island. With fifty men we could subjugate them and make them do whatever we want.

(Koning, 1991, pp. 52–3)

I say that the programmes drew upon part of this log entry. It would be more correct to say that they drew selectively upon the spirit of the entry, with the television Columbus explaining to Jodie that these were a simple people who thought the explorers had come from the sky. The dramatisation could not or would not touch upon the callous self-assurance which allows Columbus to promise to enslave or transport the Indians if their Majesties so desired. It is clear, if there was ever any doubt, that the Indians were for Columbus more of a commodity to be utilised than souls to be saved. The programme might have wondered at a society which existed without the skills of war. It might have commented scathingly on what Columbus and the Majesties who sent him did to a culture and a people who had the misfortune to have made many cultural objects from gold. But it is a programme which, despite its outward appearance of progressive pedagogy, is still caught in the Great Men of History paradigm. The programme is about Columbus first and last, and he has to be a man whose faults are minor compared to his daring. It is not about the consequences of exploration and colonialism, not about the inhumanities which are a core part of what we now call 'progress'. Jodie did not ask how Columbus and his men ensured that they could obtain gold from the Indians. She did not find out that every man, woman and boy or girl of over 14 years old had to produce a stipulated amount of gold every three months. Upon delivery of the gold or gold dust, each person was given a stamped copper token with a date on it. Anyone caught without a token was murdered by having his or her hands cut off. If the scriptwriter had consulted the work of Bartolomeo de las Casas, it would have become apparent that, on Hispaniola, some of the men, women and children were hacked to pieces, and those pieces were sold to feed the Spaniards' dogs. How would Jodie have been scripted to ask Columbus about this, and what would he have replied?

The third programme in the *Landmarks* series, *The Spanish Conquest*, shows the children something of life in contemporary Santo Domingo.

We also see a lesson about the period of conquest being taught in Seville, intercut with another being taught in Santo Domingo. The two versions of history are different but polite. The class in Seville are reassured that the Spanish took a civilised way of life to the Indians, while the children of Santo Domingo are taught of the culture and people who lived on the islands when the Spaniards came. In many ways, the commentary of the third programme is the most pedagogically challenging. It is, however, somehow lost in the flow of images and total absence of any questions in the presentation. Over images of fields, markets and brief shots of poverty, we hear:

> In modern day Hispaniola you can still see signs of the Spanish Conquest. The native people were wiped out and most of the population is now descended from the African slaves brought here by the Spanish.
>
> Large areas of land are still used to grow sugar cane for export rather than food for the local people. Sugar is just one of the crops grown for foreign markets. Pineapples and winter vegetables are also big business, grown solely for export to the United States. Very few local people own enough land to live off the crops that they grow. Many of them move to the capital looking for jobs, and end up living in desperate poverty.

Two questions need to be addressed here. How did this happen and why did it happen? A subsidiary question would be – and what has all this to do with Columbus and his explorations? Unless the teacher who uses these programmes is very critical, the representation of the Spanish Conquest will go little further than identifying that it didn't feel exactly the same in Spain as it did in Hispaniola. The irony of having an idealised statue of Columbus in the square in Santo Domingo is lost on the programme makers. Columbus is still a hero, despite everything. Such tolerance has not been exercised in Eastern Europe when histories of murder and exploitation have been brought to public light. If one considered placing such an idealised statue of Stalin in Red Square, it might provide a measure of the ideological significance of the statue of Columbus in Santo Domingo. We see in Hispaniola that the ideological power of colonialism long outlasts its period of material power.

There is an almost complete disregard, in these three programmes, for the historical scholarship which has come from Latin America about the period of Columbus and the Spanish Conquest. This cannot be explained away on the basis that we have to use 'British' sources, as we are not dealing with 'British' history. Bartolomeo de las Casa (1972) and his *Tears of the Indians* or Eduardo Galeano's (1973) *Open Veins of Latin America* should have been introduced to the children watching this programme. The concept of Eurocentrism would also have been a useful one to raise. The two semi-dramatised accounts of Columbus's voyages are Eurocentric and based on history as revolving around Great Men and Monarchs. The third programme, which is a documentary, presents the child viewer with some potentially devastating data. But it carries neither conviction nor sense of injustice. The Indians and the population of present-day Santo Domingo are still the 'others'. There is a mention at the end of the third programme of some unnamed people who are not entirely happy with celebrating the voyages of Columbus, but the modality of the statement undermines any power it might have carried:

> But not everyone feels that Columbus's journey is something to celebrate. Many people from Latin America and the Caribbean feel that they suffered much more from the coming of the Europeans than they gained.

As the title sequence comes up to end the programme we can see clearly behind the credits the cover of a book, the title of which in Spanish is *Una Historia de Resistencia*. Unless you can read Spanish are paying attention, however, this tantalising signifier will pass you by. Why is it there? What are we supposed to make of it? Why was it not mentioned in the programmes? There are indeed many people in Latin America who do not feel that Columbus's voyage is the cause for much celebration. But who are these unnamed people who 'feel' uncomfortable celebrating the voyages of Columbus? Should they be identified by age, gender, class, profession? What are the arguments they make about the negative dimensions of the Spanish conquest? Do they think it has anything to do with the way they live now, over five hundred years later? Or does it not matter much because, anyway, they are Latinos?

Conclusion

When you read a work of history, always listen for the buzzing. If you can detect none, either you are tone deaf or your historian is a dull dog. The facts are really not at all like fish on the fishmonger's slab. They are like fish swimming about in a vast and sometimes inaccessible ocean, and what the historian catches will depend, partly on chance, but mainly on what part of the ocean he chooses to fish in and what tackle he chooses to use – these two factors being of course determined by the kind of fish he wants to catch. By and large the historian will get the kind of facts he wants. History means interpretation.

(Carr, 1978, p. 23)

I began this chapter by considering some of the views of Michael Medved on the influence of film in the United States. One of the most telling and depressing points he makes is to call a film such as *Come See the Paradise* a 'gloomy guilt-inducer'. The point is telling because it is one which impedes understanding of the discourses of 'race' and racism. It is depressing because a similar view to this represents a fundamental flaw at the heart of so much educational television, particularly when it is concerned with issues of 'race'. Critical thinking is interpreted as being just too depressing and likely to make someone feel guilty about something. It is certainly true that education is not a good idea for anyone with a tendency to feel unproductively guilty. But there is another way of interpreting critical thinking – as part of a process of intellectual liberation. If we cannot teach all children to think without fear, we cannot teach them to think at all.

Several issues for further consideration come out of the discussion of these selected television programmes. Some are in the form of observations and others are hypothetical. Once again, they need to be tested until proved unworthy of further consideration. The first point to note is that the understanding of representations of 'race' in the media has to be linked to a developmental approach to media education. Critical histories are desirable. Critical viewing is essential.

A Eurocentric approach to history and to media representations of history ensures that 'others', whether exotic or not, remain the backdrop to a history in which they exist only inasmuch as the impinge upon 'we' Europeans. The central discursive platform for these histories tends to be that of the Great Man (and very occasionally the Great Woman).

The modal judgements offered in media representations of issues of 'race' for young people are likely to be qualified or softened in order that they do not become too objectionable. Hence there is talk, for instance, of people making 'an awful lot of money'. It is important to note here that the economic dimensions of racism are seldom explored with any conviction in programmes made for children. Modal judgement verbs may also be chosen which weaken the force of arguments against social injustice. Hence there are 'some people' who 'feel' that they suffered from the coming of the Europeans.

The systematic processes of historical racism are often softened to become an emotional account of harshness and cruelty. This is further highlighted because educational broadcasts which deal with issues of 'race' concentrate so much on individual figures rather than social formations; on personal faith rather than organised religion; on the characteristics of individual monarchs rather than monarchy.

The discursive mood of educational broadcasts is likely to be benedictive rather than necessitative. This means that it is more likely that one will find programmes which seek for the good which came out of something, rather than ask exactly what happened then, what we should do about it now, and what we should campaign for or defend in the future. The simple but fundamental questions which go unasked in so many history programmes such as those which I have considered are: Why did these events occur? In whose interests did they occur? What were the consequences of these events for the majority of the people who felt their impact? What is the relevance of these events for our understanding of the world today? Quite specifically, we need to ask what media representations of history tell us about issues of 'race'.

10

Unpopular popular:
Glory, *Deep Cover* and *Geronimo: An American Legend*

This chapter contains three analytical commentaries on films which I have called 'unpopular popular'. They are films made for the general cinema-going public which contain disturbing representations which resonate, for those who discuss them, in a way not often associated with popular entertainment movies. I will highlight and discuss specific aspects of each film before arguing some more general points about why such representations seldom become box-office successes, despite the fact that they often receive official praise. I will also discuss the possibility that the films are significant and problematic as much for their ideological significance as the fact that they are centrally concerned with issues of 'race'. The films are also important because they embody argument about actual social conditions and the political implications of specific courses of action. They are, without exception, concerned with questions of identity. The issue of identity, rather like that of 'race', is seldom addressed as a discrete category. The question of national identity is often interwoven with those concerned with gender, ethnicity, age and class. The complexities of debates about identity are now widely acknowledged (Bauman, 1996), Paul Gilroy (1997) has argued that there are three uses of identity which have to be recognised and recognised as problematic. These are identity as subjectivity; identity, self and Other; and identity as social solidarity. Identity as subjectivity has become more significant as certainties about one's place in the order of things have become less secure. The possibility that identity can be formed and changed through personal reflection and action is both exciting and disturbing. Identity, self and Other is bound up with concepts of sameness and difference. In relation to earlier chapters in this book, it is also concerned with concepts of what constitutes the 'normal'. Identity as social solidarity requires that we ask questions about 'specific ideas of ethnic, racialised and national identity and their civic counterparts' (Gilroy, 1997, p. 315). It also raises in a more focused way the question of the social determination of identity. Gilroy describes these ideas of identity as overlapping and interconnected. He also argues that we must disentangle them if we are to make the concept of identity useful. This is very desirable to avoid complete confusion in discussion and analysis. It should not, however, overlook the fact that identity is always multi-layered and plural in its formation and sustenance. The importance of the concept of identity lies in the fact that it is just as subject to contradiction and tension as is the issue of ideology. It is precisely these tensions and contradictions which we can observe to be in play in the films I will now consider.

Glory (1989, E. Zwick)

This film tells a story of the 54th Regiment of the Massachusetts Volunteers, a black regiment which fought with extraordinary bravery for the North in the American Civil War. The Regiment was composed of black soldiers, but their officers were white. The Colonel in charge was a 25-year-old son of an abolitionist named Robert Gould Shaw. The film is structured mainly on Gould's experience gleaned from his letters. The cinematography is exemplary and the attention to historical detail is meticulous. The film evokes the brutality and mayhem of armed combat without sensationalising. Early sequences also include a representation of surgery on the wounded troops which is contrasted with the genteel life of the rich in Massachusetts.

It was widely believed (by whites) at the time of the Civil War that black men would not make good soldiers. The film traces the process of the men's training, the abuse and racist humiliation they endured at the hands of their Irish Sergeant Major, and the way in which they proved themselves on the battlefield. There are moments of conventional macho behaviour in the film, and there are moments of intense and moving solidarity among the troops. The plot is straightforward, being nothing more than an arduous journey through the experiences of training to the destination of death and/or glory. This experience is, however, marked by moments of racist intolerance and gross social injustice. *Glory* does not raise the important matter of the economic underpinning of racism at the time of slavery. Instead, the black men who volunteer to fight are just there, just available. The voice-over of Gould Shaw (Matthew Broderick) is combined with fine close-ups of black troops to romanticise their beauty while keeping their Otherness as one of their key characteristics. At one point, while singing the praises of his men in a letter, Gould Shaw refers unself-consciously to their 'ivory teeth'. Blackness is constructed again and again throughout the film as something sometimes exotic and always different to be measured against the normality of the whites.

Different characters are carefully structured in the film in such a way as to demonstrate that African-American males do not share the same personality, interests or education. These fictional characters were written for the film, and they provide the dramatic context for the playing out of various set-piece debates or interchanges. These include the literary sensitivities of Searles (Andre Braugher) who is able to share Emerson with the white officer class as an equal, the vulnerable fury of runaway slave Trip (Denzel Washington) and the dignified wisdom of ex-grave digger Rawlins (Morgan Freeman). Trip's passionate interchange with Searles, whom he refers to as 'snowflake' and 'house nigger' is a good example of the way *Glory* highlights the contradictions inherent in either assimilationist or separatist positions:

> *Trip (Denzel Washington)*: Let me tell you somethin', boy. You can march like the white man. You can talk like 'em. You can learn his songs. You can even wear his suits, but you ain't never gonna be nothin' to him but a ugly-assed chimp in a blue suit. (*Pause*) Oh – you don't like that, do you?

Rawlins intervenes in what might otherwise become a violent situation and Trip refers to him as a nigger. Rawlins replies with a reminder that all the white soldiers who had been killed in the war up until then had been fighting 'for you'. There is a strong assimilationist logic in the argument of the older man. It is given more authority by the screen presence of Morgan Freeman:

> *Rawlins (Morgan Freeman)*: You watch who you callin' nigger. If there's any niggers around here it's you. Smart-mouthed stupid-assed swamp-running nigger. If you ain't careful that's all you ever gonna be.

The power of Washington's delivery and the icy restraint of Freeman's riposte cannot be recreated on the page. I write this as a white male who cannot and should not feel at ease as I watch such passages. There is, for white viewers, an element of voyeurism in watching two black actors say that which is usually left unsaid. They, in the context of a feature film, can bring out the discourses which are usually reserved for the racist. When articulated with fury by two African-American actors, there is a perverse pleasure on offer to the white viewer as s/he watches 'them' fight it out. There is also, whether intentional or not, a play between the historical and only pejorative use of the term 'nigger' and its private appropriation by black people as a positive marker of identity.

The film also places much emphasis on the importance of African-American soldiers deserving the same rights and treatment as their white counterparts. This is signified, however, in ways which become ideologically problematic. First, the troops have to obtain boots and socks to elevate them from their slave status. When Trip goes absent without leave in order to look for biscuits and gravy, but above all for boots, he is lashed in front of the whole regiment. When his shirt is peeled back the viewer sees the horrendous scars which have been inflicted on previous occasions. In one of the more poignant moments of the film we wait to see whether Shaw, who also observes the scars, will go ahead with the punishment. He does, of course, for the sake of the regiment and the discipline and character of the men.

When the men are first paid they received less than their white brothers in arms and Shaw saves the situation by refusing his own pay as a sign of protest. The issue of low pay is, however, transcended by concern with the wearing of the blue. The uniforms are handed out, after months of waiting, shortly after the sequence in which their low pay has been announced. The wearing of the blue uniform of the North becomes a synecdoche for recognition as a soldier and an American. When the men march for the first time in uniform the screen is filled with national pride.

When Rawlins is promoted to Sergeant Major, he indicates to Shaw that he is not too sure about whether he is happy with the responsibility. Shaw's response: 'I know exactly what you mean', is another example of the ideological work with which the film binds together those who in all other respects it keeps apart. In another scene a group of white troops are going up to the front and are barracked by Trip and respond with racist taunts. When Rawlins intervenes to stop a fight from beginning, a white soldier comments: 'Stripes on a nigger. It's like tits on a bull!' This same soldier has a strong role to play in the narrative and we see him once more before the final battle at Fort Wagner.

There is a previous combat sequence which takes place at James Island, South Carolina in which the 54th acquit themselves with honour. Afterwards, when the men are resting, Gould Shaw walks over to Trip who is sitting alone looking out over the water. Their conversation highlights once more the ideological tensions in the film, and the way in which resolution is attempted. After some preliminary, restrained conversation, Gould Shaw asks Trip if he would carry the flag for the regiment the next time they go into combat. It is a great honour from a military point of view, but Trip declines:

Trip: I ain't fightin' this war for you, sir.
Shaw: I see.
Trip: I mean, what's the point? Ain't nobody gonna win. It's just gonna go on and on.
Shaw: It can't go on for ever.
Trip: Yeah. But ain't nobody gonna win, sir.
Shaw: Somebody's gonna win.
Trip: Who? I mean you, you get to go back to Boston and big house and all that. What do we get?
Shaw: Well you won't get anything if we lose.

This is, to say the least, a bleak conversation, acted with extreme sensitivity. It seems that the film is moving towards a political awareness of the condition of black people for over one hundred years. But the scene is not over, and ideological power of the conversation will be neutralised before it is. Shaw points out that the situation 'stinks'. Trip agrees, and when Shaw asks what Trip wants, he responds with an almost mystical ambiguity that he wants to 'be clean'. When asked what he feels he has to do to be clean, Trip says, 'We ante up and kick in. But I still do not want to carry your flag.' But the film is not over yet.

Before the final battle at Fort Wagner, when more than half of the regiment are cruelly slaughtered, they stand or sit around and talk and sing. It is rather like the solidarity shown between the troops at crucial moments in Fred Zinnemann's *From Here to Eternity* (1953), but this time the actors are all black. Except for two, the officers, who are ensconced in their tent as they prepare for possible death in the manner of the 'normal' people. Outside the black troops are singing spirituals and praying and testifying. It is an evocative and moving scene, and it is crucial to the ideological thrust of the film. When some of the troops have spoken or prayed, and with the rhythmical humming and clapping very low, Trip is called forward to speak. He does this with great reluctance and shyness. After some embarrassed remarks about not being one for praying, he makes a classic pledge of allegiance to his regiment:

> *Trip*: Well I just ... Uh, uh ... You all the onlyest family I got ... and uh, I love the 54th.

He then says twice what is ideologically the most liberating and the most constraining line in the film, when musing on the possibility of being killed the next morning: 'We men, ain't we?' The proof of humanity for the black soldiers of the 54th is their willingness to face death with minimal civil rights. The next morning the 54th march up to the beach behind a splendid Stars and Stripes, fluttering in the sea breeze. The same white soldier who had derided Rawlins and almost fought with Trip is one of the white troops lining the path to the beach. As they march past, more specifically, as Trip marches past, the white soldier shouts 'Give 'em hell 54th!' It is the moment of intensely male solidarity which seals the ideological package. There is only the stamp to be put on the wax. This comes after another mystical moment when Gould Shaw looks from his horse out over the sea, before joining his troops. He then dismounts and liberates his horse which gallops off up the beach. There follows one of the most extraordinary cinematic battle scenes, during which most of the main characters in the film are violently killed. When the standard bearer is killed and the battle is at a most critical point, it is Trip who steps forward and picks up the flag he had refused for so long. The wax has been stamped. When it is all over, the men are buried together in a mass grave dug on the beach. The body of Gould Shaw is gently tossed in with his men, followed immediately by that of Trip, who rolls down in slow motion and appears to be asleep with his head on Shaw's breast. In their sleep of death there is the promise of national identity. Trip's question to Shaw, however, remains unanswered: 'What do we get?'

Deep Cover (1992, Bill Duke)

The second movie I will discuss has many characteristics of *film noir*. It is the story of a black cop, Russell Stevens Jr (played by Larry Fishburne), who goes underground to expose a cocaine smuggling ring. As a child, he watched his father gunned down while attempting a robbery and his rage and 'criminal understanding' remain with him as an adult.

Taking on the name of John Q. Hill, Stevens works under a federal agent called Carver (Charles Martin Smith). Hill eventually works for and then with a drug-dealing lawyer named David Jason (Jeff Goldblum). Through Jason he meets the people he is supposed to track down: Felix Barbosa, Anton Gallegos and finally Hector Guzman. Hill's work apparently comes to nothing, however, when the State Department decide that Guzman, the man at the top and a diplomat, is too valuable politically to be touched. They call off the investigation. Hill is, by this time, in too deep, and his actions lead to the death of several drug dealers and a religious black police officer, Ken Taft (Clarence Williams III). The DEA try to save their own face in a Congressional hearing, and to somehow exculpate Hill/Stevens. Stevens manages to avoid implicating the DEA in any illegal actions, but shows a videotape which clearly implicates Guzman and embarrasses the United States Government. The film finishes with Hill/Stevens meditating on what has happened and looking at an ideological dilemma of considerable weight.

The question of identity in this film ranges across issues of 'race' and racism and into political matters which seem to transcend both 'race' and nationality. It is shot using the language, imagery and music of the streets of Los Angeles in the early 1990s. Bill Duke, a prolific television director whose first feature film was *A Rage in Harlem* (1991), directed the film. He chose to utilise the soft-spoken voice-over of Larry Fishburne to provide the *noirish* context for a film which does much more than tell a story of criminals and the police. The tone of the film is established with the opening shots of African Americans smoking crack cocaine. The first words we hear are from Stevens:

> So gather round while I run it down, and unravel my pedigree. My father was a junkie.

On more than one occasion in this film one is reminded of the poetry of street language first used to such powerful effect by Abraham Polonsky in *Force of Evil* (1948). The two films have much in common, though Polonsky seems something of an optimist when compared to Duke's appraisal of contemporary politics. What Polonsky and others of the best *noir* directors did not represent is Duke's sense of bleakness, hopelessness and lives under constant threat of violent death. *Deep Cover* is a film which demonstrates a world-view directly related to the social conditions from which it has sprung.

The opening scene is one where the young Stevens watches his father gunned down in the snow and receives from him the bloodstained dollars which he has taken from the store. Those dollars stay with Stevens/Hill throughout the film. When Stevens is recruited for the job of going underground indefinitely, Carver, the *wunderkind* agent, who recruits him is asking all the African-American candidates the same question:

> *Carver (Charles Martin Smith)*: What's the difference between a black man and a nigger?

He receives various responses, from acute embarrassment to open aggression. Stevens simply says:

> *Stevens (Larry Fishburne)*: The nigger's the one that would even answer that question.

From this response we know that Stevens does not have too much of a problem with his identity, though the film, unlike *Glory*, is as much about the breaking down of identity as its formation. The Stevens/Hill character is increasingly unsure about his effectivity, about the morality of his own actions, and finally about the nature of morality. The narrative is structured in such a way as to take us through the excitement associated with traditional crime-busting movies, to the nausea of recognising the horrors of the drugs world. It is the African-American populace of Los Angeles who are shown to be killing each other with guns and drugs, but it is others from outside who are seen to be supplying them with the means. The middle ground of evil is attractive, in the form of Jeff Golblum's portrayal of David Jason. He represents another dimension of racism which is complicated by the fact that, as a Jew, he is also the butt of the racism of others.

Jason is someone who is sexually attracted to African-American women and also demonstrates a homo-erotic impulse towards certain African-American males. He makes his position clear enough when speaking to Hill/Stevens in the company of a cocaine-snorting black colleague, Victoria Dallard:

> You were so – like some beautiful panther or, or, or jungle storm. This is not my condescending infatuation with everything black. Those politically conservative Negroes can kiss my ass – and the anti-Semitic pricks can kiss my ass. But *you* have the gift of fury. You're like a dangerous, magnificent beast.

Jason and Stevens almost come to blows over this statement, but its narrative purpose is not as significant here as the fact that a white character is scripted to articulate a recurring erotic fantasy of some white males. In so doing it further separates off the African-American male as someone to be envied, resented – and desired. Stevens/Hill is transformed as the film progresses into Hill/Stevens. This is a direct result of his agreeing to change his whole lifestyle for a cause which, at the opening of the film, might have been described as noble. The events within the narrative, however, cause a slow but steady breakdown in Stevens' belief in himself and his disillusion with the (white) politicians who seem to control his life and the lives of his superiors. The difference between Hill and his superiors is that many of them collude with the government. The only exception is Taft, the Christian policeman. Taft is the mirror image of Hill. He works on the right side but spends too much time lecturing Hill, and the morality of Taft is too heavy for Hill, with its cloying Christian epithets.

Anti-Semitism also features as one of the racisms which this film represents. It is, however, directed only towards Jason. There are no redeeming 'good Jews' in this film. This disturbing fact is well disguised because Goldblum brings to the role an attractiveness which is akin to Milton's portrayal of Satan in *Paradise Lost*. Jason is shown as a happily married man with a very white wife and saccharin child; he also sleeps with African-American women as often as possible and likes to talk dirty with Hill. He is shown to be capable of sadistic cruelty and has a sharp sense of humour. His evil is, in short, attractive. He just happens to be Jewish, and we know that. He sits on the sofa, nursing his wounded hands. His wife says to him, 'I love you. What more do you want?' His response is intensely focused and quiet: 'I want my cake and eat it too. I want my cake and eat it too.'

The one moment in the film when multiple racisms overlap is when a corrupt policeman is telling Felix Barbosa, one of the more senior dealers, that he needs to make some arrests in order to retain credibility. Barbosa offers up Hill and Jason as sacrifices with the evocative line: 'Two niggers and a kike ... All democrats.' By this time it is clear that nobody is going to come out of this film (it is a film) very clean. One is reminded now of Trip's comment in *Glory* about the importance of becoming clean. Hill voices his dismay and confusion when he says to his superior, Carver: 'What am I doing here, man?' The answers from white superiors in *Deep Cover* are usually lies or hypocrisy. Carver begins an intense response with the line: 'John, have you ever seen a crack baby?' Being clean in *Deep Cover* means immersing oneself in the mire and desperately holding on to some beliefs for which there is minimal empirical basis in the world of the film. Hill remains an idealist, while Carver hypocritically invokes any morality which will get him his own way.

The ideological and dramatic climax of the movie comes when Hill has worked his way right to the top of the hierarchy of drug dealers and is ready to arrest Hector Gallegos, the top drug dealer. Carver says they have to leave Gallegos alone. Hill immediately realises the political implications of what is being said:

> *Hill*: You're protecting him, right? You're protecting Gallegos, this motherfucker. What is he, the new Noriega? He helps you fight communists, you let him bring drugs into the country to sell it to niggers and spics, and you use me to do that shit.

Carver makes a feeble attempt to explain and joke it away: 'It's not me. It's the State Department ... We like him now. We want him to run for President or something.' When this does not work, Carver speaks the words of a tortured liberal careerist: 'It's all shit. You know it's all bullshit. You know that. I know that.' The strength of this film is that it signifies the hypocrisy of so much contemporary political practice with a force similar to a drunkard vomiting on a parquet floor. Hill tells Carver what the viewer has already observed:

> *Hill*: You know what. This whole fucking time, I'm a cop pretending to be a drug dealer, I ain't nothin' but a drug dealer pretending to be a cop.

Hill goes through a period where he descends into a new hell as he drinks alcohol and snorts coke for the first time in his life. There is a pity in the poetry of his voice as he expresses, in voice-over, his predicament:

> You know the jungle creed
> say that the strongest feed
> on any prey it can.
> And I was branded beast at every feast
> Before I ever became a man.

As with Trip, the question of what it means to be a man comes back to haunt Hill. There is one more dramatic moment which is of particular relevance to this chapter. It occurs towards the end of the movie when Hill and Jason are meeting with Guzman and his men at the dockside. Hill and Jason are high up on the deck of the boat. Jason tells Guzman of the new wonder drug which he hopes to manufacture and which would not require the opium poppy because it would be entirely synthetic. Guzman replies with heavy irony:

> *Guzman*: You racist American. You just want to cut us poor Hispanics completely out of the market.

Jason's response is chilling. It could be read as a postmodern play on the insecurity of the signifier. Or it could be read as an acute political statement which places the economic at the centre of all exploitative relations. The popularity of making such statements is strictly limited:

> *Jason*: No, Mr Guzman. I think you know that there's no such thing as an American any more. No Hispanics, no Japanese, no Blacks, no Whites, no nothing. There's just rich people and poor people. The three of us are all rich, so we're all on the same side.

Deep Cover constantly refers to the power of money, but it is Jason's scripted words which provide the only indication that politics is about wealth as well as power. The two become virtually synonymous as the film progresses to its desolate end. The last sequence takes place in a cemetery, where Stevens has taken a young boy called James. They are there to see the grave of James' mother, who is shown throughout the film as she progressively succumbs to greater addiction. Finally she smokes herself to death on crack cocaine. James is the young innocent in all this and it is clear that we are supposed to relate Stevens' closeness to James to the former's own childhood experience. But any tendency towards a sentimental closing off of the film's narrative is undermined by Stevens' final voice-over speech. He has a considerable amount of money from all his drug dealing escapades and he is now, relatively speaking, a free man:

> *Stevens*: The money doesn't know where it came from, but I do. If I keep it, I'm a criminal. If I give it to the government I'm a fool. If I try and do some good with it, maybe it just makes things worse. Either way I'll probably just wind up getting myself into trouble. It's an impossible choice, but in a way, we all have to make it. What would you do?

Boyd (1997, p. 129) has argued that these words are a challenge to black popular culture and to black people in America today. It is important to note the screenplay was written by Michael Tolkin, who is an observant Jew. This could be read as an irony, or more persuasively as indicating that the film is a challenge with wider implications for audience understandings of issues of 'race'. It is a mark of the film's serious intent that the question is put into the lap of the audience, whoever they may be, just before they leave the cinema.

Geronimo (1993, Walter Hill)

Deputy Marshall: We want to do what's right. We'll just hang 'em.

The final film in this chapter returns to America's history. The Apache chief and warrior, Geronimo, has appeared in a host of American westerns, although he is seldom represented with reference to historical accuracy. Hill's film does at least draw upon more reliable data and attempts to show the Apache Indians as human and dignified. As with *Glory*, the story is told through the eyes of a young white officer. This time he is a second lieutenant Britton Davis, and he represents the white liberal conscience of the film, finally resigning from the army never having killed one Apache. Once again the picture signifies considerable admiration for the white man who can understand the Indians, but is less successful in representing an understanding of the Indians themselves. It is, nevertheless, a world away from those portrayals of Apaches where Jeff Chandler or Burt Lancaster represented the best of a very sorry bunch of dramatised Indians. Wes Studi, who plays Geronimo, brings dignity and authority to the part. This is further enhanced by the fact that the Indians speak Apache and there are subtitles during their conversations. This device had been used with success in *Dances With Wolves* (Kostner, 1990).

The film covers the period at the end of the nineteenth century when the Indian population were being corralled and their culture distorted or destroyed by the American government, and it marks the end of an era. The main characters in the film are based upon actual people, from Lieutenants Gatewood (Jason Patric) and Davis (Matt Damon), to General Crook (Gene Hackman) and Al Sieber (Robert Duvall) the scout. The cinematography lends scale and credibility to the film, alternating from wide shots of the vast landscape to the sweaty, stubbled faces of actors such as Gene Hackman and Robert Duvall. There is also fine horsemanship and a soundtrack which gives tactile quality to the leather and the weight of metal on both man and beast. The film begins with Geronimo's early surrender to Lieutenant Gatewood until his final surrender to General Miles, when he and the remainder of his band are sent off by train to Florida in 1886. Geronimo's dealings with General Crook are also part of the drama. Crook is a portrayed as a fair man who is not happy to see what is happening to the Apache people. In *Geronimo*, as with *Glory*, there is a narrative occasion when a meaningful conversation occurs between two central characters which pinpoints an ideological dilemma. This time it is between Geronimo and General Crook as they sit together in the hills. Crook has been reprimanding Geronimo for his raiding activities and trying to get him to live a different kind of life.

> *Geronimo*: With all this land, why is there no room for the Apache? Why does the white eye want all land?

General Crook squints and looks into the distance over Geronimo's head. He does not answer. This is one of the strongest dramatic and political moments in the film.

Lieutenant Gatewood, like Gould Shaw in *Glory*, is capable of mystical intensity as he goes about his business. Indeed, this semi-spiritual quality is one which recurs in films which are attempting a kind of mass liberal expiation for past wrongdoings. The attempt at spirituality does not always sit easily alongside the dialogue. When Gatewood is going to attempt to persuade Geronimo to surrender near the end of the movie, he leaves young Davis in charge. Turning to the younger officer he says:

> You're a fine officer. You stay noble. We're trying to build a country here. It's hard.

These lines should not, however, be dismissed as mere propaganda for the American Way. By the time the film is finished Gatewood's words have become heavy with irony, as he falls victim to the exigencies of building a new country. He is banished to a remote posting following the surrender of Geronimo. The reason for this is that the US Cavalry had been unable to find Geronimo with several thousand troops searching for him. That a small band led by Gatewood could succeed was too embarrassing to be publicised. The reminder to Davis to 'stay noble' is a plea for the retention of some idealism in a cruel world. Unfortunately, the only way which Davis has of keeping his 'nobility' is to back off, to leave the army. The price of integrity in *Geronimo* is banishment, whether for Crook, for Gatewood or for Davis. The banishment of the Apache people is interpreted, finally through the experience of this group of officers. A kind of equivalence is sought between the fates of Geronimo and Gatewood. This is established in part by the scene of male-bonding, where Gatewood trades his fine field glasses for Geronimo's 'blue stone', and by the loneliness which comes with integrity and honour.

The film does not pretend to be a history of the period, although considerable energy has been put into recreating historically verifiable characters. Inevitably, perhaps, these characters are given roles which, though based upon historical information, are changed or modified.

The characterisation of Geronimo by Studi shows him as an intelligent and careful person. The film does not, however, demonstrate his skills in the stressful negotiations which took place with the army, nor the fact that Geronimo never took decisions without a council with his fellow warriors (Debo, 1986). The duplicity of General Miles is shown in the film, but his glowing written appreciation of Geronimo is not. Nor can we know from the film that Miles had a mendacious imagination when writing up his account of the Geronimo campaign. I do not write this in order to find fault with the film, but rather to highlight the dilemmas which must be faced if one believes that it is necessary to relate representations of dramatised issues of 'race' to a world which existed and exists beyond them and which is influenced by them. The film is about legend, and it is about myth. It perpetuates both. One of the most significant weaknesses of this kind of dramatic form is that it either cannot or will not embrace the contradictions and debilitating realities of the existence of the 'hero'.

Geronimo did not die at the end of the movie or in historical time. In fact, he continued for several years, sometimes as a farmer and sometimes as an exhibit in travelling shows. He attended the Trans-Mississippi and International Exposition held at Omaha in 1898, travelling there by train from Fort Sill. When the train stopped at stations on the journey, he cut buttons from his coat and sold them to spectators. He would also sell his hat to those who wanted to pay a little more. Between stations he would sew new buttons on and repeat the process at the next stop. He was also invited and went to Washington to ride in the inaugural parade of President Theodore Roosevelt. Four days later he met with the President, who listened sympathetically to his appeals but said that there was no way he could allow Geronimo and his people to return to Arizona (Debo, 1986, p. 421). In 1909 Geronimo rode to Lawton and sold some bows and arrows. He then persuaded someone to buy him some whisky and rode home intoxicated. When almost home he fell from his horse and lay all night, partly in the water. As a result of this fall he contracted first a bad cold and then pneumonia. He asked the post surgeon to send for his children Eva and Robert. Debo succinctly summarises what happened:

> Now, in these last hours was compressed the totality of Geronimo's life and character. The post surgeon expected him to die that night, but he [Geronimo] asked that Robert and Eva be brought from Chilocco and was determined to live until they should arrive. Purington summoned them by letter instead of by wire. Thus, they did not come for two days. Geronimo had many grievances against the army, and this failure to bring his cherished Eva and his newly discovered Robert closed the circle.
>
> (Debo, 1986, p. 440)

This is not the stuff of which westerns are made. There will be those who will ask why it is necessary to bring such matters up when the film is a self-contained unit and needs to be judged by the characteristics of a genre which has now a long history in movie time. I am not concerned here with judging the merits of the genre, however, but with the representation of issues of 'race'. It is my contention that it is easier for we, the (white) audience to live with the concept of a heroic figure rather than recognising the debilitating and demeaning effect of a very particular kind of exploitation. It is true, for instance, that Geronimo sold his buttons and hats in order to make some money. It is also true that it was the appropriation of the land on which he and the Apache people lived which led to this situation. The celebration of so much of what was once a living culture now exists as a form of trading in myths whether bought with a cinema ticket, or as a cultural tourist. So much of what has become known as 'ethnic arts and crafts' is directly related to the sale of Geronimo's buttons.

Conclusion

The three films which I have discussed are very different in style and intent. *Glory* is a finely wrought narrative which tells a story of how very basic human dignity was accorded to the African-American male at a very considerable price. Trip's question, 'We men, ain't we?' is similar to that on the tobacco boxes and other decorative objects at the time of the ending of slavery: Am I not a man and a brother? The film has a much stronger contemporary ideological purpose. It is an attempt to show that the 'people' can be united under the national flag, to imagine a community (Anderson, 1991). 1989, the year when *Glory* was produced, was also the year when General Colin Powell became the first black Chairman of the Joint Chiefs of Staff. The situation of African Americans in the United States cannot be said to have benefited from either the film or the appointment. There was a brief recognition from some white audiences and the US Government that African-American people *are* human and intelligent and can take responsibility. However, if we take the film *Glory* and read it backwards from the humanity of the troops and the tragic unity in death of Trip and Gould Shaw, there is little commonality of interest, only the sombre counsel which the white officer offers to the black volunteer: 'Well, you won't get anything if we lose.' The film is not so much about the Civil War as about the anguish and conflict which exist in contemporary America. It offers a palliative symbol, the American Flag, to cover real material deprivation and injustice. The emotion which the film offers comes in a rush and does not last. The hope it offers takes the form of a (necessary) myth: that of strength through national identity.

Deep Cover is a film which, in the end, is about political identity. Stevens' closing words, quoted earlier in the chapter, pose a bleak set of questions from which, at first sight, there is no escape. It is an accurate representation of a system where money rules and meritocracy provides the bureaucratic foundations. Racism is a shared fact of life in this film world, and there is no possibility of any communal action on any issue. Stevens/Hill is asked and accepts the invitation to go it alone. This is the politics of individualism in a cruel world. Taft and Stevens are both loners and they both lose. It is of considerable ideological significance that the dramatic and political weight of the film is ambiguous. 'What would *you* do?' It comes across as a personal question. Perhaps there was no other choice, because the film would have lost its dramatic edge if it had become either didactic or called for solidarity. Nevertheless, it means that a film which has made a brilliant analysis of political corruption and social injustice, albeit somewhat metaphorically, cannot find a 'we' with which to associate.

Finally, *Geronimo* takes another small step towards the recognition that the American Indian had a way of life, a culture, which deserves respect. It also demonstrates a subtle but profound awareness of the perpetration of an enormous injustice. The price of this recognition, however, is that Geronimo must be given a comfortable heroic status and the demeaning realities of banishment and cultural assimilation must be suppressed. This film is about the identity of the viewer, not the Apache.

The above analyses are offered as a means of identifying the complexities and contradictions to be found in representations of 'race' in one sector of popular cinema. These films are not blockbusters. *Glory* grossed $26.83 million in the United States, *Deep Cover* $16.64 million and *Geronimo* $13.74 million. These figures are revealing set alongside those for films such as *Dances with Wolves* (1990) which grossed $240 million in the USA and $424 million world-wide, *New Jack City* (1991) which grossed $47.62 million and *White Men Can't Jump* (1992) which grossed $76.25 million plus $34 million on rentals (Internet Movie Database, 1997).

Nevertheless the films I have analysed are still in circulation, either as videos, or because they are shown on one of the many movie channels. It is my contention that such films carry within them a negative politics – one which cannot look to social change although their narratives often identify the need for such change. I am not arguing that such entertainment movies are *obliged* to encourage political awareness. Nor am I suggesting that it is wrong to offer a bleak dramatisation of a bleak situation (as in *Deep Cover*), or to point out that national unity is often achieved in wartime (as in *Glory*). The three films which I have chosen are not simple or inadequate as cinema – quite the reverse. This is precisely why they need to be studied for the way in which they contribute to or challenge an ideological and discursive reserve. As social change is not possible, at least in these narratives, the alternative is to concentrate on questions of identity. The irony is, that almost without exception, the identity in question is that of the dominators. In films such as *Glory* and *Geronimo*, the predominantly white audience can renegotiate a problematic relationship with their past. Far from inducing guilt, which would anyway be of little productive value, the films allow the majority audience to nod its metaphorical head with an understanding which requires no action. In many entertainment movies which deal with historical issues, there is an ideological complicity (almost certainly unintended as complicity) between the producers and the audience. The past is used as an ideological smorgasbord from which the film maker plucks a culinary mix to include richness and the shedding of an occasional tear, but which must induce no indigestion. This is why it is such a relief when Lieutenant Davis decides to resign from the army. In effect, the whole white audience can resign with him.

When the contemporary world is more directly and honestly represented, as in *Deep Cover*, there is little hope or hope for change.
Analysis of representations which can be designated as the 'unpopular
popular' needs to work from a recognition of this situation. It suggests
that research in this field of representation will have to be re-politicised
if it is to be more than a hollow enterprise. The alternative is to founder
on the rocks of ideologically complicit romanticisation – or despair.

11

International perspectives

Most of the examples analysed in this book have come either from the United Kingdom or the United States. In this chapter I will be looking at some other examples of the ways in which issues of 'race' drawn from different contexts are represented. In doing so I am attempting to begin to address the complexities of relating context and text in each situation. The purpose of the analyses which follow is to focus attention on the importance of avoiding blanket generalisations about representations of issues of 'race'. The different contexts of production and reception of media messages do not, of course, mean that racist representation is inexcusable in one context and acceptable in another. They do require, however, that we try to understand the cultural, political, economic and social implications of specific modes of representation, and do not try to 'read off' meaning unproblematically. This sensitivity to context has, always, to be set against any tendency to adopt a patronising tone in the readings of media messages: 'Oh, the Australians are so peculiar – they always show foreigners that way!' It is also important to try to identify the ideological implications of representations of 'race' in particular contexts. I will first discuss some examples from Australia, followed by a consideration of examples from Israel.

Introducing Australia

It's a bloody joke. Aborigines just sit around all day, doing nothing, with their hands out. And I've visited communities out in the bush. If they're so in tune with the land, why are they so dirty?
(Pauline Hanson, quoted in the *Sunday Telegraph Magazine*, 6 July 1997)

The above quotation comes from an article by *Sunday Telegraph Magazine* journalist Sarah Ferguson. Pauline Hanson leads the One

Nation party in Australia. Sarah Ferguson writes a piece to introduce English readers to a down home Australian racist. The readership of the *Sunday Telegraph* is estimated to be about 2 million, and it is a conservative paper. It is, perhaps, hardly surprising that the general tenor of the piece is one of tolerant condescension. There is reference to Hanson's 'barnstorming tour', a suggestion that in person 'she does not look like an extremist'. With carefully modulated sympathy, Ferguson goes on:

> Her faltering voice and quizzical, sometimes feline, look suggest a vulnerability that makes the crowd of demonstrators – the supporters of multiculturalism, after all – who stake out her rallies, look like the aggressors. Screaming abuse and threatening her supporters, they help foster the image of a lone woman at the centre of turmoil, bravely prepared to tell it like it is no matter how tough it gets.

Having suggested that it is important to consider representations of issues of 'race' in relation to the context from which they have sprung, I immediately encounter an interesting problem. My introduction to the life and work of Pauline Hanson is provided by a journalist who is certainly not hostile to her stance. I am reminded that the mediation of racism is an international phenomenon. I know, when I read this story, that I am being addressed, erroneously, as a regular reader of the *Sunday Telegraph*. I also recognise the familiar characterisation of oppositional groups as hysterical and possessing more allegedly undesirable characteristics than those whom they would oppose. Ferguson's final judgement on Hanson is, ideologically, a sobering reminder of the ways in which issues of 'race' are interwoven with a whole range of political judgements as they are re-presented:

> Whether or not Pauline Hanson will succeed in her bid to deliver a disenchanted nation from the trendies, the judges, the media and the PC politicians, remains to be seen. But, even if she dwindles into being the eccentric member for Oxley, she will have made an indelible impression on Australian politics. Whenever Australia trumpets the successes of its multi-ethnic society, there will be 'The Hanson Factor' to remind everyone that the picture is not as rosy as it seems.
>
> (*Sunday Telegraph Magazine*, p. 15)

Ferguson does not suggest that Australia is an 'allegedly' disenchanted nation. Her crass right-wing populism gathers together in one bundle representatives of both repressive and ideological apparatuses! It is not clear in fact whether what one reads is an account of the position of Hanson, or that of Ferguson. There is, of course a suggestion that Australia is, or may be becoming, a multi-ethnic society. Those who would attempt to 'trumpet' its success are presumably people who think that it is a desirable development, though the choice of the word 'trumpet' puts them somewhat in the company of the noisy demon-strators against Hanson.

I have just written about one piece of reportage which happens to deal with a right-wing populist figure in Australian politics in 1997. Pauline Hanson would not be known to the majority of people in the United Kingdom, simply because she would hardly have received any media attention. The attention she receives from this conservative English newspaper, however, suggests that white racist Australian concern over issues relating to 'race' is very similar to white racist English concern. This discourse of concern is based on an amalgam of fear and disgust with a particular group designated as 'other'. In the Australian context this has wider implications than fear and disgust about the presence of native Australians. It also includes a general anti-Asian perspective, as some Australians fear the 'influx' of immigrants and the possibility that Australia will be 'Asianised'. Hanson was elected to the Australian Parliament as an independent, having been dropped by the Liberals because of her embarrassing comments about issues of 'race'. In her first parliamentary speech she referred, in depressingly familiar language to the 'danger of being swamped by Asians'. The term Asia is used in popular media discourse in much the same way as 'Africa' can be called upon in the European context when it is ideologically appropriate. Jacubowicz *et al.* cite a newspaper placard from Tuesday 8 December 1992 which carries the banner 'Every Child to Learn Asian' (Jacubowicz *et al.*, 1994, p. 186). The precise content which might be associated with such a slogan is not as important as the ideological work it can accomplish merely by being there as a discursive marker. Asian has become a language which will, it is implied, be 'imposed' upon ordinary, normal, white Australians. The continent of Asia has been linguistically bound together, con-tained and demeaned in a simple slogan. At the same time there is the implicit assumption in such a slogan that Australia is not a part of Asia. Hanson is at pains to say so as often as possible.

This is just one media perspective upon issues of 'race' in Australia, and there are more. Racism against Aboriginal people is now well documented but less well publicised. There are many examples when such racism has either been tolerated or propagated in the Australian media. An example of this at its most callous has been researched in the report *Gambling on the First Race* (Mickler, 1994) which pays particular attention to Talk-Back Radio in Western Australia. This important report can be accessed on the World Wide Web and may be copied and distributed freely. The discussion which follows is drawn largely from that source. It concentrates on Perth's high rating morning radio programme called *The Sattler File*, presented by Howard Sattler. Recurring themes on the programme, which depends upon attracting both listeners and callers, are the allegations that Aboriginal people receive special treatment, that they drink away any money they get, that they don't deserve land rights, and so on. Talk-Back Radio, or Talk Radio as it is known in the UK and the USA, is a powerful medium for allowing the bile and bad feeling of selected disgruntled listeners to be aired to maximum effect. The selection is important here, for Talk-Radio hosts can read on a screen who is waiting to speak and a summary of their chosen topic. If any caller tries to argue with the host it is of little use because, in this case, Sattler's voice channel automatically overrides and cuts out the caller's channel as soon as he or she speaks. There is also a 7-second delay before the programme is aired – again a common practice – so that it should be possible to cut dead any speaker uttering profanities or the like before their words reach the public. One example of the particular racism which is allowed relatively free rein in the show occurred on 6 August 1990:

Caller: Good day, Howard, how are you going?
Sattler: Good, Bradley.
Caller: Answer a quick one about the Waugle (Nyoongar Aboriginal word for Rainbow Serpent).
Sattler: Yes.
Caller: Um, what do Waugles and pink elephants have in common?
Sattler: What do Waugles and pink elephants have in common?
Caller: You've got to be drunk to see either one of them.
Sattler: (in a facetious tone) Now now, now now, now now, Bradley, you shouldn't be like that. Well, I can't account for everyone.

On 31 March 1992 Sattler introduced his programme with the comment that 'The federal government has decided to throw another $150 million at Aboriginal legal aid services.' Mickler points out that this has the effect of framing all discussion which follows around factors which have been pre-established as discreditable: the possibility that Aboriginal legal services are doing a vital job; that they are not wasting tax payers' money; that the government should continue with its funding of such services. The type of comments cited need to be interpreted alongside the findings of the Royal Commission into Aboriginal Deaths in Custody (Dodgson, 1991) and the Human Rights Commission *National Inquiry into Racist Violence* (1991). Both these government enquiries found that media representations of Aboriginal people had a strong influence on both community attitudes and institutional behaviour towards Aboriginal people. Although they noted that there were examples of high quality and sensitive journalistic practice, the overall trend was as follows:

- a tendency to sensationalise crime and civil disturbances involving Aboriginal people;
- a strong emphasis on reporting court proceedings, in which the Aboriginality of offenders tends to be made known unnecessarily;
- a reliance on police sources for much of their stories, and a general failure to canvass Aboriginal opinion or cross-check police accounts of incidents;
- a failure to include Aboriginal people within the community of readers which is addressed by the paper. That is, Aboriginal people tend to be treated as outside the normal business of mainstream society (seen as Anglo-Saxon), and represented mainly when perceived as presenting a threat or a challenge to that society.
- a tendency to reproduce colonial and race [*sic*] stereotypes about Aboriginal people both by invoking Eurocentric notions of savagery, timelessness and primitivism, and by superficially treating Aboriginal social problems so as to leave readers with the impression that they are caused by something innate to Aboriginal people themselves.
- a failure to provide readers with the historical and social background which, stemming from colonisation, means that superficial 'common sense' ways of trying to understand Aboriginal affairs are inadequate.

(Dodgson, 1991)

Two points should be noted. The first is that neither *The Sattler File*, nor the findings set out above are likely to represent, in any public sense at least, the majority view on these issues. Nevertheless, they work, in the Australian context, to strengthen a discursive reserve which will be called upon if it is needed. Some would argue that, because this is a minority viewpoint, it should not be given undue attention. But racism, and racism in the media, do not depend upon occupying a majority position in order to have an ideological impact. The second point is that what the media do not say about issues of race is also of crucial significance. I will quote one more example from *Gambling on the First Race* to illustrate the point.

In January 1992, 19-year-old Louis Johnson was walking home along a quiet road in a middle-class suburb of Perth in the early hours of the morning. It was his birthday and he had been to a party. He stopped to lie down on the grass for a while. A little later a car came up to him which was carrying five young people, two females and three males. The occupants of the car came over to Johnson and two of them viciously assaulted him while the others watched. They then drove off at high speed. Moments later the car returned and deliberately ran over Johnson at high speed. They came to look at what they had done and the driver said: 'I got him, I am glad I got the black sod.' Johnson lay with a shattered pelvis and massive internal injuries until he was spotted by a passing cyclist. He was still conscious and persuaded the cyclist to call an ambulance. When the ambulance arrived, the ambulance attendants simply assumed that Johnson had been sniffing petrol and took him home rather than to hospital. His parents discovered Johnson in bed in the morning and could see that he was very ill. They called another ambulance, but Johnson was dead before it arrived. The driver of the car later confessed that he had done it deliberately, but that he had only wanted to break Johnson's legs. When asked why he did it, he answered openly: because he was black. Johnson's murder was premeditated, intentional, and carried out because he was an Aboriginal man. A bitter irony is that Johnson was a fully paid up subscriber to the St John's Ambulance Fund. The response to this attack was muted in the media in Perth. *The Sattler File* did not mention it at all.

I have quoted this example because it demonstrates that there are times when one does not need a particularly complex theory of ideology in order to recognise that media silence can also serve power relations. It is also an example of the material consequences of racist ideology, where the discursive becomes an ideologically complicit accessory to racist murder. At the time of writing this, another political contest is being fought over the question of Aboriginal land rights in Australia. Much of the media coverage of this issue is hostile to the Aboriginal case.

Meanwhile *Home and Away* and *Neighbours* continue on television in Australia and in the UK. These soap operas offer a vision of an Australia with a shared identity free from any but the most cursory references to any indigenous people. The programmes are also free from much engagement with any minority groups and certainly do not celebrate the multiculturalism which is supposedly being 'trumpeted' in some quarters. They do occasionally touch upon social problems, including drug addiction, but racism and cultural diversity are given scant attention. The question of whether or not soap operas have any obligation to engage with social issues is not my immediate concern here. What should be recognised is the ideological significance of their presence or absence. The political and ideological tension between the fictional world of *Neighbours* and the material world of the Johnson family in Perth is almost literally unspeakable. It is, however, one upon which the student of media representations of 'race' should focus.

Cinematic representations of issues concerning 'race' and identity are much more complex in Australia. A whole range of films in the 1990s, from *Muriel's Wedding* (1994) to *Strictly Ballroom* (1992) and *The Adventures of Priscilla, Queen of the Desert* (1994 – hereafter *Priscilla*), have provided an array of responses to family life, sexuality, identity and racism. I want to consider briefly the important way in which *Priscilla* offers a quiet and problematic identification with Aboriginal people through the way in which they seem at home with outsiders – in this case drag performers and transsexuals.

The film involves a journey of three characters: drag performer Tick/Mitzi (Hugo Weaving), a recently bereaved transsexual Bernadette (Terence Stamp) and Adam/Felicia (Guy Pearce) as they drive towards Alice Springs, deep in the outback, where they have been invited to put on a show at a casino. *Priscilla* is the name given to the bus in which they travel. When the bus breaks down far from the main highway, Adam repaints it with lavender paint while Bernadette goes to find help. He returns with an elderly couple, who take one look at the bus and its occupants and drive off without speaking. The three are finally rescued by a Native Australian, who invites them to join a tribal entertainment evening, where they mime to a disco hit and seem to be a big success. The remainder of the film follows their adventures as they finally reach their destination. I want to speak in some detail about the way in which the Aboriginal people are represented in the relatively short sequence mentioned above.

For convenience, I have done a selective shot breakdown of the scene where the Aboriginal man (without a name) first appears and the following scene around the open fire.

Shot Number	Shot Type	Dialogue/music	Description/effects
1.	Close up	Tick: Right. From the top	Tick
Zip Pan to	Close up		Tick's hands
2.	Mid shot	All three: Go on now Walk out the door Just turn around now You're not welcome any more	The three rehearse without music, singing quietly, without costume
Camera tracks left to show all three.			They move away from camera trying their dance steps together then turn, in synchrony, to point at the audience/camera.
		Yells of fright (all three)	The three recoil in fear
3.	Close up	Aborigine: Hello. Nice night for it.	Smiling Aborigine face
4.	Close up		Full moon with trees silhouetted.
5.	Close up	Strumming guitars	Guitar fingerboard – hands fingering simple chords
Camera tilts up to player's face	Close up	Blues chorus: I feel alright, etc.	Music continues – guitars strumming with the singing
6.	Close up		Smiling Aboriginal face.
7.	Close up		Guitar player's face. He sees the approaching group.
8.	Long shot		Approaching group – the four together come downhill screen right to left

9.	Extreme long shot – the camp		
10.	Long shot		The group, walking towards camera
11.	Mid shot	Silence	The two guitarists. They finish playing.
12.	Mid shot	Tick with the other men	Anxious looks
13.	Big close up		Guitar player
14.	Big close up		Bernadette
15.	Big close up		Young Aborigine – beautiful, gentle look
16.	Close up		The three men
17.	Big close up	Tick: I think we just crashed a party.	Tick
18.	Big close up – laughing Aborigine man (Alan)	No. Come on. You'll be alright.	
			Music and talk recommences
19.	The group walk forward	Music and talk continues	
20.	Big close up	Music and talk continues	Aboriginal face – smiling.
21.	Close up		The three men cross the frame left to right
22.	Close shot: Young child vacates seat	Music and talk continues	The three men sit.
23.	Mid shot		The Aboriginal men stand near the fire.

Tick now looks at the full moon and at the fire as the blues music continues. When the guitar music stops, Tick says: 'Well, I guess it's our turn.' We then see a close up of a jewelled and braceleted hand, turning on a decorated tape recorder and the music begins. The scene which follows shows the three performers, in full costume with wigs and make-up. They perform to Gloria Gaynor's disco hit 'I Will Survive'. The scene is shot in near darkness, with the main source of light apparently coming from the fires in the camp. As the song progresses there are several occasions when close-up shots of single Aborigines are shown, or when young Aborigines are shown sitting together, enjoying the performance. Every shot of an Aborigine face is sympathetic and shows them to be slightly bemused but enjoying the fun. Then one of the Aborigines begins to play the didgeridoo to the disco rhythm. Later in the song, the unnamed Aborigine man joins them and they have dressed him in a drag queen's costume as he mimes the rest of the song with the trio. By the time the song has finished there is a mixed sound track which incorporates both Aboriginal rhythms and voices and the disco number. The first shot of the next scene is of a panorama in the early morning, as the three men and Alan (the Aboriginal man is now named for the first time) walk across the desert. Alan is fascinated and amused by the thought that the three of them can earn a living dressed up as women.

The first point to note is that, apart from the three drag artists, everyone else in the scenes described is Aboriginal. The Aborigines are wearing casual clothing and are represented as friendly and open-faced. When the man (Alan) first speaks his greeting, it is very 'Australian' and good-natured. Once by the camp fire, the three performers, particularly Tick, are shown to develop a kind of rapport with Alan. It is significant that the music which the guitarists were playing around the camp fire is a 12-bar blues being sung with a North American lilt. The strumming guitars are then contrasted with the electronic sophistication of disco music. This, in turn, is then 'subverted' by the almost cheeky introduction of the didgeridoo. By the end of the song, we have come full circle and the American disco music, mimed to by Australian drag artists, is enriched by Aboriginal rhythms and harmonies. It is a fine example of the exuberance of cultural hybridity. As such, it is a moment of celebration and, one can argue, of mutual understanding and respect for different cultures. It is a moment when the cultural hybrid exists briefly as a new communicative form. This hybridity may also be argued to carry with it a promise of understanding and tolerance as well as celebration. Another reading might, however, suggest that this coming together of 'others' is brief, limited in potential and doomed to end as quickly as it began. This second reading suggests that issues of 'race' and racism can be read in parallel with issues relating to sexuality. A bleaker reading might suggest that the solidarity which is briefly established is the only liberatory possibility open to those who are oppressed by their societies. It is, then, a solidarity of desperation. At the same time there is a dignity in the representation of the Aboriginal people which is absent from the three main protagonists for most of the film.

I am sure that many more readings of more or less subtlety could be made of this sequence and its placing in the film as a whole. My purpose in offering a selection of possibilities is not to argue that any and all readings are of the same importance or validity. Eco has written about possible agreement that texts are *not* saying certain things:

> I shall claim that a theory of interpretation – even when it assumes that texts are open to multiple readings – must also assume that it is possible to reach an agreement, if not about the meanings that a text encourages, at least about those that a text discourages.
>
> (Eco, 1990, p. 45)

I wish to suggest, however, that there may be a semiotic tendency to evoke a common meaning behind all these readings. In this I am taking Eco's argument about the meaning that a text discourages and suggesting that once all *dis*couraged meanings have been established, there may be left some shared intended meaning which is of crucial significance. This is not mere rhetorical juggling. The common or shared meaning which is often obscured behind all these readings may be more to do with the evocation of a general mood (or discursive field) than with specific connotations. It is, I suggest, a mood of political quietism. Cultural hybridity, at least in the form presented in *Priscilla*, offers a brief respite from the daily round of 'bitching' and persecution. It speaks *for* a (potential) common humanity but not *against* injustice. The strength of the sequence I have discussed lies in its sensitivity and its blending of innocence and experience.

The world of *Priscilla* is not always one full of kindness. It is, however, tolerable because of the poetry in the fictional existence of its protagonists. This fictional world exists, for media audiences, alongside another and differently 'fictional' field of representation – that of talk radio and tabloid journalism. This, as we have seen, is less likely to offer up much poetry. *The Sattler File*, as I have noted, does not have to represent majority opinion in order to be powerful. It offers an outlet for those with bile to spare. *Priscilla* (which can be read as a metaphor for all movies which in total or in part challenge preconceptions about issues of 'race') offers some kind of strength to the oppressed. Both refer to a material world which exists in a perverse symbiotic relation to its media representation. I have also referred to a third world of representation which can be found in Australian soap operas. Each of these spheres of representation contributes to forms of understanding, but also throws up contradictions and tensions, both semiotically and materially. Political realities, especially the present struggle over Aboriginal land rights and racist persecution, demonstrate in the Australian context just how important it is for media researchers to engage with the contradictions thrown up by media discourses concerning 'race'. It also demonstrates the semiotic tensions which different contexts for reception can generate. Watching *Neighbours* in Perth may have a very different impact and ideological pull than watching the same programme in London. The absence of Aboriginal characters is unlikely to be something which the English viewer will consider. Perhaps the 'Australian' viewer might notice the absence of Jewish or Greek characters. Whatever one's cultural, national, or ethnic background, it is difficult not to conclude that *Neighbours* and *The Sattler File* provide complementary world-views. Both work, intentionally or not, to maintain waspish whiteness as the measure of all things – especially all things normal.

Contradictions from Israel

It's all been bad since the new immigrants came here. Since they came, we've watched them get ahead while we who were born here and served this country stay behind.
>   (Shoshana Ifach, speaking in Or Akiva, near Caesaria)

I want now to turn to another and very different context where the media representation of issues of 'race' is both complex and ideologically volatile. In choosing to consider brief examples from the *Jerusalem Post* I have three main aims. The first is to highlight the ways in which concepts of 'race' and national identity can generate specific forms of media discourse. The second is to consider the possibility that specific forms of discrimination may exist in representations of those who claim the same ethnic and national identity. The third is ask some questions about presences and absences in the representation of issues of 'race' in the Israeli media. It is also possible for a wider audience to engage directly with an English language newspaper. The comments offered here are exploratory and are designed to highlight areas for investigation which are sometimes beyond the scope of analysis undertaken by media researchers concerned with issues of 'race'.

The *Jerusalem Post* is Israel's English language daily newspaper. It also publishes a weekly international edition and is available on the Internet. The issue from which I have taken my examples is the international edition for the week ending 13 December 1997. The article from which the quote at beginning of this section is taken, is by Allison Kaplan Sommer under the caption 'No work, little hope'. While media reportage and anti-immigrant sentiment may be context-specific, it is remarkable how the comments of Ifach at the beginning of this section ring strangely familiar. The *Jerusalem Post* does not directly challenge Ifach's assertion that the new immigrants are able to 'get ahead' faster than those who have 'served' the country. It does, however, quote two separate sources which suggest that 70 per cent of the new immigrants are unemployed. The article begins with Ifach saying that she is so depressed by being lied to by the politicians that she is tempted to burn her Israeli identity card. The question of Israeli identity is one which recurs and is not confined to this single issue of the *Post*. It is ironic in this context that the reference is to a state-authorised identity, rather than any personal sense of worth. The reason given for possible burning of the card is the fact that Ifach feels challenged by the immigration of Russian Jews to Israel, for most of the immigrants to Or Akiva came from the former Soviet Union. It is also linked to the fact that Ifach has a son who is due for military service, and who wonders why he should serve Israel if it has nothing to offer him in return. These feelings of resentment or hostility towards new immigrants need to be set in a very particular context, for virtually 100 per cent of these 'immigrants' are Jewish, and hence have as much right to be in Israel by Israeli law as do Ifach and her family. Yet they are spoken of as outsiders, as interlopers. The problems which the Israeli media and Israeli society encounter include trying to clarify questions of identity, from who is a 'real' Jew to who has earned the rights which are in fact mandatory for all (who are Jewish) under the law. In such a debate the normalisation of 'Jewishness' is of critical ideological significance. It is something which may be invoked in times of national emergency, but somewhat overlooked when it is about Israeli new towns where there is high unemployment.

There is, of course, another dimension to this discussion of 'outsiders', and this is the existence of the Palestinian Arabs. They are reported on indirectly in a comment by Moshe Nissim, the manager of Or Akiva's unemployment bureau. He notes that there are fewer jobs for women in Or Akiva:

The industry that employed the most women, textiles, is in decline. A large facility here closed up and moved to the Palestinian Authority. I have mixed feelings about that one. On the one hand, I hate to see more women unemployed. On the other, working in textiles can be terrible – long hours, low pay, and very bad conditions.

This indirect acknowledgement of the Palestinians is linked with an implicit judgement about the kind of work and working conditions which might be acceptable for them. It may be generically inappropriate for a journalist writing a piece of straightforward reportage on unemployment to comment on this issue. Nevertheless, it is one of many examples of the normalisation of Palestinian Arabs as people of relatively minor significance. Concern over the presence of Palestinians has been temporarily replaced by concern over the presence of Russians. The same issue of the *Jerusalem Post* carries other stories which relate to Arab people, and which need to be 'read' as part of an ideological complex. It is only through a reading of numerous articles that the failure of journalists to offer analytical comment becomes of ideological significance.

The second article to which I will refer is by Elli Wohlgelertner, under the title 'Arab students' Jerusalem apartment firebombed again'. The story is, as the title suggests, about three young Palestinian women, Manal Diab, Sonia Khoury and Wafa Khouri, who share an apartment in the Musrara neighbourhood of Jerusalem. The firebombing is the second they have had to endure. Two of the Palestinian women are sisters and all three are students. They have appeared before the Knesset Interior Committee to relate their difficulties in finding an apartment in Jerusalem. The situation is sufficiently serious that the mayor of Jerusalem, Ehud Olmert visited the apartment 'to show support for the three women and to offer his help in finding another flat'. There is no suggestion in the report that three women had asked for another flat. It is reported, however, that Mayor Olmert said 'some Jews would think it's dangerous for Arabs to live among Jews'. This highly ambiguous statement is neither explored nor commented upon. Is it dangerous because the Jews are not to be trusted? Or is it because the Arabs are not to be trusted? Are the people responsible for the firebombing likely to be the Jews who think it is dangerous for Arabs to live with them? The fact that there is no comment or analysis on these issues reduces the matter to near absurdity, unless of course the ideological framework has already been established in favour of the Jews. Mayor Olmert is reported as reiterating his long-standing policy that Jews should be able to live anywhere in the city of Jerusalem, 'and so should Arabs'. The absurdity of the order in which this issue is reported, with priority given to where Jews should be able to live, is apparently unnoticed by the journalist.

The article finishes with a reference to Ashkenazi Chief Rabbi Yisrael Lau. He is reported to have condemned the attack and said that there was 'no justification for such violence'. Ideologically dictated generic convention seems to require that something more is reported, and the article finishes with the following: 'But he pointed out that no Jewish religious leader had made statements comparable to those of Sheikh Yassin, who has called for the destruction of Israel and the US.' The predicament of the three Palestinian women is thus sandwiched between a warning from the Mayor of Jerusalem, and a reprimand from a Chief Rabbi. The warning is based on what 'some Jews' might think. Neither the Mayor nor the *Jerusalem Post* reporter have any comment on this. The reprimand is not directly addressed to the three young women, but it is somehow linked in a very dubious manner with the threats of Sheikh Yassin. The ideological thrust of this piece of reportage relies heavily upon implicature (see p. 158).

The third example of how Arab people are constantly represented as second-class or inferior human beings can be found on the same page of the newspaper, in a short piece on stereotyping in Israeli school textbooks (unnamed). This time it is the stereotyping of Yemenite Jews which is under scrutiny. The Knesset Education Committee has declared that such stereotypes should be removed from school texts. In order to make sense of this suggestion, it is important to recognise that Yemenite Jews are often regarded as second-class Israelis by those who claim a European lineage. This in itself is certainly problematic and it is, once again, a moot point whether or not such an attitude should be considered as racist. The newspaper reports that the Education Committee has declared that 'Textbooks that include stereotyped descriptions of Yemenites as "thin and little" or "looking like an Arab" should be removed from the nation's schools.' The short piece, unsurprisingly, does not offer any comment on the matter. It does, however, relay a criticism of stereotyping Yemenite Jews and a normalisation of 'Arabs' as undesirables. Of course it would be possible to challenge the notion that there are some defining physical attributes which merit the description of 'looking like an Arab' (or a Jew), but this is not a concern of the Education Committee. There have, for instance, been many occasions when security forces in Israel have stopped Yemenite Israelis to check their identification because they were suspected of being Arabs. It is, of course, through the demonisation of Arabs that 'appearing to be an Arab' has become an ideologically demeaning characteristic. The potential closeness of two Semitic peoples is thus constantly undermined by an insistence on a hierarchy of difference.

I have tried to demonstrate in these brief examples from one relatively moderate Israeli newspaper that the ideological conflation of Palestinian Arabs and Arabs generally is a well-established discursive strategy. The marginalisation or demonisation of Palestinian Arabs is also a *sine qua non* of most news reporting in the Israeli media. Whether the media are responsible for the demonisation process is not entirely clear. It is much more likely that they are responsible for the marginalisation process. There is certainly a tendency in the *Jerusalem Post* for the journalist to act as simply the bearer of a message. The absence of either comment or analysis could be interpreted as an effort towards 'objective' reporting. If so, it does not work.

'Race', identity and the international audience

It is apparent from the consideration of a number of production and reception contexts that the issue of identity is often central in representations of matters concerning 'race'. It is sometimes addressed directly, as when the Israelis debate what is meant by being a Jew. It is sometimes addressed through forms of denial, such as the insistence by Pauline Hanson that Australia is not a part of Asia, and hence Australians are not to be thought of as Asians. It is sometimes addressed by marginalising or absenting from representation that which might cause ideological problems. I am referring here to the way in which the Palestinian or Aboriginal people can be excluded from media representations when the interests of the 'normal' citizens are under consideration.

In each of these examples, there is the construction or sustenance of the image of an 'other' or a 'stranger'. When qualities of Otherness cannot be sustained because the possibility of a shared humanity threatens to become dominant, the media may ignore an issue or sandwich it in such a way as to neutralise its humanising potential. The former is what happened with the death of the young Aborigine, Louis Johnson, and the latter with the three Palestinian women in Jerusalem. For those readers of media messages who are interested and able to consider representations from various regions and nations, questions of difference and universality are of paramount importance. Making sense, for instance, of the story of a firebombing in Jerusalem if one is neither a Jew nor an Arab, requires the reader to change reading positions and endure the contradictions which such changes engender. This can lead to insecurities in terms of one's own identity as well as the identities of others. It has been characterised by some as a post-modern phenomenon, which at its most acute can lead to a condition of *ambient fear*. This may include the fear of impending civil wars, or fear about job security in a world where wealth is perversely distributed, or insecurity about the nature of the social worlds which we inhabit (Bauman, 1997). Because most of the information about 'others' and 'race' is available only through the mass media, the international or global dimension of representing 'race' is even more problematic than that which is concerned with local or regional affairs. Images of issues of 'race' are likely to be multiple, fragmented and transitory. Bauman has gone so far as to argue that one's identity is today constantly assembled from overlays of easily assembled and dismantled shapes or characteristics which result in a kind of *palimpsest identity*.

> This is the kind of identity that fits the world in which the art of forgetting is an asset no less – if no more – important than the art of memorising; in which forgetting, rather than learning, is the condition of continuous fitness; in which ever new things and people enter and exit, without much rhyme or reason, the field of vision of the stationary camera of attention, and where memory itself is like videotape, always ready to be wiped clean in order to admit new images, and boasting a lifelong guarantee thanks only to that wondrous capacity of endless self-effacement.
>
> (Bauman, 1997, pp. 53–4)

Bauman is, of course, using the image of the static camera as a fertile metaphor. If we modify what he has to say and make the viewer static with the camera in constant movement, we find something very close to the condition of media consumption for many audiences. The audience experiences a kind of discursive stasis, jarred from time to time by major media events such as Live Aid, but with a tendency to return to a state of uneasy equilibrium. The art of forgetting is also something which helps to sustain what Bauman refers to as a condition of 'fitness'. It is perhaps a fitness which needs to be read ironically, because it is sustained as part of an ideological relationship. Fitness can then be recognised as a synonym for ideologically appropriate behaviour.

One more example which is both national and global might serve to illustrate the ways in which ambient fear can be melded with forgetfulness in order to produce the 'fitness' of the media audience in relation to issues of 'race'. The Italian clothes manufacturers Benetton have been running a successful advertising campaign since 1985 under the generic title of The United Colors of Benetton. The campaign has attracted a great deal of attention and critique from media and cultural studies researchers (Giroux, 1994; Ferguson, 1995). Giroux has noted that Benetton has reworked the relationship between identity formation, commerce, politics and pedagogy. I have argued that the whole Benetton campaign could be interpreted as a confidence trick or a genuine attempt to produce socially aware, concerned customers. More disturbingly, perhaps, it may be both at the same time. Most readers of this book are likely to have encountered Benetton advertisements, even if they have never bought a garment bearing the famous green trademark. I am not going to discuss the advertisements, but the magazine which Benetton publishes with the title *Colors*. Issue number 14, published as a dual language edition in English and Italian, has the title War (*Guerra*).

Colors is a magazine which is saturated with images. The War edition contains over 200, many of which are more shocking than anything which would find its way into a news bulletin or a newspaper story. Text is kept to a minimum and serves as classical Barthesian anchorage. The (postmodern) narrative can be grasped quite quickly if we consider some main headings: What is war for you? Something on TV? Part of your culture? Your business? Does it affect how you play? What you eat? Who you marry? Each of these headings act as a piece of ironic anchorage. For instance, the double-page spread with the caption 'Your business?' is composed of three images, two of which take the upper and lower half of one page, and one of which takes the whole of the second page. The first image is of what appears to be an arms fair, or perhaps an exhibition in an airport. Three white men sit on chairs on a temporary patio, at the end of which sits a red missile with a US star on it. The second image shows several black men and women in what appears to be a factory making prosthetic limbs for victims of war. The third image, a full page, shows a man in what could be Afghan costume, but might be something else, sitting in a shop full of small arms. He is apparently talking on the telephone and is seated on a decorative carpet which is covered with submachine guns. Unless you are a scholar of such things, you will not know where any of these pictures were taken, nor the conditions from which they spring. If you wish, you can try to look for further information at the end of the magazine. There is a list of photo credits which, quite literally, require a magnifying glass to read them. They provide the names of photographers and nothing else. This example is a very mild initiation into what is to come. The images simply show the tools of war and do not show the results of their use. Later in the magazine we will be shown the latter. On page 15 the question is posed, 'What is war for?' We are informed that humans spend $1 trillion a year on war, and that governments say military spending is an investment in the future. Another question is posed: 'What could this possibly mean?' In order to answer the question, a contents table is provided, with such headings as: new customers! new recipes! new fashions!

The 'new customers' section provides images of an arms fair in Aldershot in the UK. It includes some white male salespersons discussing some weaponry mounted on a jeep with uniformed Black African officers. The brief text which accompanies these images is a damning indictment of the arms trade and the named nations who sell most of the arms: 'Even a genocide is a business opportunity'. On the next double-page spread there is first a single image of a machete, then a full-page portrait of a young unnamed boy in Rwanda who carries a gigantic scar across the bridge of his nose and his cheeks, presumably inflicted by a machete blow. The text around the image of the machete points out that several victims were reported to have paid money to be shot with an AK-47 rather than be hacked to death with a machete. There is something macabre in the layout of the page and the juxtaposition with the face of the young man. More than once in the publication we observe others who show a ghoulish fascination in observing mutilated or dead bodies. We are the guests at this feast of violence and slaughter. On the next double page there is, first an image of the P90, a new type of assault rifle, which we are told, fires a bullet which, on entering the head, transfers its energy to the brain, creating an explosion that forces brain tissue through the sinuses and the seams of the cranium. On the next page is a full-page close up of an unnamed 'Gun victim in Monrovia, Liberia.' The colour image shows a full-face portrait of a person who has had the top of his/her head blown away and the contents of the skull are spilling out on the ground. The text goes on to point out that 'the wound featured here was not inflicted by the P90', but that the brochure for the weapon assures the buyer that it has been designed for 'maximum wound profile'. The next double page shows a landmine, followed by an image of two legs which have been recently severed at or below the knee. We can see blood, tendon, bone, hanging skin. It is labelled as a 'Mine victim in Quetta Hospital, Pakistan, 1995'. There is more. Later in the issue we are shown a small fashion section which, under the headings of sportswear, ready-to-wear, *haute couture* and club wear, offers us composite photomontage images of ammunition, decorative feathers, machine guns, rifles, prosthetic limbs and night vision goggles on a range of composite military figures. It is, I suppose, an attempt at wit. The issue finishes by making some suggestions, in line with the thinking of Mr Toscani, the inspiration behind the main photographic campaigns at Benetton, that anti-war advertising could be sponsored by major brand names like Coca Cola or Marlboro. By this time the magazine has become either politically naïve or cruelly cynical.

The reason for this brief consideration of one issue of *Colors* is that it provides, once again, an example of how Otherness is represented, even in death. It cannot be an accident that all the mutilated bodies and corpses in the magazine are black. It cannot be an act of solidarity with black victims of war to show their dismembered or mutilated unnamed bodies in order to work for international peace. If the mutilated bodies had been white and named, and shown in the same horrendous detail, what might have been the consequence? For white and named is at one end of a representational spectrum, at the other end of which is black and unnamed. The new globalisation, the new internationalism, the new sensitivity to war is highly colour (in)sensitive.

Conclusion

I have tried to argue that an international perspective to representations of issues of 'race' has to be considered along two parallel semiotic trajectories. First, there are, indeed, common factors in the representation of Otherness which are produced in different social and political contexts. This commonality is that of the marginalisation or demonisation of others. Second, where an international perspective on such issues is claimed, a key factor in deciding upon what can be represented and the gruesome detail with which it can be shown, is often that of 'race'. If this hypothesis holds up, it suggests that there is much work to be done before the media can claim to have transcended a racialised prioritisation of human dignity and worth. The cruellest totalising irony which stems from all the ambient fear which the privileged may have to endure is that it points towards the need for a form of media representation which 'recognises the diversity of peoples and the unity of the human race at one and the same time' (Todorov, 1993, p. 353).

12

Paradigms for the future?

I have never been persuaded, however, that racism is as all-pervasive as Professor Williams seems to claim – or that making us ever more conscious of it will help it to go away. I suppose I am of the old-fashioned school that thinks that it is good to be unconscious of racial differences and to think of people in other ways.

(Roger Scruton, visiting Professor of Philosophy, Birkbeck College, University of London)

Of course, you're saying that as a white male, aren't you?

(Sue McGregor, Broadcaster)

(From the discussion of Professor Patricia Williams' Reith Lectures, BBC Radio 4, 1 January 1997)

On ideology ...

Professor Scruton begins his contribution to this radio discussion with a fundamental confusion between racism and what he describes as 'racial differences'. The two points which he makes are, however, very relevant to this closing chapter. First, he is right to say that making people more aware of the existence of racism does not necessarily make it go away. It is unlikely, however, that many serious thinkers would argue that it is therefore better to be unconscious of such things. Scruton's position might help to explain why there is very little serious theoretical or empirical research on issues of 'race' and the media from conservative thinkers. Second, 'racial differences' are only of consequence because of racism. They have no serious basis in science, and to continue to use the phrase as a conversational gambit accepts as foundational something which is, in the end, merely inflammatory. The third point, which I would add is that it is so much easier to think this way if you are a middle-class white male. The fact that the statement was made on the radio by a prominent conservative philosopher in 1997 suggests that the ways in which issues of 'race' are addressed in the media are in still need of urgent investigation. I began this book by arguing that we cannot stand outside ideology when researching representations of 'race' in the media. I further suggested that the value of recognising the ideological dimensions of media messages and media research was that it could establish a sense of *productive unease*. I wish to explore a little further what this might mean by looking back over the ground I have attempted to cover and relating it to some developments in media research.

The relationship between ideology and the media has been on the research agenda for a long time, although it is occupying a back seat at the moment. It has been addressed specifically and in detail and it has been discussed at a more general level (Hall, 1978; Thompson, 1990). As previously noted, however, there is less work which specifically addresses issues of 'race' and the media. It is for this reason that such pieces as Hall's 'The whites of their eyes: racist ideologies and the media' remain so significant (Hall, 1981). In this work, Hall distinguishes between inferential and overt racism and suggests that the former relates to 'those apparently naturalised representations of events and situations relating to race, whether "factual" or "fictional", which have racist premises and propositions inscribed in them as a set of *unquestioned assumptions*' (Hall, 1981, p. 28–52). I have tried to extend this argument about representations based upon unquestioned assumptions. In doing so I have drawn upon a range of possible analytical devices, including the concept of implicature and the suggestion that there is in a given social formation a *discursive reserve* which is built, sustained, and occasionally challenged in a number of ways.

... and contradiction

I have also suggested that the concept of *contradiction* is important if we are to research media representations of issues of 'race'. This can be illustrated if we consider certain specific discourses which may together constitute the discursive reserve. The media, for instance, may have suggested that certain groups (often called 'immigrant' groups) are less inclined to work than others. This same group may then be represented on another occasion as willing to 'stay open day and night' if they happen to own a shop of some kind. At the same time comedy shows will be made where the lazy and unproductive lives of the indigenous (white) population are celebrated. The contradictions thrown up by these representations are played off against each other in a kind of miniature cultural *episteme* where they tend to sustain ideological relations of power and subordination rather than challenge them. Racist ideology, and probably ideology in general, can draw upon a discursive reserve which allows for all these different positions to be adopted as part of a unitary (if brittle) world-view. If the contradictions become too gross they will either be avoided in 'serious' programmes or, in comedy programmes, used as a means of attacking critics of such comedy for having an under-developed sense of humour. Behind these apparently contradictory positions, however, there are dimensions of racism which remain relatively stable.

It is important to note the difference between recognising contradiction when it is used to justify ideological relations or recognising contradiction as a signification of ideological power plays. It is, for instance, the utilisation of 'common sense' (that great flattener of contradiction) which can allow the viewer, listener or reader to balance out contradictions in daily life; and it is a sense of professional practice which can allow the media producer to know which topics or themes can be raised at the same time or associated one with the other. Where contradictions are highlighted in a media representation, we find confusion, embarrassment, and sometimes hostility. In Chapter 8 we saw how Jon Snow wrestled unsuccessfully with the contradictions brought up in a programme concerned with the far right in Europe. A different and much rarer example would be Nana Mahomo's documentary *Last Grave at Dimbaza* (1974), in which economic exploitation and white privilege are highlighted and contrasted with the suffering and death of children under the apartheid regime. In this case the contradictions which are highlighted are those between the 'civilised' comfort of the benefactors from apartheid, as they sit in cafés and sip their coffee or beer, and the small empty graves awaiting the bodies of the next children to die in Dimbaza. Such contradictions were sufficiently poignant to keep the film from the television screen for a long time. When it was shown in the UK, it was immediately followed by a documentary made by the apartheid regime, showing happy black citizens living in pleasant houses, wearing suits and driving cars. It was the ideological concept of 'balance' which worked towards reducing the political and economic implications of the representations of 'race' shown in *Last Grave at Dimbaza*. The concept of balance in relation to media representations of 'race' is mechanical and too often dependent upon crass binary thinking.

Audience research and issues of 'race'

There are three main approaches to the identification, study and research of issues of 'race' and racism in the media. None of them presupposes a singular research method. The first is that of the interpretation of texts; the second is concerned with the audience for media representations; and the third is concerned with the production contexts and their economies. There continue to be variations on this theme but the circuit of culture so elegantly theorised by Richard Johnson and recently developed by Paul du Gay is still most relevant (Johnson, 1986; Du Gay *et al.*, 1997). I have concentrated in this book on questions of textual interpretation. This has been a matter of choice and prioritisation, and it does not indicate any disregard for the importance of studies of the production context or for audience research. I wish to say something about the latter because I believe it to be most significant for future research into issues of 'race' and the media.

A great deal of research in the last two decades has been concerned to demonstrate the ways in which audiences interact with the media. Some of the research has gone to great pains to show that the audience actively makes sense of media messages (Ang, 1985; Ang, 1991; Buckingham, 1987; Morley, 1986; Fiske, 1989; Fiske, 1994). In part, this could be argued to have occurred as a response to heavy-handed and over-determinist researchers who had suggested that the viewer was a helpless victim of the text. The main culprits here were allegedly people called *Screen* theorists because they had written for the British journal of the same name. There is some truth in the fact that some of the writers associated with *Screen* were over-zealous about mass powerlessness, and the elite role of the intellectuals in lifting the veil of ideological domination. Those researchers who moved towards what is often called the 'new' audience research often did so, however, with a similar zeal. They had discovered that the audience could think and that making meaning was something socially negotiated. James Curran (1990) has pointed out that many of their ideas were not exactly new.

More recently, Virginia Nightingale (1996) has examined developments in audience research. She notes that the new audience research seeks to demonstrate a sympathetic and understanding rather than derogatory orientation to the audience, and that David Buckingham, as one of its more prominent practitioners, has 'strategically changed the thrust of the cultural studies audience experiment' (Nightingale,

1996, p. 90). Nightingale argues that Buckingham reduces the power of the text to carry meaning and concentrates instead on its power to orchestrate discourse. It is thus by utilising the text that the audience speaks and negotiates meanings. The problem with this is that it does not allow any space for what Nightingale calls the text's 'discursive commitment'. The text's 'discursive commitment' would seem to be some kind of euphemism for its ideological positioning. The relegation of textual significance is graphically and regrettably illustrated in one of Buckingham's more excessive claims about television and children. I quote it here because it illustrates the way in which a refusal of the ideological, on the basis that one has rejected crass ideological determinism, can lead one down unproductive or counterproductive byways. It is also arguable that Buckingham's reading of the example which follows is somewhat preconditioned by his relationship with the audience which is the subject of his research. Buckingham is here discussing the children's television entertainer Timothy Mallett who appeared in a programme called *Wacaday* which was produced by the now defunct TV-AM. Buckingham notes that Mallett 'carries the clownlike persona of the children's presenter to its extreme. His typical outfit will include a luminous striped T-shirt and clashing, equally luminous Paisley shorts' (Buckingham, 1995, p. 54). Buckingham makes some heavily ironic judgements about Mallett and then lets his own sense of irony run away with him. He discusses the fact that *Wacaday* was a programme with 'educational pretensions'. Each week the programme took a different country as a theme. In 1991 Mallett visited South Africa where we

> saw Timmy dressed in a Zulu warrior outfit and pith helmet, consulting a witch doctor, and then attacking the tribesmen with his mallet; beating the locals in an ostrich race; and telling the story of the 'heroic bravery' of the British soldiers at Rorke's Drift.
>
> (Buckingham, 1995, pp. 56–7)

Buckingham links this sentence with an endnote which highlights his own way of dealing with contradiction through sardonic humour and heavy irony.

> Further examples of Timothy Mallett's acute political analysis may be found in *Timothy Mallett's Utterly Brilliant History of the World* – needless to say, a book regularly promoted on *Wacaday*. While not

recommended for readers of an ideologically sensitive disposition, it has all the credentials for a National Curriculum History textbook.

(Buckingham, 1995, p. 61)

Whatever one thinks of this, the key point to note is that Buckingham is forced by his own irony to pronounce upon the meaning of the programme in a way which exceeds in interpretative certainty the claims of most other contemporary commentators:

> The point here, however, is not simply that Timothy Mallett is right-wing, or patronising towards other cultures, or even that he trivialises important political issues. While I personally find this offensive, I don't believe it makes very much difference to the children who watch the programme ... It seems absurd even to entertain the idea that Timothy Mallett is a kind of political Svengali, mesmerising innocent children into ideological torpor.
>
> (Buckingham, 1995, p. 57)

Buckingham is clearly not of an ideologically sensitive disposition. He is also able to make judgements as an adult about television programmes which he is confident will have no effect on children. Those with whom Buckingham disagrees are never granted that privilege. The catalogue of faults (I assume that is what Buckingham thinks they are) in Mallett's programmes can be dismissed by reducing the complexities of ideological analysis to 'mesmerising children into ideological torpor'. The reference in the endnote to the National Curriculum in History is another ironic swipe at the deficiencies (real enough) of history curricula in the United Kingdom. But it is all the subject of ironic or sardonic dismissal. I have tried to argue throughout this book that we have to be sensitive to all forms of 'normalising' signification. To this I would certainly add the sardonic normalisation of the world of Timothy Mallett, and the discourses of those who would normalise ideological insensitivity or incomprehension as virtues. I do not think that Buckingham's analysis demonstrates a sympathetic and understanding orientation to the audience – particularly if they happen to be on the receiving end of racist signification and behaviour. He is, however, pronouncing upon issues which are very much concerned with representations of 'race'. Much of the contemporary audience research simply skirts round such issues in its search for evidence of the audience's patterns of active media consumption and utilisation.

On the collection and analysis of data ...

Audience research relies, in major part, upon the collection of data about its subject. This very often takes the form of interviews of one kind or another. The first point to note is that, in order for such research to be analysed or commented upon, the interviews are turned into text. The researchers' analysis of the medium as text is thus replaced by the analysis of the audience as text. The second is the nature of the interviews or discussions, which are usually recorded and transcribed before analysis. Although they may run into hundreds or even thousands of pages of transcript, individual contributions are often rather brief and fragmented. They are further fragmented by the selection which the researcher makes in order to be able to manage the weight of the data. They are then interpreted by the researcher, often without the methodological rigour associated with traditional discourse analysis, or the slightly more adaptable approach to interpretation of the social semioticians (Hodge and Kress, 1988). They are, in effect, commented upon. This is not necessarily a weakness if the research is somehow rooted in a more general theoretical commitment to questions of, for instance, power or epistemology, or even communicative efficacy. Commentary on small sections of interviews cannot, of itself, tell us much about the audience and their relationship with the society of which they are a part, or of their detailed or long-term understandings of media messages. It can, in part, offer us insights into the ways in which meanings are negotiated in a particular context. To take the analysis any further, the researcher has to import a wide range of judgements which are not part of the research, usually not part of the experience of the research subjects, and seldom directly related to the research methodology. There are exceptions, and examples of productive analyses of this kind would include those undertaken by Fowler and by Potter and Wetherell, and commented upon in Chapter 2.

One possible clue as to how audience research into questions of 'race' might be productively developed has been provided by Rae Sherwood in *The Psychodynamics of Race* (1980). The research is based upon many hours of interviews with families. Their attitudes to matters concerning 'race' are allowed to emerge as they tell stories about their lives and their feelings. It is a lengthy process and is based on unstructured interviews. The interviewers tried to refrain from giving responses which would either praise or condemn anything which was said. Interviewees were allowed to explore their understandings of issues relating to 'race' and identity at length. They were also sufficiently relaxed or unthreatened to speak in a manner which is much more open and extended than that found in a great deal of audience research. The resulting transcripts are much less constrained or hemmed in with qualifications than those often found in comparable situations where the research is about issues relating to the media. It also means that many of the subjects make statements which make explicit their fears and insecurities as well as their judgements about various 'others'. The comments which the subjects offer are also only a part of a larger narrative in which they speak of just about every aspect of their lives which they consider to be important. I offer this as an example without prejudging the nature of the textual analysis which has to take place in order to comment on the responses of the subjects. The complexity of responses in relation to the overall social, economic and emotional situation of the subjects demonstrates just how careful one has to be about interpreting audience responses to the media, and how limited so much data collection has been.

To illustrate the point I offer just a small section of one subject's comments. He is a Mr Chattaway (a fictional name, as is the area of London in which he lives) from Athol and he is speaking *amongst many other things* of his thoughts about Indians as motorists.

I get irritated by Indian motorists. They turn left or right without any indicators and that's what get up my back. [*sic*] And if the lights are green and I'm going across in my car and they walk in front of me, I drive for them. I know it's wrong. [Laughs] My missus gets scared [laughs] because when the light says green for me I go, and if they walk across then, they're taking a chance. They're in the wrong because they shouldn't cross. I've had some near misses – ooh yeah ... regularly every morning, down here at the end of my road, I don't stop for them. I tell you my missus gets worried about it and says 'You'll kill one of them one of these days'. As I say, I've got the lights in my favour, I've paid my insurance and road tax and I obey all the rules and regulations and they must do the same. What's good enough for me is good enough for them. So if they want to walk in front of me and take a chance, well that's up to them. So far I've only skinned them. [Laughs] They get away with murder. If the lights are in my favour I do everything I should do. Whites automatically stop, they don't take chances like that, but the Indians just walk across ignorantly as if you have to stop for them. Well, I don't,

I'm afraid, I don't. If they want to live in this country, then they've got to do the same things as I do. If the lights say 'Go', I go – if it says 'Stop' I stop. They must do the same instead of just turning left and right without indicators. They just get up my back. You just look at their cars – they've got bashes and bangs on them where people have hit them. It's because they just don't bother – it's like their own country, all run to wrack and ruin.

(Sherwood, 1980, p. 134)

The above transcript offers rich soil for the discourse analyst. It also reads as though written by Johnny Speight as a rejected script for Alf Garnett. But it is neither. It is part of a narrative told by Mr Chattaway about his youth, his wartime service, his feelings about the price of housing and a host of other things. It is very clear that they all have or had an impact upon his understanding of the world, and his racist outlook. For the audience researcher such information is rarely if ever available or taken into account. If each viewer is as complex as this, and I suggest that most are much more complex, then the investigation of the audience requires much sensitivity and patience. It seems absurd to ask subjects for their responses to media representations and 'interpret' their responses without taking the complexities of their daily lives into account, without *situating* their readings. This is not an argument for abandoning audience research based upon interviews – far from it. It is, however, a plea for a reconsideration of how the media researcher/ethnographer might approach her/his subjects. Nor is it an argument for abandoning detailed research into and interpretation of media texts.

The 'Rocky' road to the audience

I want first to comment on a now deservedly well-known piece of research which points another way forward, though it is also fraught with difficulties. I am referring to Valerie Walkerdine's 'Video replay: family, films and fantasy' (Walkerdine, 1986). The research is not specifically concerned with issues of 'race'. Walkerdine recounts her experience at the home of the Cole family, where she has gone because she is engaged in a research project concerned with 6-year-old girls and their education. It just happens that the Cole family are viewing *Rocky II* on video, and this becomes the spur which leads Walkerdine on a research path which she had not planned. She recognises that she has almost stumbled into a piece of small-scale audience research, and that such research has a strong voyeuristic potential. The data which she collects is based largely on notes written up after the viewing. The interpretation of the data involves a considerable amount of self-interrogation. Walkerdine is very aware of the need for empirical work which reasserts 'the importance of the creation of subjectivity as active, even if the subject is caught at an intersection of discourses and practices' (Walkerdine, 1986, p. 188). Walkerdine's own methodology leads her to engage with psychoanalytic theory, and to include elements of her own childhood and family history in the interpretations of her data. I am not concerned to appraise this dimension of her work, however, but to highlight two important points. The first is that Walkerdine realises that her research gained considerable impetus due to the fact that the Cole family thought she was researching something else! The problem with so much contemporary audience research is that it is carried out in such a way that the subjects are likely to prepare their personae in advance. In effect, the researcher is usually finding out how a subject will behave if they become part of a small research project. How they might have behaved otherwise remains a relative mystery. There are also numerous ethical issues which are raised by the possibility that research might be undertaken surreptitiously. The second point is that Walkerdine is still struggling with the question of whether and how much the text determines the subjectivity of the audience and hence their potential response. In the sentence quoted above she seems to be reformulating the suggestion that we may make our own history, but not in the conditions of our choosing. I wish to argue that audience research, particularly that concerned with issues of 'race', should not become trapped in the 'textual determination' versus 'active creation of subjectivity' circle. The importance of reintroducing the question of ideology into research about representations of 'race' is that it is based upon the assumption that meaning is negotiated socially, struggled over, and occasionally contested. Responses to and understandings of representations of 'race' can then be conceptualised as a relationship in which all parties are conscious, thinking beings. Ideology is not something which is *done* to someone or some group. Ideology, as I have argued throughout this book, is a relationship of power and subordination. Audience researchers have still a long way to go before they unravel how that relationship is constituted and sustained.

The above issues are not a digression from the main theme of this book. They have been mentioned because the new audience research has been notable for the way in which it has not addressed issues of 'race' in the media. It may be that the question of 'race' and racism is something to which the new audience research will eventually turn its attention. It may also be that investigating such questions would require some methodological reappraisals. If benign or malevolent racism exists, it will seldom manifest itself directly in an interview session with a researcher. If racism is perceived in texts or if the interviewees wish to express anti-racist or racist sentiments, this is more likely to occur when the interviewees feel secure, whether they be perpetrators or recipients of racism. Nightingale reminds us of Eco's perceptive judgements, almost a quarter of a century ago, about the dangers of equating what is said by an audience with what they may have understood. She also refers to the problem of what is said and what remains unspoken (Nightingale, 1996, p. 99).

On interpretation

Silverman and Torode (1980) argue that interpretation involves a widespread practice of linguistic mastery. They also argue that this is not confined to the academy, but can also be found in linguistic practice in such settings as schools and hospitals. To this we must also add the linguistic practices of the media. Interpretation is something which is all-pervasive and, they suggest, needs an interruption of 'the conventional setting, text, and debate' in order to identify the ways in which this linguistic mastery is utilised. This concept of interruption is important for two reasons for those studying representations of 'race' in the media. The first is that it allows us to ask questions about the modalities and genres of the significations under scrutiny. The second is that it facilitates the continuous investigation of the relationship between language and reality:

> For us interruption is the attempt to reveal the interplay between 'appearance' and 'reality' within language itself. As against the view of language as a reality *sui generis*, whether transparent or opaque, we insist that language necessarily refers, as appearance, to a reality other than itself. But, we propose, the way in which it does this is to refer *to other language*. Thus plurality is inseparable from language, and it is the play of reference from one language to another language that suggests the reference of language to a reality other than language.
>
> (Silverman and Torode, 1980, p. 8)

If they are right in suggesting that material reality is apprehended by a reference or cross-reference from one language to another, we are very close to the concept of intertextuality. I have tried to show in the examples chosen in this book that media texts do indeed refer to each other in important ways. Rather than referring to an external world, however, they can sometimes seem to be engaged in a complex semiotic exercise of keeping the world at bay. Instead of addressing the relationship between specific modes of signification and the material world, representations of issues concerning 'race' sometimes lose that material world and the material experience of those of us who inhabit it.

On modalities and generic forms

I hope that I have demonstrated, through my choice of examples from the press and the cinema, that specific media genres tend to adopt certain modal judgements in their representations of 'race'. The certitude of the tabloid headline can be contrasted with the implicature through which certain columnists can sustain xenophobic or racist discourse. In the cinema we can find propagandist exercises in identity building, or liberal narratives of (white) progress. We can also find generic forms that do problematise 'race' issues and leave the audience with many deliberately unanswered questions. What is required is both the study of individual genres and modalities, plus comparative studies of the ways in which similar issues are handled through different genres. Our understanding of representations of 'race' needs to develop through a recognition of the tensions, the overlaps and the contradictions which comparative study brings out. It is likely that comparative study will establish recurrent discursive patterns in the media representation of 'race', but considerable variety in the ways in which such patterns are embellished or improvised upon for contextually relevant effect.

On history and historiography

I have given some time to a consideration of the ways in which educational television approaches history and the representation of 'race'. The question of historiography is one that I think needs to be on the agenda of media researchers and students as a matter of some urgency. The histories which have been constructed in *Schindler's List*, in *Malcolm X*, in *Geronimo*, in talk radio shows, are just some examples of significant discursive and narrative fields which work to provide a sense of identity to a range of audiences. They also work to sustain, or sometimes challenge, relations of power and subordination in specific societies. In considering the discursive strategies which such media adopt, we must also work to avoid them being considered as *only* struggles over language, including audio-visual language. Historiography and media representation demonstrate at one and the same time the central importance of language, and the need to ensure that we never lose sight of the referents which exist beyond the intertextual.

On narrative

Most of the media examples included in this book are strongly narrativised accounts, whether they purport to be fact or fiction. Narratives of 'race' are also part of the discursive reserve. It is interesting to hypothesise that implicature may be more concerned with *narrative* propositions than with other propositional forms. Some of the narratives associated with race have been investigated by Van Dijk (1987; 1993b). His work and that of Sherwood may provide useful pointers for future audience research, though at the moment there is little evidence of detailed and penetrating analysis of audience perceptions of issues of 'race' and their understanding of the ideological dimensions of narrative structures. This is not meant to imply that any audience member should necessarily become involved in unravelling the complexities of narratology. What is does mean is that researchers need to establish whether and how audience members negotiate the ideological dimensions of, for example, the narrative structure of *Glory*. The challenge is to develop a methodology for such work which is not dogged by the kinds of weaknesses I have mentioned earlier. The narratives of news also need to be studied in relation to representations of 'race'. It is now arguable, for instance, that the narrative structures of the news in the 1970s in the UK can be recognised through relatively simple recurrent motifs. Black people were seen as 'the problem'. Muggers were the real threat to a stable society. News of black people meant news of trouble. These and other simple structures were struck like chords on a guitar, sometimes with the regularity of strumming, embellished with the details of the latest newsworthy occurrence. The turn of the century is likely to hear different narrative rhythms, but the ideological significance of representing fundamentalisms, national-isms, and essential identities will need most careful scrutiny and analysis.

Conclusion

I argued in Chapter 3 that there are serious problems for the media researcher in adopting uncritically the concept of difference when studying representations of 'race'. This does not imply that questions of identity and difference are somehow insignificant. Shelves of theo-retical and historical and textual analyses testify to the contrary. Nevertheless, representations that celebrate, for instance, cultural dif-ference can be seen to complement, and sometimes to encourage racist discourses where the concept of difference is condemnatory, vindic-tive and essential. The tensions between these apparently opposed discursive and representational fields need constant attention.

The question of identity is one that has been very important to the development of theories associated with postmodernism. Debates about the fluidity of identity and cultural hybridity are now a central part of many cultural and media studies courses. I have tried to indicate that cultural hybridity is an interesting and sometimes excit-ing concept, and one with considerable ideological importance. The celebration of identity and cultural hybridity could be read as a liberatory break from the shackles of determinism. It could also be read as the last gasps of the socially and politically disempowered. The representation of many issues relating to 'race' takes place within the discursive fields associated with these social, political and semiotic tensions. Research into the representation of 'race' as we approach the end of the twentieth century will need to grapple constantly with the contradictions which textual analyses will throw up, and to relate these to the contexts in which they have been produced and the contexts in which they will be 'read'.

The identification of contradiction and tension does not conjure up any specific paradigm for research. This is all to the good. I have, however, given some attention to audience research in this chapter because I think it is a field which has yet to deliver on its promise and potential. The sense of 'productive unease' about which I wrote at the beginning of this book is a necessary prerequisite for the study and research of representations of issues of 'race'. It requires a tireless engagement with theories of ideology, whether one is researching at the macro or the micro level. It also requires, as I have implied many times, an engagement with universalism over the particularisms which have become so much a part of media, philosophical and now political discourses (Eagleton, 1996, p. 121).

The historian Eric Hobsbawm has summarised the issue very precisely in relation to the study of history. What he writes is particularly appropriate if we may be permitted to substitute the study of media representations of 'race' for the concept of history:

> Historians, however microcosmic, must be for universalism, not out of loyalty to an ideal to which many of us remain attached but because it is the necessary condition for understanding the history of humanity, including that of any special section of humanity. For all human collectivities necessarily are and have been part of a larger and more complex world. A history which is designed *only* for Jews (or African Americans, or Greeks, or women, or proletarians, or homosexuals) cannot be good history, though it may be comforting history to those who practise it.
>
> (Hobsbawm, 1997, p. 277)

Filmography

Note: The film title is followed by the date of release, the production company and the name of the director.

Amistad, 1997, Dreamworks, Steven Spielberg
A Rage in Harlem, 1991, Miramax Films/Palace Pictures, Bill Duke
Cat Ballou, 1965, Colombia Pictures Corporation, Elliot Silverstein
Come See the Paradise, 1990, Twentieth Century Fox, Alan Parker
Cry Freedom, 1987, Universal Pictures, Richard Attenborough
Dances with Wolves, 1990, Majestic Film, TIG Productions, Kevin Costner
Deep Cover, 1992, New Line Cinema, Bill Duke
Force of Evil, 1948, Enterprise/MGM, Abraham Polonsky
From Here to Eternity, 1953, Colombia Pictures Corporation, Fred Zinnemann
Geronimo: An American Legend, 1993, Colombia Pictures Corporation, Walter Hill
Glory, 1989, TriStar Pictures, E. Zwick
Guess Who's Coming to Dinner, 1967, Colombia Pictures Corporation, Stanley Kramer
Last Grave at Dimbaza, 1974, Morena Films, N. Mahomo
Malcolm X, 1992, 40 Acres & A Mule Filmworks/JVC Entertainment/ Largo International N. V., Spike Lee
Mississippi Burning, 1988, Orion Pictures Corporation, Alan Parker
Muriel's Wedding, 1994, CiBy 200/House & Moorhouse Films/ Miramax Films/Australian Film Finance Corporation
Rocky II, 1979, Chartoff–Winkler Productions, Sylvester Stallone
Schindler's List, 1993, Universal Pictures, Steven Spielberg
Strictly Ballroom, 1992, M&A Film/Rank, Baz Luhrman
The Adventures of Priscilla, Queen of the Desert, 1994, Gramercy Pictures, Stephen Elliot

Bibliography

ALTHUSSER, L. 1970: *Reading Capital*. London: New Left Books.

ALTHUSSER, L. 1971a: Ideology and ideological state apparatuses: notes towards an investigation. In *Lenin and philosophy and other essays*. London, New York: New Left Books, Monthly Review Press, 121–73.

ALTHUSSER, L. 1971b: *Lenin and philosophy and other essays*. London, New York: New Left Books, Monthly Review Press.

ALTHUSSER, L. 1977: *For Marx*. London: New Left Books.

ANDERSON, B. 1991: *Imagined communities*. London: Verso.

ANG, I. 1985: *Watching Dallas: soap opera and the melodramatic imagination*. London: Methuen.

ANG, I. 1991: *Desperately seeking the audience*. London: Routledge.

BARTHES, R. 1972: *Mythologies*. London: Jonathan Cape.

BARTHES, R. 1977: *Image, music, text*. London: Collins.

BARTOV, O. 1997: Spielberg's Oskar: Hollywood tries evil. In Loshitsky, Y. (ed.), *Spielberg's Holocaust*. Bloomington: Indiana University Press.

BAUDRILLARD, J. 1991: The reality gulf. *Guardian*. London, 11 January.

BAUMAN, Z. 1989: *Modernity and the Holocaust*. Cambridge: Polity Press.

BAUMAN, Z. 1992: *Intimations of postmodernity*. London: Routledge.

BAUMAN, Z. 1996: From pilgrim to tourist. In Hall, S. and Du Gay, P., *Questions of cultural identity*. London: Sage.

BAUMAN, Z. 1997: The making and unmaking of strangers. In Werbner, P. and Modood, T. (eds), *Debating cultural hybridity*. London: Zed Books.

BENTON, T. 1984: *The rise and fall of structural marxism*. London: Macmillan.

BERNAL, M. 1987: *Black Athena*. New Brunswick, NJ: Rutgers University Press.

BILLIG, M. 1982: *Ideology and social psychology*. Oxford: Basil Blackwell.

BILLIG, M. 1990: Stacking the cards of ideology: the history of the *Sun Souvenir Royal Album, Discourse and Society*, I(1): 17–38.

BILLIG, M. 1991: *Ideology and opinions*. London: Sage.

BILLIG, M. *et al.* 1988: *Ideological dilemmas*. London: Sage.

BOCOCK, R. 1986: *Hegemony*. Chichester: Ellis Horwood.

BOYD, T. 1997: *Am I black enough for you?* Bloomington: Indiana University Press.

BREITMAN, G. (ed.) 1965: *Malcolm X speaks*. New York: Grove Weidenfeld.

BRONNER, S. E. and KELLNER, D. M., (eds) 1989: *Critical theory and society: a reader*. London: Routledge.

BRUNER, J. 1963: *The process of education*. New York: Vintage Books.

BUCKINGHAM, D. 1987: *Public secrets: Eastenders and its audience*. London: British Film Institute.

BUCKINGHAM, D. 1995: On the impossibility of children's television: the case of Timothy Mallett. In Buckingham, D. and Bazalgette, C. (eds), *In front of the children: screen entertainment and young audiences*. London: British Film Institute.

CALLINICOS, A. 1989: *Against postmodernism*. Cambridge: Polity Press.

CALLINICOS, A. 1990: Reactionary postmodernism. In Rattansi, A. and Boyne, R. (eds), *Postmodernism and society*. London: Macmillan.

CAMPBELL, C. P. 1995: *Race, myth and the news*. London: Sage.

CARR, E. H. 1978: *What is history?* London: Pelican.

CASAS, D. L. 1972: *The tears of the Indians*. New York: Oriole Chapbooks.

CERTEAU, M. de 1988: *The practice of everyday life*. London: University of California Press.

CURRAN, J. 1990: The new revisionism in mass communication research: a reappraisal. *European Journal of Communication*, 5(2): 145–51.

DEBO, A. 1986: *Geronimo: the man, his time, his place*. London: Random House.

DODGSON, P. 1991: *Royal Commission into Aboriginal deaths in custody: Regional report of inquiry into underlying issues in Western Australia*. Vol. 2. Canberra: AGPS.

DONESON, J. 1997: The image lingers: the feminisation of the Jew in

'Schindler's List'. In Loshitsky, Y. (ed.), *Spielberg's Holocaust*. Bloomington, Indiana University Press, 140–52.

DU GAY, P., HALL, S., JANES, L., MACKAY, H. and NEGUS, K. 1997: *Doing cultural studies*. London: Sage.

DUNAYEVSKAYA, R. 1973: *Philosophy and revolution*. Brighton: Harvester Press.

DYER, R. 1997: *White*. London: Routledge.

EAGLETON, T. 1991: *Ideology: an introduction*. London: Verso.

EAGLETON, T. 1996: *The illusions of postmodernism*. Oxford: Basil Blackwell.

EBERT, R. 1996: *Cinemania*. Bath: Future Publishing.

ECO, U. 1990: *The limits of interpretation*. Bloomington: Indiana University Press.

ELLIOTT, P. and GOLDING, P. 1979: *Making the news*. London: Longman.

FAIRCLOUGH, N. 1989: *Language and power*. London: Edward Arnold.

FERGUSON, B. 1985: Children's television: the germination of ideology. In Drummond, P. and Lusted, D. (eds), *TV and schooling*. London: BFI/Institute of Education, 47–52.

FERGUSON, R. 1995: Race, gender and a touch of class. In Prentice, R. (ed.), *Teaching art and design*. London: Cassell, 50–64.

FERRO, M. 1984: *The use and abuse of history*. London: Routledge and Kegan Paul.

FISKE, J. 1989: *Reading the popular*. London: Unwin Hyman.

FISKE, J. 1994: *Media matters: everyday culture and political change*. London: University of Minnesota Press.

FOUCAULT, M. 1980: *Power/knowledge*. London: Harvester–Wheatsheaf.

FOWLER, R. 1986: *Linguistic criticism*. Oxford: Oxford University Press.

FOWLER, R., HODGE, R. KRESS, G. and TREW, T. 1979: *Language and control*. London: Routledge and Kegan Paul.

GALEANO, E. 1973: *Open veins of Latin America*. New York: Monthly Review Press.

GALTUNG, J. and RUGE, M.H. 1965: The structure of foreign news. *Journal of International Peace Research*, 1, 64–90.

GARNHAM, N. 1990: *Capitalism and communication*. London: Sage.

GILBERT, R. 1984: *The impotent image: reflections of ideology in the secondary school curriculum*. Lewes: Falmer Press.

GILROY, P. 1997: Diaspora and the detours of identity. In Woodward, K. (ed.), *Identity and difference*. London: Sage.

GIROUX, H. 1994: *Disturbing pleasures: learning popular culture*. London: Routledge.

GOODING-WILLIAMS, R. (ed.) 1993: *Reading Rodney King: reading urban uprising*. London: Routledge.

GORDON, P. and ROSENBERG, D. 1989: *The press and black people in Britain*. London: Runnymede Trust.

GRAMSCI, A. 1971: *Selections from the prison notebooks*. London: Lawrence and Wishart.

GUERRERO, E. 1993: *Framing blackness: the African American image in film*. Philadelphia: Temple.

HALL, S. 1977: Culture, the media and the 'ideological effect'. In Curran, J. *et al. Mass communication and society*. London: Edward Arnold.

HALL, S. 1981: The whites of their eyes: racist ideologies and the media. In Bridges, G. and Brunt, R. (eds), *Silver Linings*. London: Lawrence and Wishart.

HALL, S. 1982: The rediscovery of 'ideology': return of the repressed in media studies. In Curran, J. *et al.* (eds), *Culture, society and the media*. London: Methuen.

HALL, S. 1983: The problem of ideology: Marxism without guarantees. In Matthews, B. (ed.), *Marx 100 Years On*. London: Lawrence and Wishart.

HALL, S. 1988: The toad in the garden: Thatcherism amongst the theorists. In Nelson, C. and Grossberg, L. (eds), *Marxism and the interpretation of culture*. London: Macmillan.

HALL, S. 1991: The west and the rest. In King, A.D. (ed.), *Culture, globalisation and the world system: contemporary conditions for the representation of identity*. Basingstoke: Macmillan.

HALL, S. 1992: The question of cultural identity. In Hall, S., Held, D. and McGrew, T. (eds), *Modernity and its futures*. Cambridge: Polity Press, 274–313.

HALL, S. 1996: Signification, representation, ideology: Althusser and the post-structuralist debates. In Curran, J., Morley, D. and Walkerdine, V. (eds), *Cultural studies and communications*. London: Arnold.

HALL, S. 1997: The spectacle of the 'other'. In Hall, S. (ed.) *Representation*. London: Sage.

HALL, S., CURTI, L. and CONNELL, I. 1976: The unity of current affairs television. *Working Papers in Cultural Studies 9*. Birmingham: Hutchinson.

HALL, S., CRITCHER, C., JEFFERSON, T., CLARKE, J. and ROBERTS, B. 1978: *Policing the crisis: 'mugging', the state and law and order*. London: Macmillan.

HAMMOND, P. (ed.) 1997: *Cultural differences, media memories: Anglo-American images of Japan*. London: Cassell.

HAMMOND, P. and STIRNER, P. 1997: Fear and loathing in the British press. In Hammond, P. (ed.), *Cultural differences, media and memories*. London: Cassell.

HAWKES, T. 1977: *Structuralism and semiotics*. London: Methuen.

HEATH, S. and SKIRROW, G. 1977: Television: a world in action. *Screen*, 18(2): 7–77.

HEBDIGE, D. 1988: *Hiding in the light*. London: Routledge.

HOBSBAWM, E. 1997: *On history*. London: Weidenfeld and Nicolson.

HODGE, R. and KRESS, G. 1988: *Social semiotics*. Cambridge: Polity Press.

HODGE, R. and KRESS, G. 1993: *Language as ideology*. London: Routledge.

HOLQUIST, M. (ed.) 1981: *The dialogic imagination*. Austin: University of Texas Press.

hooks, b. 1994: *Outlaw culture: resisting representations*. London: Routledge.

HOROWITZ, S. R. 1997: But is it good for the Jews? Spielberg's Schindler and the aesthetics of atrocity. In Loshitsky, Y. (ed.), *Spielberg's Holocaust*. Bloomington: Indiana University Press, 119–39.

HOWE, D. 1987: *Washington Post*, 6 November.

HUMAN RIGHTS COMMISSION 1991: *National inquiry into racist violence*. Australia.

HUNT, D. M. 1997: *Screening the Los Angeles 'riots'*. Cambridge: Cambridge University Press.

INTERNET MOVIE DATABASE http://uk.imdb.com/

JACUBOWICZ, A., GOODALL, H., MARTIN, J., MITCHELL, T., RANDALL, L. and SENEVERATNE, K. 1994: *Racism, ethnicity and the media*. St Leonards, New South Wales: Allen and Unwin.

JAMESON, F. 1991: *Postmodernism, or, the cultural logic of late capitalism*. London: Verso.

JAY, M. 1984: *Marxism and totality*. Berkeley, California: University of California Press.

JHALLY, S. and LEWIS, J. 1992: *Enlightened racism*. Boulder, Col.: Westview Press.

JOHNSON, R. 1986: What is cultural studies anyway? *Social text* (16): 38–80.

JOHNSTON, A. 1991: Families at war. In Prinsloo, J. and Criticos, C. (eds), *Media matter in South Africa*. Durban: University of Natal, 87–94.

KENNEDY, G. 1978: *The death of Captain Cook*. London: Duckworth.

KONING, H. 1991: *Columbus: his enterprise*. London: Latin American Bureau.

LARRAIN, J. 1979: *The concept of ideology*. London: Hutchinson.

LEE, S. 1992: *By any means necessary*. New York: Hyperion.

LUSTED, D. and DRUMMOND, P. (eds) 1985: *TV and schooling*. London: British Film Institute.

MACKENZIE, J. 1995: *Orientalism: history, theory and the arts*. Manchester: Manchester University Press.

MALIK, K. 1996: *The meaning of race*. Basingstoke: Macmillan.

MARCUSE, H. 1972a: *Reason and revolution*. London: Routledge and Kegan Paul.

MARCUSE, H. 1972b: *One dimensional man*. London: Abacus.

MARX, K. and ENGELS, F. 1973: *Selected Works*. Volume 3. Moscow: Progress Publishers.

MARX, K. and ENGELS, F. 1976: *The German ideology*. London: Lawrence and Wishart.

MCLENNAN, G. 1992: The enlightenment project revisited. In Hall, S., Held, D. and McGrew, T. (eds), *Modernity and its futures*. Cambridge: Polity Press.

MCLEOD, J., KOSICKI, G.M. and ZHONGDAN, P. 1991: On understanding and misunderstanding media effects. In Curran, J. and Gurevitch, M. (eds), *Mass media and society*. London: Edward Arnold, 235–66.

MEDVED, M. 1992: *Hollywood versus America*. New York: HarperCollins.

MERQUIOR, J. G. 1985: *Foucault*. London: Collins.

MICKLER, S. 1994: *Gambling on the first race: a comment on racism and talk-back radio – 6PR, the TAB and WA government*. Louis St John Johnson Memorial Trust Fund: http://kqli.murdoch.edu.au/cnfinwm/CRCC/fellows/mickler/reports/g-index.html.

MORLEY, D. 1986: *Family television: cultural power and domestic leisure*. London: Comedia.

NICHOLS, B. 1991: *Representing reality*. Bloomington: Indiana University Press.

NIGHTINGALE, V. 1996: *Studying audiences: the shock of the real*. London: Routledge.

NLB (ed.) 1977: *Aesthetics and politics*. London: New Left Books.

NORRIS, C. 1990: Lost in the funhouse: Baudrillard and the politics of postmodernism. In Rattansi, A. and Boyne, R. (eds), *Postmodernism and society*. London: Macmillan.

NORRIS, C. 1992: *Uncritical theory: postmodernism, intellectuals and the Gulf War*. London: Lawrence and Wishart.

NORRIS, C. 1993: *The truth about postmodernism*. Oxford: Basil Blackwell.

OLLMAN, B. 1973: *Alienation: Marx's conception of men in capitalist society*. Cambridge: Cambridge University Press.

PAJAKOWSKA, C. and YOUNG, L. 1992: Racism, representation and psychoanalysis. In Donald, J. and Rattansi, A. (eds), *Race, culture and difference*. London: Sage.

PECHEUX, M. 1982: *Language, semantics and ideology*. London: Macmillan.

PENDERGRAST, M. 1993: *For God, country and Coca-Cola*. London: Weidenfeld and Nicholson.

PIETERSE, J. N. 1992: *White on black: images of Africa and Blacks in western popular culture*. London: Yale University Press.

POSTMAN, N. 1986: *Amusing ourselves to death*. London: Heinemann.

POTTER, J. and WETHERELL, M. 1987: *Discourse and social psychology: beyond attitudes and behaviour*. London: Sage.

POULANTZAS, N. 1965: *Political power and social classes*. London: New Left Books.

PRICE, M. 1980: *The peasants' revolt*. London: Longman.

ROSE, P. 1989: *Jazz Cleopatra: Josephine Baker in her time*. New York: Random House.

SAID, E. 1978: *Orientalism*. London: Routledge and Kegan Paul.

SCHLESINGER, P. 1987: *Putting 'reality' together*. London: Methuen.

SEARLE, C. 1989: *Your daily dose: racism and the Sun*. London: Campaign for Press and Broadcasting Freedom.

SHERWOOD, R. 1980: *The psychodynamics of race*. Brighton: Harvester Press.

SHOHAT, E. and STAM, R. 1994: *Unthinking Eurocentrism: multiculturalism and the media*. London: Routledge.

SILVERMAN, D. and TORODE, B., 1980: *The material word: some theories of language and its limits*. London: Routledge and Kegan Paul.

SOMMER, A.K. 1997: No work, little hope. *Jerusalem Post*, 13 December.

STUART, L. 1966: *A course in British history: 1688 to the present day*. London: Arnold.

STURROCK, J. 1979: *Structuralism and since: from Lévi-Strauss to Derrida*. Oxford: Oxford University Press.

THOMPSON, E.P. 1978: *The poverty of theory*. London: Merlin.

THOMPSON, J.B. 1990: *Ideology and modern culture*. Cambridge: Polity Press.

TODOROV, T. 1993: *On human diversity*. London: Harvard University Press.

TWITCHEN, J. (ed.) 1990: *The black and white media book*. Stoke-on-Trent: Trentham Books.

VAN DIJK, T. 1987: *Communicating racism*. London: Sage.

VAN DIJK, T. 1991: *Racism and the press*. London: Routledge.

VAN DIJK, T. 1993a: *Elite discourse and racism*. London: Sage.

VAN DIJK, T. 1993b: *Stories and racism*. In Mumby, D.K. (ed.), *Narrative and social control*. London: Sage.

VAN LEEUWEN, T. and KRESS, G. 1994: *Reading images: the grammar of visual design*. London: Routledge.

WALKERDINE, V. 1986: Video replay: families, films and fantasy. In Burgin, V., Donald, J. and Kaplan, C. (eds), *Formations of Fantasy*. London: Methuen.

WETHERELL, M. and POTTER, J. 1992: *Mapping the language of racism: discourse and the legitimation of exploitation*. London: Harvester–Wheatsheaf.

WHITTAKER, R. 1997: Television production: newsworthiness. The Virtual Institute of Information, World Wide Web.

WILLIAMS, R. 1974: *Television: technology and cultural form*. London: Collins.

WILSON, T. 1993: *Watching television*. Cambridge: Polity Press.

WOHLGELERNTER, E. 1997: Arab students' Jerusalem apartment firebombed again. *Jerusalem Post*, 13 December.

WOODS, D. 1987: *Asking for trouble*. Harmondsworth: Penguin.

WOODWARD, K., (ed.) 1997: *Identity and difference*. London: Sage.

WRIGHT, W. 1975: *Sixguns and society*. Berkeley: University of California Press.

Index

Stalin, J. 204
Stam, R. 174
Stamp, T. 243
Stern, I. 118
Stone, O. 197
Stirner, P. 140
Strictly Ballroom 243, 273
structural analyses 67
Stuart, L. 200
Studi, W. 230, 232
Sturrock, J. 66
Sun 130, 135, 152
Sunday Telegraph 237, 238

Tahiti 209
Tarantino, Q. 197
teachers 33
Tebbit, Lord 146–53
Terreeoboo 209
Thatcherism 33, 37
Thaw, J. 113
Therborn, G. 81
Thomas, T. 160
Times, The 145
Thompson, J. 46–50, 162, 259
Todorov, T. 257
Tolkin, M. 229
Torode, B. 268
truth 12, 24, 27, 35, 59, 61–3, 91, 107, 162
    Foucault on 63
Twitchen, J. 175
Tyler, W. 200

universe of discourse 26, 29, 39
unification 50

Van Dijk, T. 129–32, 270
Van Leuween, T. 133
video diary 192
Volney, Comte de 72

Wacaday 262
Walkerdine, V. 266, 267
Washington, D. 110, 221
Watch 206
Wearing, H. 243
Wetherell, M. 55, 56, 57, 264
Whittaker, R. 176–8
White House 98
whiteness 125, 172, 181, 183, 184, 248
Wilberforce House 202
Wilberforce, W. 205
Wilder, B. 111
Wiley, R. 96
Williams III, C. 225
Williams, P. 258
Williams, R. 155
Wilson, E. 181
Winfrey, O. 4, 51, 85–107, 185
Woods, D. 109
Woodward, K. 81
World Bank 189
Wright, W. 67

Yassin, Sheik 251
Yemenite Jews 251
Yorkshire Television 201
Young, L. 206

Zephenia, B. 190
Zinneman, F. 223, 273